10 MINUTE TECH

VOLUME 2

10-Minute Tech

VOLUME 2

More Than 600 Practical and Money-Saving Ideas from Fellow RVers

TRAILER LIFE BOOKS

Editorial Director: Bob Livingston
Copy Editor: Kristopher Bunker
Production Director: Christine Bucher
Production Manager: Carol Sankman
Interior Illustrations: Bill Tipton/CompArt Design
Cover Design: Brian Burchfield
Interior Design: MSA Digital Graphics Group

This book was set in Aachen BT, Berkeley Oldstyle ITCby BT, Bookman
ITCby BT and Futura BT and printed by Ripon Community Printers.

9 8 7 6 5 4 4 3 2

ISBN: 0-934798-72-9

CONTENTS

SAFETY

APPLIANCES

MAINTENANCE

AUTOMOTIVE

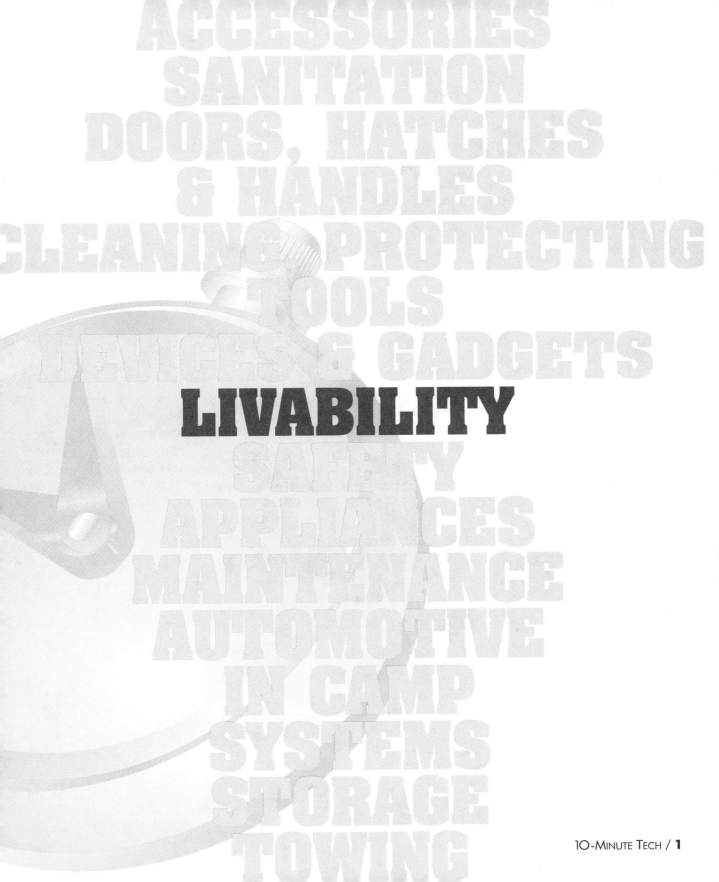

ACCESSORIES
SANITATION
DOORS, HATCHES
& HANDLES
CLEANING PROTECTING
TOOLS
DEVICES & GADGETS

LIVABILITY

SAFETY
APPLIANCES
MAINTENANCE
AUTOMOTIVE
IN CAMP
SYSTEMS
STORAGE
TOWING

SNAZZY FLOOR REGISTERS

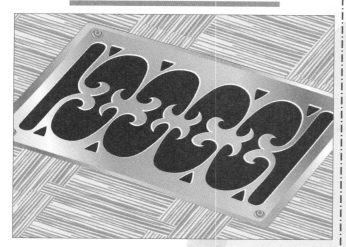

Most units come with plain louvered floor registers. Well, it's time to have snazzy floor registers! I recently purchased three antique brass decor registers from Home Depot. They fit exactly into the hole that was already cut into the floor of our unit. You just have to remove the top register from the adjustable louver-door unit with a screwdriver and screw the new top into the original holes. Be sure to measure your register opening before purchasing the new registers, as they come in several sizes.

ARLENE CHIAROLANZIO, FLORHAM PARK, NEW JERSEY

ADD-A-SHELF

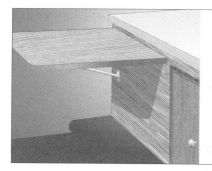

If your motorhome could use a table near a chair or a couch, as ours could, here's a project that works well. I purchased a 12-inch countertop extension from Camping World. It can be easily attached to the wall, using the provided hardware. When I need an end table, I put it up; otherwise it travels flat against the wall. No more spilled drinks and cans of soda on the rug! It works great for small areas. When I'm parked in a campground, I put a lamp on it, which looks great in the window and provides a light when we're returning to the coach after dark.

ARLENE CHIAROLANZIO, FLORHAM PARK, NEW JERSEY

A HOT TIP

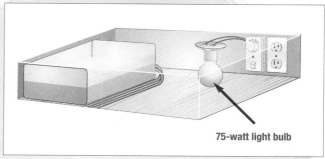

75-watt light bulb

A 75-watt light bulb, mounted in a porcelain fixture, can go a long way toward keeping tanks and pipes from freezing. Placed in the compartment near the tanks and hoses, enough heat will be given off to keep the temperature at an acceptable level. You could even add a timer to the circuit. I turn mine on when it's 20 degrees F or colder.

SAM MOLLOY, LEXINGTON, KENTUCKY

CLOSEUPS ◆ CLOSEUPS ◆ CLOSEUPS ◆

A BEAR MAKES YOUR BED

The bed in our unit is confined by walls on three sides and, in addition, has a wardrobe over the foot of the bed. Needless to say, it is a grizzly to make. To ease the job, we sewed the plain top sheet to the fitted bottom sheet, across the foot of the bed. Now both sheets are put on in one motion and they never become untucked.
HEBERT SUTTON, SUN CITY WEST, ARIZONA

CLOSEUPS ◆ CLOSEUPS ◆ CLOSEUPS ◆

A COLORFUL SOLUTION

There are so many keys to carry while motorhoming, I had to find a solution for quickly identifying which key goes with each lock. I painted the surface around each keyhole a different color and painted the corresponding key head to match. I used white correction fluid, nail polish, paint, etc., which made it easy to replace if time wore the paint away.
HELEN VAUGHN, PANACEA, FLORIDA

AIR DEFLECTORS

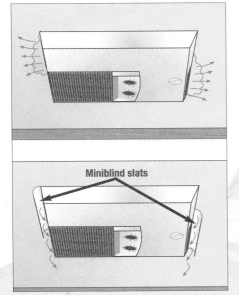

Miniblind slats

To prevent dark stains from soiling the ceiling material due to the flow of air from the air-conditioner vents, I enlisted the help of miniblind slats. I took two 1-inch-wide slats and super-glued them together lengthwise. When they were dry, each slat slipped into the space between the vent shroud and the ceiling.

The slats direct the air flow away from the ceiling and there is no more discoloration of the material.

DANNY TODD, DUNNELLON, FLORIDA

A SHORT STORY

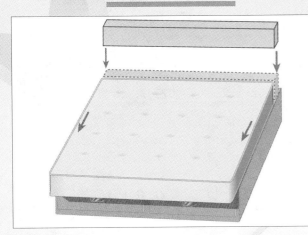

As in most other RVs, our queen-size bed is short. In order to accommodate a 6-foot 4-inch man, we cut a piece of firm foam 6 inches wide, the width of the bed by the height of the mattress. I covered it with a color-coordinating fabric.

At night, we pull the mattress down, toward the foot of the bed. We insert the bolster in the space created at the top of the bed. This will not interfere with the bed linens.

In the morning, we remove the bolster and push the mattress back up so that the full width of the aisle is restored.

CHARLOTTE CARPENTER, WESTMINSTER, COLORADO

BLOCK THE HEAT

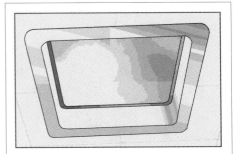

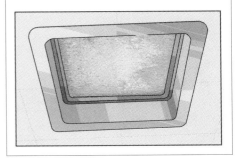

I love the skylight in the shower, but not the sunlight and heat it generates in the motorhome, so I decided to make a cover for it.

Since there is a space between the outside dome and the inside cover, I was told sun-reflective material would trap the heat and crack the plastic. Therefore, I used a color-coordinated piece of light canvas and sewed pockets on two sides for adjustable curtain rods. After inserting the two rods, I adjusted them to fit into the skylight opening.

Now we still have light, and my 6-foot-tall husband has plenty of headroom. The cover is also very easy to remove, should we want the heat.

DONNA WELCOME, SUN CITY, CALIFORNIA

CLOSEUPS ◆ CLOSEUPS ◆ CLOSEUPS ◆

A LITTLE GOES A LONG WAY

I use fluorescent paint in many ways. On outside door locks and their keys, a dab glows in the dark. While watching television, the remote-control unit is hard to see, so I highlight the buttons that are used often.

The stairs can also be seen more easily with a line painted along the top of the step and an even larger line drawn across the stair tread. The paint can also highlight the end or switch of your flashlight, making it easier to find in the dark. Various light switches tend to blend into their surroundings, so a tiny dab makes it easier to find them at night.

Use just a little, because the paint goes a long way.

ARLENE CHIAROLANZIO, FLORHAM PARK, NEW JERSEY

AWNING-ROD ACCESS

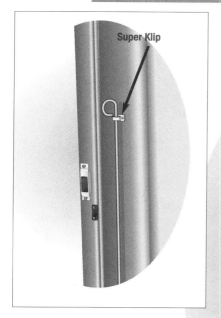

Super Klip

Storing the rod that is used to extend the awning has always been a problem for us. We seem to never have it accessible when we need it. I found a device called Super Klip at a local hardware store and it fits the bill perfectly for storing this elusive rod. I mounted two of these clips inside the rig, adjacent to the entrance door for easy access. The only modification was to drill two small holes in the clips so they could be screwed into the wall. I found the adhesive tape provided with the clips to be inadequate.

GERALD F. TODD, ELLIOTT LAKE, ONTARIO, CANADA

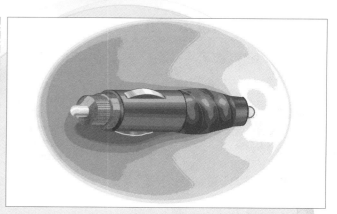

A SOFT GLOW

When we take the grandkids camping, we need some minimal light in the coach. We need lights that are not too bright and do not put a serious drain on the battery.

Our answer? I purchased a male cigarette-lighter plug and a small 12-volt pilot lamp at RadioShack. I soldered the leads from the plug to the terminals of the light as close as possible. I then carefully taped each soldered connection and wrapped tape around the entire unit to strengthen it and to give a more uniform appearance to the whole assembly.

I can plug this light unit into any cigarette plug in the dash or wherever, and have a soft glow (enough to see the kids and walk around the coach) without ending up with a dead battery. The lamp has a very low mil-amp draw and can be left on for several days without a noticeable drain on the battery.

PAUL DIEHL JR., SPRING GROVE, PENNSYLVANIA

◆ CLOSEUPS ◆ CLOSEUPS ◆ CLOSEUPS ◆

A NEW USE

Recently, we were about 900 miles from nowhere when I noticed a minor leak in the roof of our fifth-wheel (at the TV antenna). No RV supply houses were in the area and I did not have roof coating with me, but I remembered something I had used to repair a leaking chimney on our house.

I went to an auto-parts store and got a can of spray undercoating. Ten minutes later I had repaired the leak sufficiently to allow the completion of our trip without water damage. Just spray the undercoating on a dry surface as you would spray paint, taking care not to over-spray onto unwanted areas. Spray undercoating dries quickly, and when I returned home I cleaned it off with mineral spirits and made the permanent repairs. I have made a can of spray undercoating a permanent addition to my take-along emergency tools.

JERRY JONES, BONNEAU, SOUTH CAROLINA

Editor's Note: *This can only be used on metal or fiberglass roofs and is not safe for use on rubber.*

◆ CLOSEUPS ◆ CLOSEUPS ◆ CLOSEUPS ◆

$2 ICE BUCKET

A couple of years ago we were camping and I needed something to keep extra ice in. I didn't want to spend a lot on an ice bucket, and a cooler was too large. We were at a store and I spotted a Styrofoam bait bucket for less than $2. I bought a round one with a nylon cord for the handle; the lid attaches to the cord.

My husband laughed when I first bought a bait bucket for ice, but now he thinks it's great! I used that bucket for two years and this spring I decorated one with stickers that can be bought almost anywhere. Everyone that sees my ice bucket has positive comments, and several have gotten their own "bait buckets." The cord handle is very handy, as you can take the bucket to the picnic table or wherever very easily.

MARY DUTTON, MOBERLY, MISSOURI

CABINET LOCK-UP

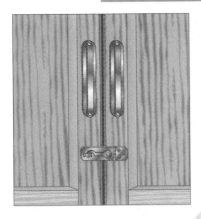

Many owners complain about securing the drawers and cabinets in fifth-wheels with rear kitchens. For cabinets, consider using a brass hasp that's available at hardware stores for $3 to $4. Before we installed the hasps on our cabinets, one door was pushed open by stored items inside and was damaged by the slideout room while it was moving to the open position. Now that problem is solved.

Drawers require a different approach. The constant jarring causes the hardware to loosen, which eventually prevents the drawers from moving in and out smoothly. Our fix was to install a brass drawer pull in the cabinet face above and below the drawers. These $3.50 parts are available at any hardware store; try to match the existing drawer pulls. We then used a 1-inch-wide piece of strapping and installed snaps at each end. Snaps and the appropriate tools are available at fabric stores. Before we hit the road, we thread the strap through all the drawer handles and the upper and lower cabinet pulls, and snap each end tight.

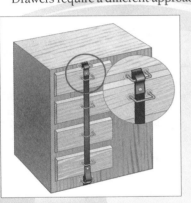

DONNA AND PETER VAN KLEECK, DOVER, MASSACHUSETTS

CLOSET SECURITY

For those of you who have full-length, passage type closet doors in our RV that are equipped with dummy door knobs and marginal-quality latches to keep them closed, here's a simple fix. Pick up a First Watch brand security door lock at a hardware store and install it right above the knob on each closet door. These Swing Locks can be installed in minutes and only cost around $2 each. Once in place, all you have to do is pull up and rotate the Swing Lock into position.
CLIFF LEESE, SALEM OREGON

CLEAN COFFEE

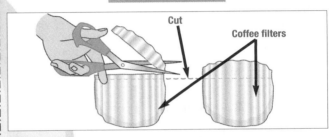

Cut

Coffee filters

Iwould like to share an easy and clean way to make coffee while RVing. I make coffee pouches out of regular drip filters. Put one scoop of coffee in each filter, stacking then (open on top of each other. Stack them in deep bowls for easy transport to your sewing machine. Carefully fold a filter in half, scrunch the top together and sew a seam across the top, sealing the coffee. Don't cut the threads between filters; leave a little space and slip the next under the feed-dogs (without raising them). Continue doing this, making a chain. When the last one is sewn, simply cut them loose and you have a very neat coffee pouch. Trim the excess filter above the seam to take up less space.

Store the pouches back in the can. When it's time to make coffee, just use the same number of pouches that you would use scoops. No spilled coffee grounds and clean up is a snap. Also, there is no risk of pouring used coffee grounds into the drain.

We use a percolator-type pot, and these pouches work beautifully. If you have the drip style, put a clean filter in the holder first to help hold the water around the pouches during the drip process.
DIANA L. BRADLEY, MUNCIE, INDIANA

CHIPPED, CRACKED OR BROKEN

Tired of chipped or broken dishes? There is an easy solution to this problem.

First, purchase some plastic foam or paper plates and bowls, which are approximately the same size as the dishes and bowls you want to protect. Also, purchase a spool or two of hook-and-loop fasteners for each stack of dishes (available at RV supply stores). Next get some four-pack cardboard wine containers from the supermarket. Stack the dishes and bowls in an alternating pattern with the paper or Styrofoam plates. Wrap the hook-and-loop fasteners around the stacked dishes in a cross pattern with each strip at right angles to the other. Next, place the glasses in the cardboard four-pack containers. Finally, place everything in the cupboards and you are ready to hit the road.

CLIFFORD RODGERS, APPLE VALLEY, CALIFORNIA

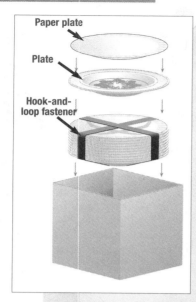

Paper plate

Plate

Hook-and-loop fastener

CLOSET FIX

In both rigs that we have owned, hanging clothes in the closets has been a frustrating experience, until we modified the system. It's almost impossible to use strong plastic hangers in the metal rail provided due to the proximity of the holes to the ceiling, and it's hard to move the clothes around when retrieving items if the closet is packed tight. We solved the problem by utilizing 1-inch eye snaps, metal closet rods and rod ends, together with end brace boards. We use the metal rail to hook the snaps with the rod positioned in the loops. Brace boards can be used on one or both sides of the closet. Now our clothes are easy to hang and they stay in place while on the road.

ROBERT E. GEIGER, MENA, ARKANSAS

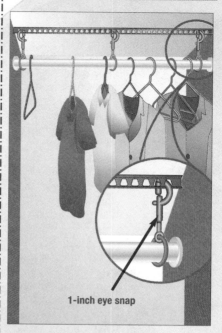

1-inch eye snap

DINETTE LOUNGING

One of the best places to watch television in my RV is from one side of the dinette booth, but sitting bolt upright for hours is uncomfortable, so I devised a "recliner." I purchased a child's bean-bag chair from a toy store and stuffed it in the back corner of the dinette. Since Pooh doesn't go with my RV décor, I wrapped a bed sheet of an appropriate color around it. A matching extra bed pillow on top can be scrunched comfortably under my neck while my back and elbows are supported by the malleable little bean bag. To support my legs, I purchased an 18 × 36-inch shelf, which matches the interior wood-grain trim on the dinette, to use under the seat cushion. I pull the shelf halfway out to support my legs when I curl up to watch the television. Now, I can slump in comfort and even nap on my dinette.

JANET CARTER, DALLAS, TEXAS

COOL IT

I am among those who are uncomfortable leaving the LP-gas on while towing our fifth-wheel. However, I worry that our refrigerator might reach unsafe temperatures. This becomes a bigger concern when we travel in hot desert climates.

To address this, I purchased eight lunch-size freezer gel packets and keep them in our fifth-wheel's freezer compartment. They are small and take up very little space. Before we hit the road, I place them in various locations inside the refrigerator, close the door and enjoy peace of mind. We have never had a problem, even when the outside temperatures hover in the triple digits.

Once we settle in at a campground, I simply toss the gel packs back into the freezer and they are ready for next time.

DIANE SIMS, ALBANY, OREGON

CUP HOLDERS

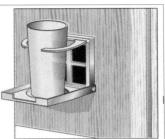

We drink large amounts of water throughout the day and night. Our fifth-wheel does not have bedside tables, so we had to improvise in order to have a handy glass of water during the night. We purchased cup holders from a marine store and mounted them at a convenient height on the closet walls on either side of the bed. Come morning, we have coffee-cup holders while we watch the morning news. The cost of the holders was $3 each.

BOB DEAN, NANAIMO, BRITISH COLUMBIA

COVER STORAGE

My pots and pans are stacked with plastic-foam sheets between each of them. I had no place for the covers, so I bought cup hooks and short bungee cords. I mounted the covers on the inside of the cabinet doors where they ride safe and secure. The pan covers ride out of the way and stay put during travel.

JEAN COUGLER, WATERTOWN, NEW YORK

◆ CLOSEUPS ◆ CLOSEUPS ◆ CLOSEUPS ◆ CLOSEUPS ◆ CLOSEUPS ◆

AN ILLUMINATING IDEA

_T_ired of dimly lit RV parks and a 12-volt DC exterior light that puts out very little illumination? I came up with a simple, inexpensive solution. The kitchen in our fifth-wheel is on the same side as the front door where we wanted more outdoor lighting. I noticed that the microwave was plugged into a double 120-volt AC outlet inside the overhead cabinet, leaving one receptacle empty.

At the hardware store, I purchased an exterior 120-volt AC dusk-to-dawn lamp fixture and an outside extension cord (with a ground wire) that plugs into the outlet. These lights can be found in white, which will match most exteriors.

Using the kitchen window as a guide, as it could be seen outside as well as in, I measured the desired location, and drilled a ⅜-inch hole just through the exterior wall skin. Using a flashlight and a small screwdriver, I probed through the hole to make sure there were no other wires in the way. Still from the outside, I then drilled on through the interior wall. I cut the extension cord near the male end, leaving it long enough to reach from the 120-volt outlet inside the cabinet, to the new exterior fixture. I then threaded the section of extension cord through the hole, from the inside out, attached the wires to the fixture, screwed the light to the RV side wall (pre-drill the mounting holes), caulked the fixture and all the drilled holes and plugged it in.

When the sun goes down, the light comes on and it can be unplugged when not needed.

RON GARDNER, ATWATER, CALIFORNIA

Editor's note: _Please be courteous to your fellow RVers and confine your lighting to your campsite. It can be very annoying to try to sleep while a nearby vehicle has its exterior lights on, unfortunately causing your interior to be well lit. Be sure you don't also cause a side-clearance problem with a fixture that protrudes too far from the side wall of the rig and be cautious when drilling through the walls._

◆ CLOSEUPS ◆ CLOSEUPS ◆ CLOSEUPS ◆ CLOSEUPS ◆ CLOSEUPS ◆

CLOSET DRILL SERGEANT

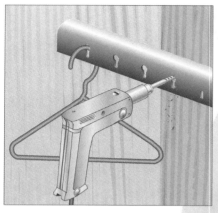

Many of our RV closet rods consist of a metal strip with a row of holes to insert the clothes hangers into. These are great for keeping hangers in place while in transit. But the holes are too small to insert the plastic hangers many of us like to use. The quick fix is to make the holes larger with a drill.

CHARLES MCAFEE, HALEYVILLE, ALABAMA

GREAT HANG-UP

*W*e just purchased a new motorhome. I was putting clothes into the closet, which has a metal hanging rack, and I found it was impossible to get the hangers out after I had put them in. My solution is very simple: Put the hangers in backward! They are easy to remove without cutting off the tips or making any other adjust

STELLA SHERER, THOUSAND OAKS, CALIFORNIA

COOKING TILES

*T*he oven in our RV has always burned cakes and other foods, unless they get my undivided attention. I picked up an idea on a television show that really works. All you have to do is lay unglazed 6-inch tiles on your oven rack. I cut the tiles to fit around the side and front, leaving a ½-inch space for air circulation. I found that it does not take longer for food to cook and I can bake a 9-inch square cake in 21 minutes at 350 degrees F. I leave the oven rack in the center position. The tiles sell for 19 cents each at the home center — that's only $1.40 for the whole project.

AVA NORMAN, DESERT HOT SPRINGS, CALIFORNIA

CUSTOM WINDOW SCREENS

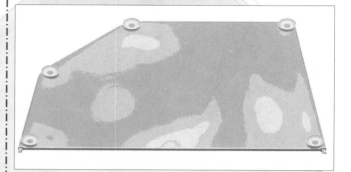

I have a Class C motorhome. I replaced all the screen material on the windows with solar screening for improved sun protection.

I wanted to extend this benefit to the cab area, so I made a pattern of the cab's side windows. Then, using a sheet of solar screening, I cut two pieces to cover the glass area. I cut small slits in the five corner areas and inserted suction cups through the holes on the side of the screen to be fastened to the window. I secured the suction cups by looping and tying a few turns of monofilament line to the back side of the cups.

The screens can be attached to either the inside or the outside of the side windows and can be removed or reinstalled easily.

JAMES KUCABA, ORANGE, CALIFORNIA

DIRECT THE RUNOFF

When our trailer is not in use, we always park it with the curbside wheels on a raised platform. This tilts the body away from the curb, opposite the normal crown of the street, and directs most of the rainwater and snow melt to the streetside of the roof. Since the awning serves as a trough on the curbside, we hope that directing most of the runoff to the other side will prolong the life of our awning.

BRUCE TRUDGEN, WILLIAMSBURG, MICHIGAN

FOOL THE KID

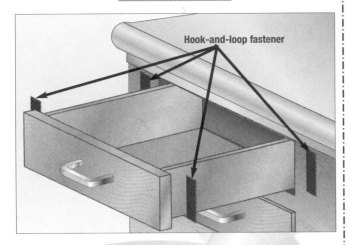

Hook-and-loop fastener

I have a child who likes to pull drawers open. I fixed the problem by mounting hook-and-loop fasteners to the back side of each drawer face and the front of the cabinet. To install, simply apply a section of hook-and-loop tape (with adhesive backing) to the inside of the drawer face, leaving the opposite portion of the material attached. Peel off the protective paper from the exposed section of hook-and-loop material and close the drawer. This will give you the proper position for the matching hook-and-loop tape. Now the drawers open with a heavier pull, foiling the kid's access attempts. Side benefit: The drawers stay secure on rough roads.
RICHARD E. RICE, PORT HURON, MICHIGAN

GET A LEG (OR TWO) UP

Our fifth-wheel has no space for a recliner, but has a comfortable sofa bed in the slideout. Thinking of the sofa recliners that I've seen, I came up with my own version. I took a sheet of ⅜-inch plywood cut to 3½ feet by 14 inches and covered it with contact paper.

I simply slide it under the sofa cushion with enough left in front to put on a pillow to comfortably prop up my legs. For support in front, I added two legs hinged to the plywood. The legs fold up on the hinges and the whole recliner can be stored under the sofa when not in use.
DEBBIE PASELL, ESSEX JUNCTION, VERMONT

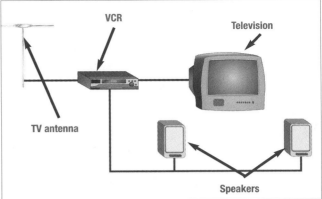

VCR · Television · TV antenna · Speakers

HEAR YOUR TV

The space provided for a TV set in my fifth-wheel is enclosed, which inevitably muffles the sound from the television.

As we always have a VCR along, I purchased a stereo-to-mono adapter (part no. 274-387B) from RadioShack. Plug the adapter into the audio-output jack on the VCR. Then plug in a pair of computer speakers into the adapter.

Place the speakers anywhere you want and can hear plainly without having to turn up the television sound overly loud. The VCR must be wired between the antenna and the television and turned on and tuned to the desired station.
BILLIE HURLEY, SHERMAN, TEXAS

Editor's Note: Look at the back of your television. Most late-model sets have audio-output jacks, so all you would have to do is run the computer speakers from them to completely eliminate the VCR from this set-up.

GREAT POTLUCK RECIPES

*O*ne of the best parts of any camping trip is the food. My group of friends always has a potluck on one night of our trip. Through the years, I have gathered a number of recipes that lend themselves nicely to cooking in camp. I purchased a small photo album and used my computer to print out my favorite camp recipes onto 4 × 6-inch cards and put them in the album. The cookbook is compact and the recipes are protected in the plastic sleeves. Now our favorite recipes are always with us and I have blank cards in the book so that I can collect more recipes along the way.
LINDA S. MARTIN, LAKEWOOD, CALIFORNIA

DISH CUSHION

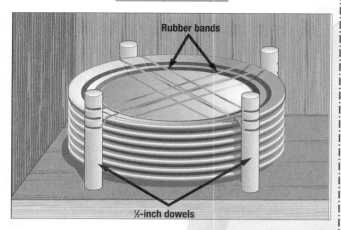

Rubber bands

Front

½-inch dowels

We had a problem with the dishes breaking in our fifth-wheel's rear kitchen. To keep the dishes in one piece, I cut a piece of ⅜-inch plywood into four pieces. Each one has the same depth as the inside of the cabinet and is slightly wider than the dish or plate. I then drilled four ½-inch holes in each piece, half the thickness of the plywood and glued ½-inch dowels in the holes. Each dowel should be as long as the stack of dishes it is to hold in place. I then cut four or five ⅛-inch-deep notches on the outsides of the dowels. The dishes are placed on the plywood pieces and two rubber bands are stretched across, forming an X pattern. Hook-and-loop strips are used under the plywood and on the shelf to keep the dishes from moving. I haven't broken a dish in five years and more than 30,000 miles of traveling.

HENRY BARRY, TACOMA, WASHINGTON

DRAWER SUPPORT

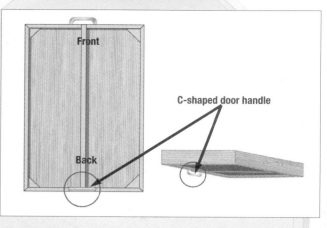

Front

Back

C-shaped door handle

When the plastic slide locks on our kitchen drawers broke and allowed the drawers to hang precariously when pulled out, I made a unique repair; I went to the local hardware store and brought some inexpensive C-shaped door handles. By removing the drawers below each one in need of repair, I was able to gain access to install the handles. Each handle is attached so that it is placed under the slide rail in the back of the drawer and attached with the provided screws. This makes a very secure lock, so the drawer does not tilt when opened, and the repair does not interfere with drawer operation. This can be used on the other drawers of the same type throughout the RV. It only costs about $1 per drawer to make the repair.

CHARLES E. REEVES, PORT ARKANSAS, TEXAS

EASY TO TACKLE

I have a large assortment of earrings, and I needed a way to organize them while traveling. I found that clear plastic tackle boxes, available at a variety of stores (including mass merchants and hardware), are great for this. They come in many different sizes and have adjustable dividers. I can store all of my earrings, with each color in its own compartment. They are easy to see and travel well because they cannot fall out of the containers, and the containers can be stored on top of each other.

I also use this type of storage container for necklaces and my makeup. My husband uses them for screws, miscellaneous hardware, bulbs, fuses and assorted batteries.

PAT PULLUM, ROGERS, ARKANSAS

DO THE TWIST

We needed a convenient place to hang our plastic grocery bags that we were going to use for trash. I decided the ideal place was to hang them on the side of a cabinet. I bought two single garment hooks and fastened them to the cabinet about 14 inches apart. By pulling the back of the bag tight between the hooks and then twisting the bag handles around the hook, the bag will hang open in the front.

ROGER WESTERMAN, AUTAUGAVILLE, ALABAMA

ELIMINATE NECK STRAIN

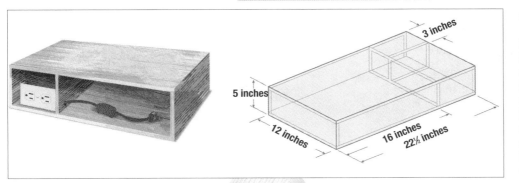

3 inches
5 inches
12 inches
16 inches
22½ inches

The overhead TV compartment in our Class C motorhome, although functional, left us with a bit of neck strain after watching television for a period of time. That was because we had to tilt our heads back to view the set while sitting on the couch. We needed a better and more natural viewing level.

Our cab area isn't used while camping and it is the right viewing height for our television set, so it became the ideal location. The fun project was building the portable TV/VCR stand for about $25 with materials from our local building-supply store.

The TV/VCR stand is made from a 2 × 4-foot piece of ¼-inch oak plywood cut to the proper dimensions. After nailing and gluing the pieces together, I sanded, stained and polyurethaned the whole thing, which gave it a professional look that matched the rest of the cabinetry.

To dress up the front edge of the cabinet, I used contact cement to glue on the gold-and-black plastic door-edge molding, which I purchased at an automotive store. In the rear of the videocassette-storage compartment of the unit, I mounted an electrical-outlet box wired with a 16-gauge extension cord.

The new TV/VCR stand fits snugly between the cab seats on the armrests, which hold it in place at a comfortable viewing height, and it is easily stored under the dinette table while traveling. The cab's privacy curtain merely swings behind the TV/VCR cabinet while we're viewing television.

So, not only did we not use any valuable space inside our motorhome, but we actually gained another cabinet for storage!

MARVIN YEAKEL, WAVERLY, NEW YORK

CLOSEUPS ◆ CLOSEUPS ◆ CLOSEUPS

EASY FOOTREST

If you don't have a recliner in your RV, but really like putting your feet up while relaxing, try using a camping stool. These stools have a canvas seat and aluminum folding legs. They can be found in almost any camping or outdoor store. These stools not only make great footrests at the right height, but also provide extra seating when necessary. We also use one while working on the computer, as it happens to be a good height for that purpose.

CARL AND PAT PULLUM, ROGERS, ARKANSAS

CLOSEUPS ◆ CLOSEUPS ◆ CLOSEUPS

FINDING THE REMOTES

We used to misplace the remotes for our two televisions in our RV. To fix this, we purchased a couple of cheap desktop pencil holders at Wal-Mart. We then drilled a small hole in the top back of each holder and screwed them to the wall in convenient locations — one in the living area and one in the bedroom — where the televisions are located. We now have no problem finding these remotes. You can also adhere the new "remote holders" using double-sided tape if you prefer not to drill into the wall.

CARL AND PAT PULLUM, ROGERS, ARKANSAS

CLOSEUPS ◆ CLOSEUPS ◆ CLOSEUPS

FINDING THE REMOTES II

We had quite a problem keeping the remote controls with their various electronic devices. We solved the problem by using a strip of hook-and-loop fasteners. A short strip was cut, the paper backing was removed and then applied to the back of the remote. The other half of the hook-and-loop fastener was applied to the television, VCR or whatever. We discovered less dirt stuck to the tape if the loop part of the tape is applied to the remote.

HAROLD AND MARGARET LEED, SHIPPENSBURG, PENNSYLVANIA

I Can See Clearly

In the rear of my bathroom closet, I placed a see-through plastic caddy. Each pocket is filled with items that are used frequently and difficult to store in other places (for easy access). The caddy is attached using a center hanger and is stabilized at the bottom with hook-and-loop tape; this keeps the caddy from swinging while traveling. Now my husband never has to ask where the items are stored.

HELEN VAUGHN, PANACEA, FLORIDA

Instant Counter

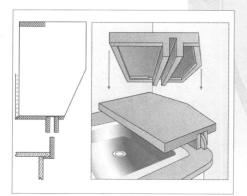

We bought a new motorhome and everything is perfect except that there's not enough counterspace, and the sink is too close to the end of the galley. Our solution was to build a splash guard that serves as a base for the additional counter. After finding Formica that matched the kitchen décor, we cut out a splash guard and attached it to the end of the counter using the appropriate-length screws. Then we cut a piece of wood — determining how wide it needed to be so that it would not interfere with the use of the sink and not be in the way of the person sitting on the adjacent sofa. We also had to make cuts to go around the miniblinds that cover the kitchen window.

In order to give added support, we finished off a piece of oak with polyurethane and screwed it into the wall. We added screw hooks to the piece of oak and hung decorative items so it would look nice when the counter extension is not in use. The counter is fairly simple to make if you're handy with wood and the dimensions will vary, depending on the configuration of your galley.

LORETTA AND JOSEPH FOSTER, CANTONMENT, FLORIDA

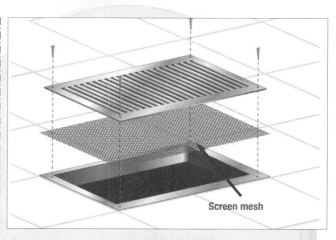

Screen mesh

Junk Screen

We have always been concerned about dropping small items into the floor-mounted heating vents in our RV. We came up with the idea of removing the vents, laying screen mesh — similar to the type found in a screen door — over the opening and screwing the covers back in place. The screen keeps the ducts clean year-round. Vacuuming the vent area removes any dirt, dust, food and other items that may accumulate on the screen.

CARL AND PAT PULLUM, ROGERS, ARKANSAS

◆ CLOSEUPS ◆ CLOSEUPS ◆ CLOSEUPS ◆

KEEP YOUR
BOTTOM WARM

*N**ot full-timers yet, we extend our RVing season as early in the spring and as late in the fall as possible, depending on local conditions. (In northern Michigan campgrounds close.) I have found several hints to make these extended summers much more enjoyable.*

Having a fifth-wheel with extra insulation, we still found that the bed in front would be chilly in cold, windy conditions. Adding more blankets warmed the top but did not keep the coldness from seeping up from the bottom of the trailer. I purchased a dual-control heated mattress pad. Now, when parked with electric hookups, each of us can take the chill out.

Likewise, with the door and windows tightly shut, we had condensation problems. We researched and found a small, freestanding dehumidifier, which ended the condensation problem. An added bonus is that the dehumidifier releases heat when it is running and helps keep us warm.

CHERYL SEDERQUIST, GAYLORD, MICHIGAN

INCOGNITO LITTER BOX

We just purchased a new fifth-wheel and were looking for a place to put the litter box for our two kitties. Under the refrigerator is a louvered door that provides access to the hot-water tank and is open to our basement storage, which has outside doors. We removed half of the louvers in the door and braced those that remained; a pet door was placed into that opening. In the basement, under the compartment, we closed in the area for the litter box with coated wire sections. One of the wire sections can be opened to service the litter box from the outside. Now we don't take up valuable space inside the rig and the best part is that the kitties use their "hidden" litter box.

BERNARD INGRAM, GOODMAN, WISCONSIN

HOT STUFF

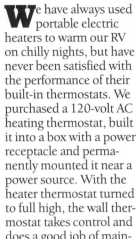

120-volt AC heating thermostat

We have always used portable electric heaters to warm our RV on chilly nights, but have never been satisfied with the performance of their built-in thermostats. We purchased a 120-volt AC heating thermostat, built it into a box with a power receptacle and permanently mounted it near a power source. With the heater thermostat turned to full high, the wall thermostat takes control and does a good job of maintaining a constant temperature.

BRUCE TRUDGEN, WILLIAMSBURG, MICHIGAN

Editor's note: Make certain the thermostat you use is rated for 120 volts AC; ordinary thermostats, like those used in the home, operate on low voltage.

HIDE AND SEEK

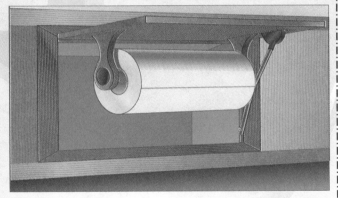

Our RV has no under-the-counter space for mounting paper towels. I tried using an upright holder on the counter, but it would fall over, especially when grabbing for a towel in an emergency. It also took away valuable counterspace. I came up with the idea of mounting a metal spring-loaded paper-towel holder on the inside of one of the overhead cabinet doors. This has worked perfectly for me, and when I am finished in the kitchen, I just close the door and things are neat and tidy again. I only lost about 6 inches of space from the inside of the cupboard, but gained the space back with a clear countertop.

ISOBEL MCKENZIE, SEBRING, FLORIDA

LIGHTING A DARK CABINET

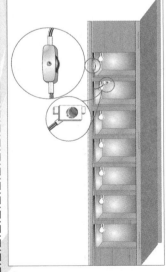

Our trailer has a five-shelf cabinet that is used to hold cooking supplies and utensils. The dark corners of the cabinet made it hard to locate what we needed.

I made a string of 12-volt DC lamps and mounted one on the upper left corner of each shelf, shining onto the shelf area below. Next, I mounted a "momentary-on" switch so the lights go on when the cabinet door is opened and they turn off when the door is closed. Also, I included a regular line switch to use when we need to make sure the lights stay off. (For example, the door might accidentally swing open during travel or storage.)

The necessary 12-volt DC lamp, sockets, 18-gauge wire and switches are all available at your hardware store, home center store or RadioShack.

A. A. RAMBIKUR, DALE, TEXAS

LESS EDGE WEAR

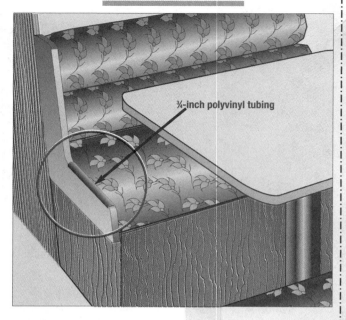

¾-inch polyvinyl tubing

The upholstered frames on the outsides of the dinette benches in our motorhome began to show evidence of excess wear due to our sliding in and out of the seats. To reduce the wear, I purchased a section of ¾-inch polyvinyl tubing, cut it to the appropriate lengths, split the tubing lengthwise and installed a section over each top edge of the upholstered framework. The protective tubing stays securely in place despite the constant use and the upholstery stays in good shape.

M.G. VANCURA, CINCINNATI, OHIO

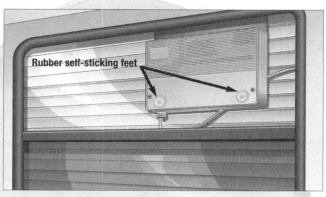

Rubber self-sticking feet

LIGHT UP MY SPACE

Being disappointed with the single, dim, 12-volt DC light fixture on the exterior of my trailer, I found that I could modify a fluorescent light, mount it on the inside of the window frame and create the light I needed. This provides an enormous amount of light, is easy to control and is protected from the weather. The fixture I used was a GE under-cabinet compact fluorescent light, model UC13; it's available in hardware and home-improvement centers.

I cut a flat piece of aluminum from a roll of roofer's flashing, also available at building-supply stores. I bolted the aluminum plate to the metal body of the light fixture, creating a 3-inch flange. I then carefully marked the positions of the two window mounting screws in relation to the flange and drilled the holes. I installed two large rubber self-sticking feet to the window-side base of the light fixture; this keeps the light from scratching the window during travel. I completed the installation by mounting the light using the window-frame screws. The light is plugged into the nearest 120-volt AC receptacle using the existing chord. It's now very easy to reach inside the blinds, switch it on and light up my campground space.

DON DEJARNETTE, TUSCALOOSA, ALABAMA

LESS IS MORE

*A*fter meals and at various other times, I've found it necessary to heat all six gallons in the water heater, when a much smaller amount was actually needed. Think of the LP-gas or electrical energy that was wasted and the time spent waiting for the water to heat.

One day it dawned on me that I had been overlooking a fast, simple, economical way to heat just the right amount needed — the coffeemaker! Now I simply fill the carafe with the amount needed (less the coffee, of course) and let it run through. The hot water is ready in a flash and you have saved time, water and energy.

ALTA JERRELL, HOMOSASSA, FLORIDA

KEEP BED SHEETS WHERE THEY BELONG

*P*illow-top mattresses pose a problem for fitted bottom sheets. By morning the sheets are usually pulled out. A simple solution is to buy a pair of men's suspenders. Snip the threads holding the straps together and clip them to each edge of the sheet, across the underside of the mattress, at each end. Voilá! No more slippage!

DARYL LUCAS, ADA, MICHIGAN

LOST AND FOUND

Carry your motorhome keys on rings with brightly colored markers attached. The colorful markers will help you find the keys when they are inevitably dropped at the campsite, on the trail or in the coach. We chose colored key hooks that attach to our pants' belt loops (to keep more stuff out of our pockets). By having different colors for each set (and habitually using the same color), you know which set you are looking for and can retrace your steps if keys become lost. Spare sets are useful to loan to guests and in case of real loss.
ALLAN BENNETT, FOUNTAIN HILLS, ARIZONA

LET THERE BE LIGHT

Every time I wanted to do something in the battery compartment of my fifth-wheel, I found that my body blocked the light, which would have to come in through the compartment-door opening. I tried to use a lantern, but it didn't work well, as it wasn't bright enough. My unsatisfactory solution was to use a flashlight, which of course, involved the use of one hand.

I purchased three 12-volt DC ceiling lights (two would work, but I like things bright) and a 12-volt extension cord with battery post clips on one end. The lights were then wired to the extension cord. I prefer the clip-end-style cord, so I can completely disconnect the system from the batteries and there will be no chance of accidental use of battery energy when dry camping.

I mounted the lights to the metal support running the length of the compartment ceiling, using plastic wire ties. The lights were wired in parallel. If you are using 6-volt DC golf cart-style batteries, remember to connect the lights across a series set, otherwise the lights will be very dim.
CLIFFORD RODGERS, APPLE VALLEY, CALIFORNIA

LIGHT-SWITCH INDICATOR

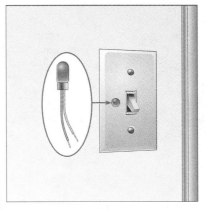

It has always been difficult to find the 12-volt DC light switch on the far wall of the bathroom at night. To solve the problem, I installed a pilot light in the panel next to the switch. I used a RadioShack light-emitting diode (LED), part no. 276-209, since it only draws 0.01 amp. It's very important that the LED draw very little current, especially if you can't cut the power from the batteries before storing the rig, or when boondocking.

Wire the LED across the switch's contacts. Make sure you do not wire the LED in series, or you'll be going back for another light. No need to be concerned with polarity; just hook it up temporarily; it should light when the switch is off. If not, reverse the leads. Drill a hole in the switch plate to mount the LED using a press fit or a dab of epoxy.
ROBERT VAN BODEGON, POMPTON LAKES, NEW JERSEY

LOW-DRAW LIGHT

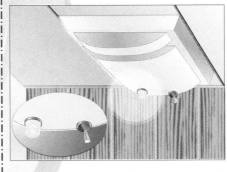

At night when we dry-camp, we still like some light in the motorhome (especially in the bathroom), but do not want to run the batteries down. So, I purchased a miniature toggle switch and a low-amp-draw pilot lamp at RadioShack for less than $5. I drilled holes in the bathroom light lens to accommodate both the lamp and the switch. Black and white wires connect the switch and the new lamp, wired in series, to the power-supply wires for the original lamp fixture.

The original light functions as it originally did, and the new lamp works whenever the miniature switch is turned on. Its soft glow enables us to use the bathroom at night.

The new lamp is a low-mil-amp bulb, drawing minimal current. It can be left on for several days without a noticeable effect on the battery.
PAUL DIEHL JR., SPRING GROVE, PENNSYLVANIA

MINI TRASH CONTAINER

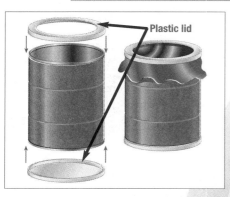

Plastic lid

For a neat mini-countertop trash container, use a large coffee can as a base. Cut out the center of the plastic lid, leaving a ½-inch rim. Place a plastic vegetable bag in the can and use the lid to hold it in place. When another empty coffee can is available, use that lid for the bottom of the mini-trash container to prevent scratching of the counter surface. The container can be painted, papered or stenciled to match the décor of your RV.
TINA LUKE, EMERY, SOUTH DAKOTA

NO MORE FRAYING

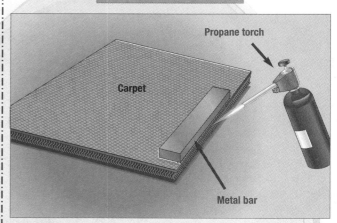

Propane torch

Carpet

Metal bar

Many RVers use carpet remnants to fill in places on the floor, but after a short while the ends become frayed and create additional cleaning chores. The trick to a neat and permanent edge is very simple and easy. After cutting and fitting the carpet, lay it on the garage floor or another concrete surface. Secure a metal bar 1½ inches or more in width. Place it along the cut edge, exposing approximately ⅛ inch of the carpet. Using a propane torch, apply the flame to the exposed edge only long enough to melt the carpet fibers. The carpet cannot be made of only natural materials. I suggest that you practice on scraps until you get the timing down. Also, it's very important to do this with plenty of ventilation; the fumes from certain materials can be very toxic.
ANTHONY D. BEQUETTE, VANCOUVER, WASHINGTON

NIGHT LIGHTS

In our travels, we use night lights, powered by 120-volt AC shore power, for a soft glow in our motorhome. One night light is positioned in our vanity area; the other is in the receptacle under the dinette. Thus, if we ever need to get up in the middle of the night, the brighter lights do not have to be turned on. How pleasant this is when you're half-asleep!
KATHY BAXTER, LOUISVILLE, TENNESSEE

MARKING TIPS

When taking showers in my trailer, I cannot see the HOT and COLD markings on the mixer valve without my glasses; the transparent knobs blend into the wall. I finally painted a large blue dot on the COLD handle, which is easy to see from a distance.

I also painted large blue marks on each awning brace so that I know which hole to allow the handle to lock in place, providing the proper height of the canopy.
KATHY LAVIGNE. ENFIELD, CONNECTICUT

MAKE A DEHUMIDIFIER

I found an easy, inexpensive way to make a dehumidifier. Get two 5- or 6-gallon buckets with lids from the local hardware store (or inquire at a restaurant, which may have empty lard buckets you can get for free). New or used, clean them well. At the hardware store, get a 50-pound bag of rock salt and divide it between the buckets. With the lids off, place the loaded buckets inside the motorhome, one forward and one in the rear. When not in use, put the lids on tightly and store. When the rock salt becomes saturated with moisture, spread it out on a piece of plastic and dry it in the sun. Store it in the sealed buckets until the next use. It should last for years. I've used this method since 1987 and have not had a mildew problem.
PETE VAN HEE, OCALA, FLORIDA

PERCH AND SUCH

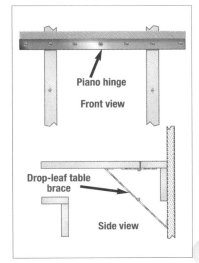

Piano hinge

Front view

Drop-leaf table brace

Side view

I have a cat that likes to look out the bedroom window, so I built a platform for it to hang out on. To make my folding shelf, I bought a 1 × 12 × 36-inch board, an 8-foot-long piece of 1 × 2-inch board, a 36-inch continuous hinge (piano hinge), five 2-inch wood screws, seven 2-inch metal screws and a 10-inch drop-leaf table brace. I cut the 1 × 2-inch board into two 36-inch sections. One section was sanded and drilled (the 2-inch width) to fit five wood screws. The sections were glued and screwed together (see drawing). The 1 × 12 × 36-inch board was already presanded, so I only had to stain and varnish it to match the interior wood. The hinge was attached first, and then the board was secured to the wall, making sure at least two of the metal screws went into studs. Check to see that no wires are behind the area where the shelf is being mounted. By the way, the shelf makes a great working "counter" mounted in any convenient location inside your rig.
RICHARD PREVALLET, LIVINGSTON, TEXAS

PAN HOLDER

Looking for a place to store our cookware, we found the inside of the closet door right next to the stove to be very handy. Cup hooks are used to hang the pans and wide elastic is tacked into one side and attached to the other side using a hook and small eye-screw. The cookware doesn't swing around and it wont get scratched from stacking. It's a great space saver, too.
DORIS PEMBERTON, CANTONMENT, FLORIDA

CLOSEUPS • CLOSEUPS • CLOSEUPS

PLATE PROTECTION

To protect plates, bowls, glasses and coffee mugs from breaking, I have an idea that really works and does not take up extra space in our cupboard — which is really important to us.

Buy one or two yards of semi-plush corduroy material. Cut the material in circles a little smaller than the plates and bowls and put one piece between each plate and bowl. For glasses and mugs, cut a rectangle 1 inch larger than the width and the exact height of the individual piece. Sew the width and slide the corduroy over the glass or mug. If you use pinking shears to cut the material, the edges will not unravel. After 10 years of boating and 20 years of RVing, I have never broken any china or glasses.
MARILYN PORTNOY, FELTON, CALIFORNIA

CLOSEUPS • CLOSEUPS • CLOSEUPS

NON-ROLLING ROLLS

Throughout my years of RVing, I have seen a number of ways to secure the paper towels while on the road. Here's my idea: Use a shoe string and tie it around the roll. It works for toilet paper, too.
NELLIE MANSELLE, URBANA, ILLINOIS

CLOSEUPS • CLOSEUPS • CLOSEUPS

MODIFIED SHOWER HEAD

On a new camper I purchased, the shower head required such a large flow of water that the pump supplied only enough for a weak spray. A huge amount of water was required for a shower. I gradually glued the shower head holes shut with household cement until I got a good spray. I ended up with only six holes open. Now I have a vigorous spray, and I use less than a gallon of water to take a good shower.
CARL RADCLIFFE, PARKERSBURG, WEST VIRGINIA

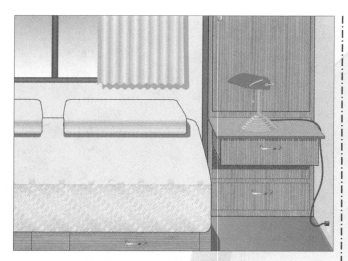

PORTABLE NIGHTSTAND

My brother and his wife have a beautiful travel trailer with wonderful cabinetry. The first time out, however, they realized something was missing. The floor-to-ceiling cabinets that flanked each side of their queen-size bed left no room to place an alarm clock or a glass of water. There was no nightstand or shelf. The large picture window above the head of the bed allowed no room to install an overhead shelf.

My brother (being a very clever guy) came up with a great solution, which required no modification of the existing cabinets. The upper half of this storage unit is a cabinet, but the lower half has drawers. He merely cut a piece of finished shelving material about a foot in length. With the drawer open, the shelving material fit perfectly over the width of the drawer, straddling both sides. Closing the drawer slightly gave the new nightstand a snug fit. Having used a finished piece of shelving material gave it a nice professional look, but any old board will work. The shelving stores inside the upper cabinet for travel or when not in use.

JUDY CAMERON, SANTA CRUZ, CALIFORNIA

MORE SHOWER ROOM

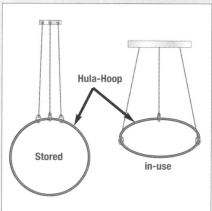

When our son and daughter-in-law bought their first pop-up, they made sure it had a shower. Having a shower is great, but lacking room inside, the shower presented a problem for even the smallest campers. We came up with a very easy and simple remedy for this by purchasing a Hula-Hoop at a local toy store. Using nylon string with plastic loops, we suspended the Hula-Hoop halfway down the shower curtain. This holds the shower curtain open to provide additional room. It stores easily by sliding the plastic loops to one side and letting the Hula-Hoop hang down vertically. Attaching it to the ceiling can be done in a variety of ways.

PAT AND DENNIS BAUER, MUSKEGO, WISCONSIN

PORTABLE CEILING FAN

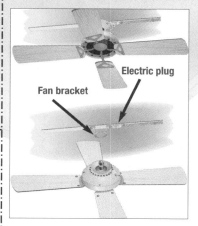

We wanted to install a ceiling fan, but lacked the necessary clearance when the slideout was retracted for travel. To solve the problem, I installed a fan bracket into the ceiling and modified the decorative cup to handle the wiring. First, I opened the room and determined the appropriate location for the ceiling fan. Once the bracket was in place, I drilled a hole in the decorative cup and installed a rubber grommet. Then I connected the wires to the fan leads with a male plug extending from the decorative cup. With the fan in place, I ran an extension cord from an outlet in the side wall to an appropriate location near the ceiling fan. The cord was secured to the wall and ceiling using special wire straps. Now all I do is install the fan when the slideout is extended and plug it in. I reverse the process before I retract the slideout.

ROBERT D. SHAFER, BOCA RATON, FLORIDA

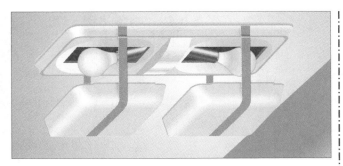

POOR MAN'S BUG-ZAPPER

One evening when we went into our motorhome, about 100 gnats came inside with us. I noticed they were attracted to the lights, so I lowered the lenses and hung them below the bulbs with masking tape. The gnats would touch the hot bulbs and fall into the lenses. Later I cleaned and replaced the lenses, and from then on we have been bug-free.
ALEX LABAC, YORBA LINDA, CALIFORNIA

PREVENT WATER PUDDLING

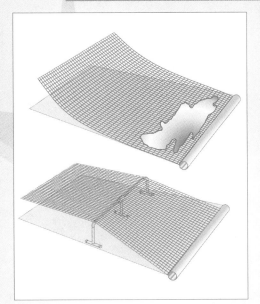

Water collected on our slideout room awning. To eliminate these puddles, we used ¾-inch plastic pipe and fittings to construct a support bar between the roof of the slideout and the awning.

Purchase a section of ¾-inch plastic pipe, four ¾-inch T-fittings, six ¾-inch end caps, two ¾-inch right-angle fittings and a can of PVC cement.

Cut two sections of ¾-inch pipe so that when they're assembled together, they will span the width of the awning. Assemble the three support legs, as shown in the drawings.

To use, open the slideout and awning and slip the support bar assembly between the two. This will cause the awning fabric to rise and allow the rain to drain away instead of puddling.
REBECCA ALLEN, MOCKSVILLE, NORTH CAROLINA

PUDDLE ELIMINATOR

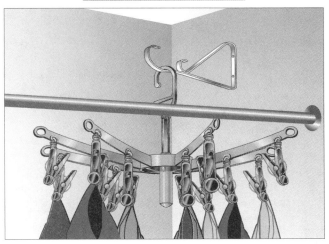

Our fifth-wheel has a tub/shower combination and I was tired of the puddles of water that found their way to the floor whenever we hung wet items, such as swimsuits, over the shower rod to dry. We first mounted a plant hanger high on the wall, opposite the shower head. Then we hung a plastic umbrella-style clothesline to the plant hanger. These clotheslines are inexpensive and have their own clothespins attached. It's out of the way when it's not being used and does not interfere with the shower; it can be easily removed since it is suspended from a clothes-hanger-type of hook. Now any wet clothing drips directly into the tub.
RITA DANIELS, SUNDANCE, WYOMING

QUICK NIGHT-LIGHT

We often camp in places with no electrical hookups, but with three children in our trailer, we needed a night-light that would run off the trailer's batteries and not draw too much power. I purchased a no. 303 lamp from an electronics supply house and inserted it in place of the regular bulb in one of the trailer's incandescent light fixtures. Since the lamp is rated at 28 volts DC, it burns about half as bright on 12 volts DC, and the one bulb uses a minimum of power. Any lamp with the same size base rated at a higher voltage should work. The higher the rated voltage, the dimmer the light.
CRAIG WOLFE, BROOKLYN PARK, MINNESOTA

PREVENTING CABINET FLIERS

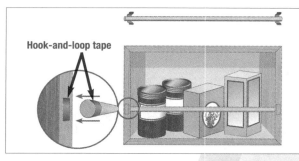

Hook-and-loop tape

To keep items from tumbling out of the cabinets when the doors are opened after a day on the road, I devised a simple system. I cut a ⅜-inch diameter dowel to fit the inside cabinet measurement. I wrapped each end of the dowel with the loop side of sticky-back hook-and-loop tape. I cut a ¾-inch length of the hook side and placed it on the inside edge of the cabinet at the desired height; repeat for the other side of the cabinet. The rod is held in place with the hook-and-loop tape.

To enhance the appearance, the dowel can be stained to match the color of the cabinet.
PENNY REPH, ASTORIA, OREGON

REVISITED MEDICINE CABINET

(Two more solutions to an old problem)

In my RV, after a day's driving, I had a problem keeping the articles in my bathroom medicine cabinet from falling out when I opened the cabinet door. I solved this by using ⅛-inch plastic sheeting held in place with double-sided foam tape.

Cut the plastic long enough to cover the width of your shelves, high enough to retain the contents and low enough for you to be able to reach in and remove what you need.
BILL HOLTZ, BERLIN, MARYLAND

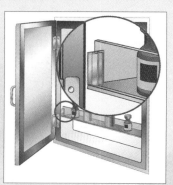

To keep the items in your medicine cabinet in place, consider using a "fence" for each shelf. Using ⅛- or ¼-inch plastic sheeting, cut to height and length. Cut four pieces (per shelf) of square Plexiglas (or wood) to the height of the "fence." Glue one piece on the front edge of each side wall, at each end of the shelf. Then glue the next two pieces back from the first two, the thickness of the Plexiglas fence. Slide the "fence" into place. The "fence" can be left in place or removed when you are parked.
PAUL ANNDERSON, KANKAKEE, ILLINOIS

REFLECTING IDEA

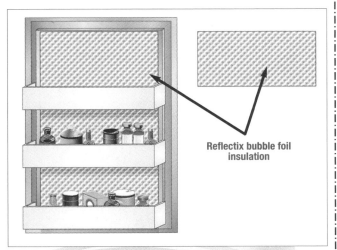

Reflectix bubble foil insulation

Cans and bottles kept sliding around the trays in the door of our refrigerator as we drove down the road. Not only did things turn over, but the cans also caused black scuff marks on the white interior. We cut pieces of Reflectix bubble foil insulation to fit against the inside of the refrigerator door. Each piece fits into the door tray and extends to the bottom of the tray above it. The pieces fit snugly in the trays so no adhesive is needed. Not only do our cans and bottles stay put, but the extra insulation has increased the cooling efficiency. This project cost less than $3 and took less than 15 minutes to complete. Reflectix can be found at hardware stores and RV supply centers.
KIM R. GRAY, FRANKFORT, KENTUCKY

STICK 'EM UP

*N*eed a bulletin board, but don't have the wall space to hang one? Convert your refrigerator/freezer door into a message center. Replace the decorative front panel with cork-like material from an inexpensive bulletin board bought at a discount center. The top edge of the frame holding the decorative panel on the refrigerator will unscrew, so you can slip the old panel out and the new one in.

The brown color of the new bulletin board blends with most wood-grain RV interiors. Use pushpins to stick on notes, just like you would a regular bulletin board. It provides a handy place to tack lists, messages, photos, camping cards and even a favorite poem.
COLEEN SYKORA, RAPID CITY, SOUTH DAKOTA

SECURING VALUABLES

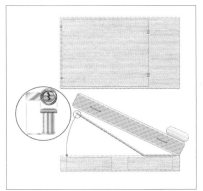

As full-timers, my wife and I have been very concerned about securing our valuables and important papers when taking our RV in for service or repairs. Since our RV has a storage area under the bed, which is accessed only by raising the hinged plywood platform that supports the mattress, we opted to lock it down. To do this, buy two identically keyed file-cabinet locks from a lock shop or hardware store. They need to be about a half-inch longer than the thickness of the platform.

Install them vertically at the end of the platform so that they latch into the inside of the bed box. The keyholes are out of sight under the mattress and if the locks are properly adjusted, the bed platform will give the impression that it is of solid construction and immovable.

Of course this will not stop a determined burglar, but it will prevent snooping and pilfering.
J.D. DOUGH, MIDDLESBORO, KENTUCKY

SERIOUS READER

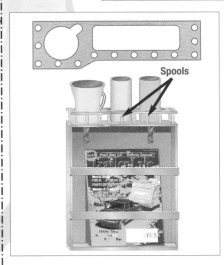

Spools

I do a lot of reading in the bathroom and there's not much room for books and maps, so I decided to install a rack that stores magazines, a coffee cup and reading glasses. I built a rack using ½-inch-thick wood stock, spools from the woodworking store and a couple of angle brackets. The entire project is screwed together. The magazines fit into a 10 × 14-inch structure and the top is cut to accommodate the coffee mug (and handle) and the glasses. Size and type of wood can be changed to meet any individual's taste.
WES WILSON, GALESBURG, ILLINOIS

SCREEN DOOR TO STORM DOOR

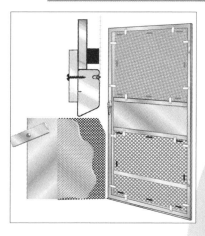

During the air-conditioning and/or heating season, a problem arises: What to do with the motorhome door? If you leave the door open to enjoy the scenery and/or extra light, it's hard to maintain the inside temperature. If you close the door, you say good-bye to the view and the light. To solve this dilemma, we made Plexiglas storm windows to fit over the motorhome's screen door.

Either measure carefully, or take the screen door to your local glass company or hardware store and have ⅛-inch-thick Plexiglas cut to fit over the existing screen openings. Purchase at least six to eight screen clips per opening. Attach the screen clips to the edge of the door openings by drilling holes one size smaller than the diameter of the screen-clip screw. Be careful not to drill all the way through the door frame. Set the Plexiglas in place and tighten the clips. To remove the Plexiglas, loosen the clips, turn sideways, remove glass and retighten the clips.

To prevent the Plexiglas from rubbing holes in the screen during movement of the coach, attach small squares of hook-and-loop material to all four corners, top and sides of the screen.
LOIS TAYLOR, LARGO, FLORIDA

SECURE THOSE HANGERS

Spring extension rod

We have a closet located at the rear of our fifth-wheel and occasionally the hangers will bounce off. My solution is to take a small spring extension rod (refrigerator size) and extend it wall-to-wall right against the hanger tops. It does not take much tension and the hangers will not bounce off the permanent closet rod.
SHARON HARGUS, HIGHLAND, ILLINOIS

SLIDEOUT TABLE

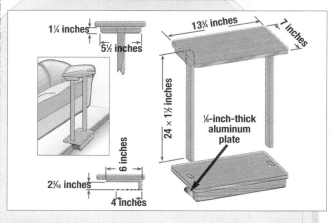

My wife needed a place to set her drink while sitting on the couch in the slideout room. So I designed a small stand which attaches under the slideout floor. The table does not interfere with the slideout seal and can be easily repositioned or removed as needed.

The table is made from ⅜-inch oak stock and is 7 × 13¾ inches. An aluminum plate, ⅛-inch-thick, is used to make the hardware that fits under the slideout's lip and is attached to the table base. Two 24 × 1½ inch legs are used to connect the table to the base. The setup looks ice, is fairly inexpensive, easy to build and it works great.
MAX WESSON, WILLIAMSPORT, PENNSYLVANIA

STOPPING THE SPLATTERS

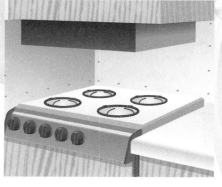

To help our new rig stay fresh, we set about making little improvements. Here's one: To protect the wall area around the stove, we placed ⅛-inch clear Plexiglas sheeting along the side wall and behind the stove. This sheeting extends from the top of the backsplash surrounding the stove to just underneath the range hood. Screws are used at intervals around the edge of the Plexiglas to hold it in place. The same type of Plexiglas has been used around the bathroom washbasin. To add to your coach, measure to suit your particular configuration. This protection makes cleanups a snap, and saves your wall covering.
PHYLLIS INGHRAM, FORT JONES, CALIFORNIA

SLIP SLIDING AWAY

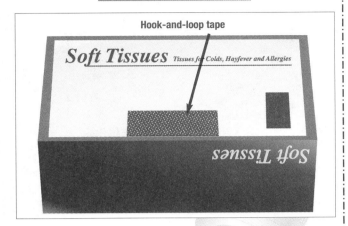

I got tired of the tissue box sliding off the drivetrain hump and around the floor in the vehicle. My solution was to cut two parallel 1-inch slits in the bottom of the tissue box, about 3 inches apart. Then I fed the ends of a piece of hook-and-loop tape, hook-side exposed downward. The hook-and-loop tape is not glued to the box, but it stays in place. When the box is empty, the hook-and-loop tape can be reused.

RALPH FREDLUND, LAKEVILLE, MINNESOTA

SOAP-DISH FIX

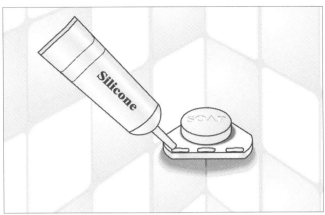

Our one-piece fiberglass shower is terrific, except for the angle of its built-in corner soap dish; it's impossible to keep a bar of soap on it. To solve this problem, we applied a thick bead of good-quality silicone sealant across the edge of the soap dish. We left two gaps near the center to allow the water to drain properly, but still keep the soap in place. It works great and it has not become moldy or unsightly during more than a year of use.

PAULA M. HARMER, LONGWOOD, FLORIDA

◆ CLOSEUPS ◆ CLOSEUPS ◆ CLOSEUPS ◆

THOSE SHORT "QUEEN" BEDS

With otherwise excellent RV equipment, there are still frequent complaints by tall people about short queen beds (60 × 75 inches). As a 6-foot 1-inch (73 inches) person who likes to sleep flat on my back, I found the 75-inch bed caused foot cramps and toe pressure problems. My wife and I teamed up for an easy solution.

Realizing that the way I lay on a normal pillow "wasted" about 6 inches between my head and the wall, we decided to make a narrower pillow. A fiber-filled pillow (shredded foam, feather or other filled pillow will also do) was opened enough to remove about a third of the filling and then sewn back to about two-thirds of its original width, yet keeping its original length and thickness.

Now the top of my head is about 1 inch from the wall (an inch miss is as good as a mile) and I sleep as comfortably as in our regular queen-size bed at home.

PAUL BINDER, SARASOTA, FLORIDA

◆ CLOSEUPS ◆ CLOSEUPS ◆ CLOSEUPS ◆

SOFTENING THE BLOW

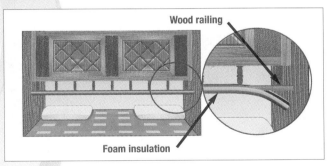

Our queen-size bed has a row of storage cabinets above the head of the bed, requiring us to dip under them when we lie down on the pillows. Getting up in the middle of the night was a real head-banging experience — it certainly wakes you up in a hurry. We would hit our heads on the front edge of the 3-inch decorative wood railing that hangs below the bottom of the cabinet structure. We purchased a 6-foot length of the round, gray foam used to insulate ½-inch copper tubing. This type of insulation is slit lengthwise from the manufacturer, so all I had to do was slip the foam over the edge of the wood railing. Now when we hit our heads, the blow is cushioned.

BILL MCANALLY, PALM DESERT, CALIFORNIA

TIRED OF WATER

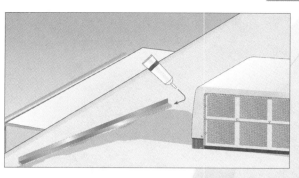

I got tired of the roof air-conditioner condensation water running down onto my slide-topper awnings. As it collects it causes these rather small awnings to get slightly stretched and stained. Hardware stores sell ¾-inch, clear plastic, 90-degree-angled material (wall corner protector molding) in 4- or 8-foot lengths. I butted a 4- and an 8-foot section together to form the 12-foot length I needed (the length you need may vary depending on your rig). The idea is to have the molding redirect the condensate to where you want it to flow.

I put a bead of rubber roof caulking on the bottom of each molding, laid them on the roof, inside angle facing toward the air-conditioning unit, to collect and direct the water. Starting about 18 inches in from the roof edge beside the air conditioner, I decreased the line so the end of the molding was only about 4 inches from the roof edge near the rear of the rig, creating an angle to encourage runoff. I then put a bead of caulking along the full length to seal the edge of the molding to the roof.

Now the water runs harmlessly down the side of the rig as it would without slideouts and I don't have to sweep water off my slide toppers every other day.

Dennis Lees, Livingston, Texas

SOUND CONTROL

I have a small television in my rig. The sound comes out of a small speaker on the side and hits the nearby wall. To hear the sound, I had to turn up the volume so that my neighbors could listen with me, or find a better solution.

I bought a pair of powered computer speakers from Wal-Mart, 20 feet of stereo headphone extension cable (⅛ plug to ⅛ jack) from RadioShack (part no. 42-2462) and, since the extension cable had a stereo plug, I purchased an audio plug (⅛ stereo plug that fits into the ⅛ monaural jack on my television, part no. 274-368). If your television has stereo outlets, this adapter will not be necessary.

The above-mentioned parts have allowed me to run the extension cable from the television, up the wall and across the ceiling, with adjustable cable clips (RadioShack part no. 274-368) holding the cable and ending with the speakers behind the sofa. The speakers are powered by an adapter plugged into a 120-volt AC outlet. To keep from having to turn the speakers off and on every time I use the television or unplug the adapter from the wall, I purchased a GE plug-in cord switch (part no. 5365-21D) that plugs into the outlet and then the adapter plugs into the switch. I found the GE switch at an Ace Hardware store.

Now I can watch television without having to share the sound with my neighbors.

Richard Prevallet, Livingston, Texas

TV PERCH

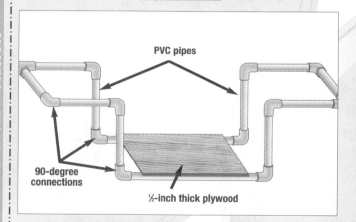

PVC pipes

90-degree connections

½-inch thick plywood

My Class C motorhome did not have an entertainment center or a provision for the television, and we didn't like the viewing angle when the television was positioned on one side of the cabover bunk. To improve the viewing angle and to take advantage of unused space, I built a lightweight stand that puts the television at a more reasonable viewing level and stores easily on the cabover bunk when traveling. The stand is assembled using schedule 40 PVC pipe.

To build, I made the appropriate measurements and determined that I needed one 14-foot section of 1½- or 1¼-inch PVC pipe, 12 90-degree PVC connections, PVC glue, ½-inch-thick plywood cut to 16 × 24 inches and four wood screws.

Once you cut the PVC pipe into lengths to fit your particular cabover-bunk opening, the rest is like putting together an easy puzzle. In no time, you can have a TV stand that makes use of otherwise wasted space.

Albert E. Dean, Hico, Texas

STEP AID AND SHOE CLEANER

We needed a step to assist in getting in and out of our RV, plus we wanted something to help clean the dirt off our shoes. We made a 24 × 18-inch wooden platform that is 4 inches high (measurements can be adjusted to suit individual needs). I used 1 × 4-inch wood for the sides, ends and underneath cross supports. The frame was covered with ⅜-inch plywood. The step was painted with marine varnish, which provides good weather protection. Outdoor carpet was used to cover the step — folded over the ends and tacked from underneath. The carpet can be easily replaced when it gets worn.
CARL R. HARTUP, FORT WAYNE, INDIANA

TWO IDEAS FOR WET TOWELS

Although my 32-foot motorhome has a large bathroom, there is only one towel bar and no convenient place to add another. When we have to dry more than one or two towels, we run out of bar space. In order to hang up damp towels so they will dry by morning, we use the large, vinyl-covered sun visors in the front of the coach. We take showers at night just before bedtime, so the towels are hung up when we go to bed and taken down in the morning. They are not even in the way when we turn the front-passenger seat around to sit in, as the visors hold the towels over the dash.

This requires no cost, no drilling of holes, no coach modifications and no time to set up or take down!
JOE ROULEAU, LAGUNA NIGUEL, CALIFORNIA

My husband and I are enjoying our fifth RV, and from the most humble little trailer to our current luxury 40-foot diesel pusher, without exception, the manufacturers have never provided enough towel racks in the bathrooms. The obvious solution is to install more towel racks from a hardware store, but there are other alternatives available.

I found that wreath hangers work as additional towel holders. These hangers are available in plastic or metal. When placed over the top rail of the shower stall, inside to hold a bath scrubbie or a wet washcloth, or outside to hang a wet towel, they are instantly available as an additional rack, which can be moved to any location.
EILEEN HARTEL, FALLSTON, MARYLAND

STRANGE AND HELPFUL

*E*rrand Bag — I hang a shoe bag by the door and put letters and other things in it that need to be taken when I go out the door.

*F*oot Soak — I use a rubber sink stopper to block the drain when I shower, being careful not to allow the water to rise above the lip of the stall. This gives me a quick foot soak every time I shower.

*B*lanket Storage — I store an extra blanket on top of the mattress, under the sheet, so I always have an extra blanket.

*C*lothes Pole — If I am drying clothes inside, I use my hiking pole balanced between two chairs to hang garments on plastic coat hangers.

*H*air-Color Bottles — I rinse out used haircolor bottles and fill them with wood glue, which comes out the nozzle in a narrow bead. I put a bit of crumpled foil on the tip to keep it from drying out.

*P*lastic Shower Cap — I use disposable shower caps when I am painting to keep paint out of my hair.

*W*ashing Clothes — A new toilet plunger can be used to wash clothes in a large clean plastic garbage bag. This is a handy way to wash clothes if you are not near a Laundromat.

*C*ampfire — To light a fire when the wind is blowing, crumple newspaper inside a paper bag and lay it on the ground with kindling on top. Light the paper inside the bag and the flame will be protected from the wind.
LINDA BUTLER, CHILLIWACK, BRITISH COLUMBIA

SWIVEL STAND

The accompanying illustration shows the swivel stand my husband made for our television so it could be viewed from two different areas. We have a rear bedroom. He put the swivel shelf in the living-room area, but at bedtime, all that needs to be done to see it from the bed is to rotate it around. This also creates extra room on the cabinet where it used to sit, since the television is now above it on its own shelf.

SUSIE SCHENK, VERNON HILLS, ILLINOIS

SUCTION-CUP SEALING

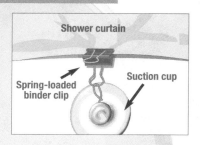

Shower curtain

Spring-loaded binder clip

Suction cup

Having trouble with water leaking onto the floor around your shower curtain because it doesn't seal well? An easy solution can be found at many office-supply and hardware stores. Spring-loaded binder clips and hooks attached to suction cups are available in many different sizes and work nicely in keeping the shower curtain under control. To use, securely fasten one end of a binder clip to the hook on the suction cup and clip the assembly onto the shower curtain where needed. A little moisture on the suction cup will securely hold the assembly to the shower wall, thus keeping the curtain close to the wall, preventing those annoying water leaks all over the bathroom floor.

BILL JONES, IRVINE, CALIFORNIA

TRAVEL FILE

Keeping track of maps and brochures while traveling is always kind of messy. They probably end up in a drawer or a cabinet and get very mixed up. My solution to this problem is to use a full-page-size accordion-pleated file folder, available from any store selling office supplies. Be sure to get the one that has alphabetical dividers so every item can be filed for quick retrieval. And while you're at it, why not buy two more file folders and get your maintenance and financial records straightened out?

B.C. MCCREA, PORT ANGELES, WASHINGTON

STUMBLE NO MORE!

I got tired of stumbling over the trash can on the floor of the kitchen area of our RV, so I made two hooks to mount any plastic grocery or other store bag on our oven-door handle. The two hooks were made by bending two short lengths of 10- or 12-gauge Romex electrical wire (available at any hardware store). These wires are plastic-coated and easy to bend and, when formed into the hook shape, will slide along the oven handle to fit any of the plastic bags in which stores pack your purchases. After filling with trash, unhook the bag, tie the bag handles together, and you're "out the door."

ALMON HANAGRIFF, LAKE CHARLES, LOUISIANA

THROW SOME LIGHT ON THE SUBJECT

We have a lot of storage room under the bed in our RV and have found it a great place to store our files. However, we soon found that access to the paperwork in the evening hours was hampered due to insufficient light.

To solve this problem, we purchased a small battery-operated tap light, similar to those advertised on television, and fixed it under the lift-up bed over the storage area. Now, whenever we need anything from the files, we have a light for better viewing.

CARL PULLUM, ROGERS, ARKANSAS

SPICE IT UP

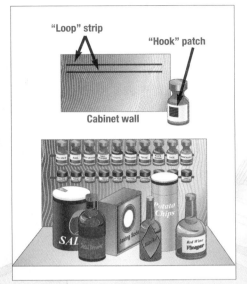

"Loop" strip

"Hook" patch

Cabinet wall

As an avid cook, I have accumulated quite an assortment of spices in small plastic bottles. These were invariably in a jumble after a day's journey on rough roads. It was also difficult to locate a particular spice when needed. I solved this problem, and added much needed storage space, by utilizing 1-inch hook-and-loop fastener strips along the side and back walls of the storage cabinet. I first glued the loop side of the strips to the wall and cut the hook side into 1-inch pieces (approximately). These pieces were glued onto the back of the spice containers. Hanging the spices on the wall allowed the use of previously unused cabinet space. Using this approach, I was able to install two rows on the back of the cabinet; one for tall bottles and one for shorter bottles. The arrangement will vary depending on the cook's spice assortment.

ELIZABETH BLASDEL, LIVINGSTON, TEXAS

STOVE-TOP SAVER

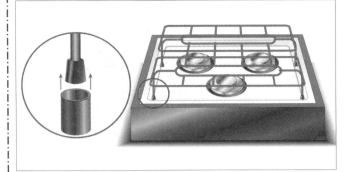

Due to a manufacturing error, the grid on our Atwood Wedgewood stove sits too close to the burners. Since the burners are not adjustable, even the lowest setting will overheat the enamel top and the paint will flake off. Atwood replaced my top and said that they were working on a new design.

To ensure that this didn't happen again, I tried this quick fix, which did the trick. At the hardware store I purchased a 9-inch filler tube, used for toilet repair. I cut it into four equal pieces, which I used for spacers, slipping them over each grid foot. This allowed the grid to be raised ½ inch, which in my case worked great. Using high-temperature paint, you could even paint the spacers black to match the rest of the stove.

BOB GOODNOW, WEST BOYLSTON, MASSACHUSETTS

TOO-BRIGHT LIGHTS

CLOSEUPS • CLOSEUPS • CLOSEUPS

When we took delivery of our new motorhome, we were delighted to see many light fixtures. We soon learned that more is not always better. These lights were just too bright! I removed all the plastic light covers and took them to a shop that had a glass-bead blaster (used for cleaning small parts). You might try auto-parts stores that have machine-shop service; a sandblaster would also work. The insides of the light covers were blasted until a frosted effect was achieved. With very little work, we got all the fixtures to give off a muted, glare-free light, a much more comfortable look.

MIKE HIGGINS, BAKERSFIELD, CALIFORNIA

WARM UP

CLOSEUPS • CLOSEUPS • CLOSEUPS

We have a twin-bed arrangement in our trailer (beds against the outer walls, aisle in the center). We really like this layout because of the ease of making beds and being more open. The mattresses are installed on a plywood base with storage under both beds. The only problem we have with this arrangement is the cold temperature that is transmitted through the walls and from under the beds.

We solved this problem with two 4 × 8-foot sheets of 1-inch-thick foam insulation. We cut them into pieces, so each bed had a sheet of foam under its mattress. We had enough left from each sheet to line the rear and side walls (adjacent to the bed) with pieces 15 inches high. The easy way to cut the foam is to use a hacksaw blade (no handle).

We, in effect, isolated the mattress from the cold, and were surprised at how much warmer it became.

B.C. McCREA, PORT ANGELES, WASHINGTON

TWO TIPS FOR THE ROAD

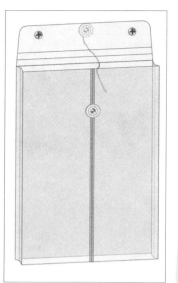

In order to store a calendar, bills to be paid, snapshots needing to be filed, etc., we bought a plastic expandable 9¾ × 11¾-inch envelope from an office-supply store. By using the existing screws from the window frame, I screwed through the flap and hung one for my husband and another for myself, alongside our kitchen between the table and the wall. I also have pens and highlighters clipped to the plastic envelope.

These are unseen and the inside dinette chairs don't bump them at all, nor do active grandkiddies.

Betty Hecker, Pensacola, Florida

If you don't have room in your RV for a filing cabinet, try using a magazine rack. We use the kind that can be found at camping stores. They come in three sizes, and the middle size is just right for regular-size file folders.

They can be attached to the wall or to the inside of a cabinet or closet door. They really help keep things organized.

Coleen Sykora, Rapid City, South Dakota

WANT TO BE A BAG LADY?

Easily found in craft shops and generally sold in packs of 100, I purchase small (4-inch) zippered plastic bags (the kind beads or jewelry are sold in). I use the bags to keep a small supply of spices for the galley, including small quantities of less-used spices from stores that sell them by the ounce. Each bag is labeled, put in alphabetical order and stored in a suitably sized plastic, oblong container. Twenty or more spice packets will fit into such a container.

Ann Piper, San Diego, California

WHERE SHOULD WE STOP?

Before we enter a new state, I obtain one of its highway maps and color-code it with highlighters. We use a different color for each of the campground organizations we belong to. Public dump stations have another color, while scenic areas/places of interest have still another. Other colors could highlight additional things of interest to you.

This way, we know where everything is before we begin and can plan our trip accordingly, without having to check a number of books every time we travel.

Susanne Smith, Salmon, Idaho

USE THE OL' NOODLE

For years, we have camped with RVs that are have dinettes with seat and back cushions that fold down into a bed. I have told my wife how uncomfortable the seat is to sit in because it forms a right angle with improper support in the lower back, and should have some kind of wedge behind it. She suggested, "Why not use a round foam noodle like the kind the kids use for swimming?" We bought a couple of them, cut them the length of the back cushion, and placed them at the bottom behind the back cushions. It worked perfectly!

Donald Shurte, Flint, Michigan

VENT FILTER

*O*ne of my furnace vents, located at the top of our entry stairs, was constantly collecting dirt as we went in and out of our motorhome. No amount of foot-wiping solved the problem. Cleaning required removal of the vent to vacuum.

At Home Depot, I found disposable fiber furnace-vent filters that really work great. All I do is remove my RV vent, lay the filter over the opening and replace the vent. The filters fit perfectly, right out of the package. Now our vacuum picks up through the vent, plus I get some filtering action while the furnace is in use.

A package of 12 filters costs less than $3, and each one lasts about three months.

RICHARD GABE, ATLANTA, GEORGIA

TRAVELING WITH GLASS

*M*y husband and I like to use drinking glasses (real glass, not plastic) while traveling in or RV. I found an inexpensive way to safely carry these glasses while on the road. Place each glass in a child-size tube sock. This keeps the glasses from rattling while you drive down the road and if one should break, all the pieces of broken glass will remain in the tube sock. The socks stretch, conforming to the size and shape of the glasses. I have even carried water goblets this way for several years and have never broken one.

VIRGINIA SMITH, FLINT, MICHIGAN

TWO WAYS TO TREAT YOUR HANGERS

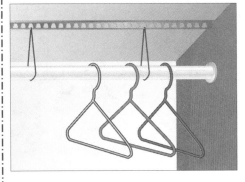

1 We like using plastic clothing hangers, but hate the punched-metal hanging racks many motorhomes have. To allow us to use more hangers and get them on and off more easily, we cut a length of ¾-inch PVC pipe to hang below the existing metal rack. The PVC was cut ½-inch shorter than the width of the closet. We glued a piece of foam at each end of the pipe to protect the sides of the closet. Then we purchased some metal shower-curtain clips. Starting 4 or 5 inches in from each end of the metal rack, we hung the small end of a clip about every 12 inches. We slipped the PVC pipe through the larger part of the metal clips, and now we have a good, sturdy and inexpensive clothes rod.

DONNA RAINEY, CAPE CORAL, FLORIDA

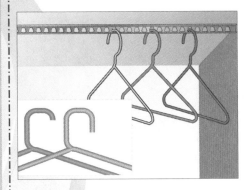

2 It's very difficult to put clothes hangers on the metal hanging racks many of the motorhome manufacturers use. I purchased plastic clothes hangers and cut the tip off to about ¼ to ½ inch. Measure the tip first, so you don't get it too short, or the hanger might fall off while you are driving.

KARL KUHN, GAINESVILLE, FLORIDA

WATER RETENTION ISN'T ALWAYS BAD

*T*o keep the dog's water from spilling over on the carpet while my motorhome is in motion, I took a plastic 5-gallon bucket, cut it off 2 inches taller than the water dish, and placed the dish inside the cut-down bucket. The water dish is 9 inches in diameter and 4 inches tall. The cut-off bucket is 11 inches in diameter and 6 inches tall. Now, when the water spills, it is caught in the bucket. The carpet stays dry, the dog has water, and the spillage only has to be emptied every three or four days.

LUTHER STRUVE, POCATELLO, IDAHO

What Goes Bump in the Night?

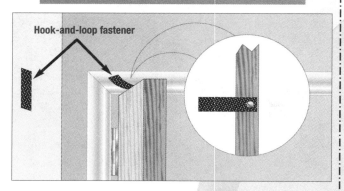

Hook-and-loop fastener

We have a trailer with a center bath. The door from the bath to the living room/kitchen area is a hinged door. If the trailer is not perfectly level, the door does not stay open and may slowly swing part of the way closed. This is very dangerous in the middle of the night. To prevent this I bought a pack of hook-and-loop fasteners. I cut a 1-inch piece, and stuck it on the wall behind the door, where the top edge of the door touched the wall. I then thumbtacked a 3-inch piece to the top of the door in line with the spot of the wall where the other piece of hook-and-loop fastener is. Now, when the door needs to stay open, just fasten the two parts together.

Don Roesler, Ottawa, Illinois

Your Toast is Ready!

*O*ur toaster sits directly under the smoke detector. I've heard many folks complain that they are tired of the smoke alarm indicating that their toast is ready.

A simple solution is offered by Kidde Corporation. I replaced my factory-supplied smoke detector with the Kidde product that has a hush button. When we start up our toaster each morning, we push the hush button and get seven minutes with no alarms. The detector does chirp about every 30 seconds to remind us of its inactive state. After seven minutes, it returns to normal operation.

The smoke detectors come in both 9-volt battery and 120-volt AC (hard-wired) models. The battery version sells for less than $15 at most hardware retailers.

Walter Roeske, Mebane, North Carolina

SANITATION
DOORS, HATCHES
& HANDLES
CLEANING, PROTECTING
TOOLS
DEVICES & GADGETS
DIVABILITY

SAFETY

APPLIANCES
MAINTENANCE
AUTOMOTIVE
IN CAMP
SYSTEMS
STORAGE
TOWING
ACCESSORIES

A Helping Hand

We had a partially disabled friend who needed help to get into our motorhome. An assist bar next to the door seemed to be what was needed. We wanted to install one of those that folded back against the side of the coach when not in use. But, with our awning bar in the way, it couldn't be used.

Instead we found a grab bar, which is made to assist a person in and out of a bathtub. Made of steel, it is very sturdy, and you can grab it at almost any height. The grab bar can be purchased at any hardware store or home center for a lot less money than the fold-away type.

To install the bar, drill short pilot holes for the mounting screws into the wood frame that surrounds the door opening (behind the fiberglass or aluminum side wall). If you are not sure where the frame is, contact your motorhome manufacturer. Squirt silicone sealer into each screw hole before mounting to keep the area waterproof.

George Olmstead, Huron, South Dakota

A Key Answer

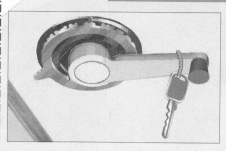

At one time or another, most RVers have forgotten to lower the crank-up TV antenna. A sure cure is to use a two-part key chain. Keep the ignition key on one part and the rest of the keys on the other. Now, when raising the antenna, hang the ignition-key part of the key chain on the crank handle.

Deryle Schlier, Fridley, Minnesota

CLOSEUPS ◆ CLOSEUPS ◆ CLOSEUPS ◆

Be Warned

A large-size orange-colored detergent jug can be an excellent safety-warning device when set at the rear of a stopped vehicle during the day or night. For greater nighttime visibility, wrap a strip or two of reflective tape around the jug. When well-rinsed, it can be filled with water or sand to keep it stable. The use of several of these jugs will provide even greater protection, using one in front and one or two at the rear.

Delilah Houseworth, Eagle Harbor, Michigan

CLOSEUPS ◆ CLOSEUPS ◆ CLOSEUPS ◆

CLOSEUPS ◆ CLOSEUPS ◆ CLOSEUPS ◆

Another Clothespin Reminder

I have taken the "clothespin reminder on the gearshift for your antenna" one step further. I put a mini-clothespin on our refrigerator's sliding switch. When we pull into a gas station I always remember to turn off the LP-gas to the refrigerator. But too many times, as we were pulling into our campsite at night, I'd realize that I had forgotten to turn the LP-gas back on.

Now I just hook the clothespin on my clothes in a conspicuous and/or annoying spot, and I remember to turn the LP-gas back on as we're leaving the gas station.

Connie Smith, North Canton, Ohio

CLOSEUPS ◆ CLOSEUPS ◆ CLOSEUPS ◆

Anybody Seen Our Heater Cover?

After losing our water heater's cover in a desert windstorm, we discovered the small clip holding the cover in place had flipped sideways during the last time we washed our fifth-wheel.

Now when we walk through campgrounds and rest stops, we notice that many RVs don't have the clip turned horizontally and snapped down to hold it securely. Checking this before leaving your RV site could save you the high cost of a new cover.

Bonnie Maus, Livingston, Texas

CHEAP FLASHER

Flasher

Trailer umbilical cord

Although there are expensive gadgets on the market to provide emergency lighting when your trailer must be left along the highway, there's a very inexpensive and easy method to provide flashing lights. Either carry an extra heavy-duty emergency flasher or simply borrow the one in your existing tow-vehicle fuse panel (it must have two prongs). Assuming that your trailer's umbilical-cord plug is wired using the industry-standard seven-way schematic, just insert the two-pronged flasher into the two slots as shown. The trailer battery supplies the 12-volt DC power. Your trailer's clearance and tail-lights will flash like Christmas lights. The flashing lights also make a good locating "device" for late arriving guests, especially if you're camped in a primitive area.
VIRGIL E. GAUL, WEST COVINA, CALIFORNIA

BRIGHT IDEA

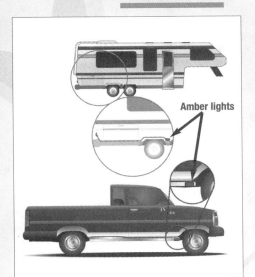

Amber lights

For obvious safety reasons, I mounted an amber light at the front corner of the aluminum running boards on my pickup. In this position — and wired to the front turn signals — the light flashes and reflects off the bright aluminum when the turn signals are used. This gives other drivers more notice of an intended turn.

I mounted an additional amber light in the middle of the molded fender cover on each side of the trailer. These lights are connected to the brake and turn-signal lights in the rear, and the wire is concealed along the edge of the aluminum siding behind the fender covers.
DICK MEUNIER, LA SALLE, ONTARIO

CHILD IN CAPTIVITY

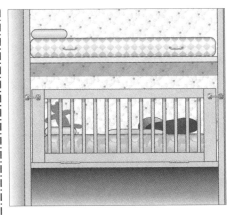

Like so many young families with children, we purchased a double-bunk style trailer, but we faced a problem when our 7-month old started camping. We needed a safe way to keep him in the bottom bunk without falling out. A folding gate would work, but we wanted something more permanent. I fabricated a wood frame from 1 × 3-inch pine and used ⅜-inch dowels for spindles. The frame looked much like his crib sides. Two hinges allow the frame to swing down and two-barrel bolts keep the gate safely closed. The total cost of the project was less than $20. The dowels should be close enough so that an adult's fist cannot get through the space. The height of the gate should be shorter than the dimension from the floor the bottom of the gate so it will swing down. Make sure you use clean wood and that any stain or paint used is safe for children.
SCOTT W. SHAW, TONAWANDA, NEW YORK

HOLD IT!

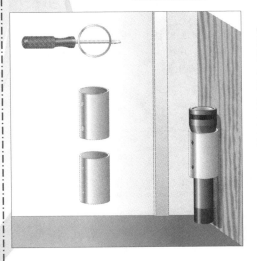

Ahandy holder for a flashlight can be easily made from a 2-inch section of PVC pipe. Drill two ¼-inch holes in the front side of the PVC for screwdriver access, and two smaller ones in back for the mounting screws. Fasten the pipe vertically to the side of a cabinet or wall, and slip the handle of the flashlight into the top opening. When it's mounted close to the entry door, near the steps, you don't have to enter your vehicle to get the flashlight when you want to use it outside.
RONALD VELDHUIZEN, NEW FRANKLIN, WISCONSIN

CLOSE IT

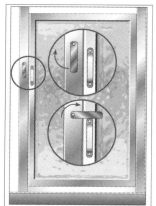

A magnetic strip along the opening edge of the shower door in our fifth-wheel latches the door. This is fine when parked, but it does not stay closed during travel. I took a brass nameplate from an old award (or you could get a small brass or chrome plate at a hardware store) and drilled a hole slightly larger than the sheet-metal screw I used to mount it on the RV shower door.

I mounted it in such a way that it hangs down without interfering with the door opening when we are parked. I also left enough slack in the snugness of the screw to let the plate rotate freely. I put a drop of epoxy glue on the screw shaft before inserting it to act as a lock washer and to prevent it from loosening.

When we get ready to travel, we simply rotate the brass plate across the front of the door, letting it rest on the shower-door handle. This has proven to be a fail-safe system during thousands of miles of travel.

Ray Joyner, Corvallis, Oregon

LOOSE LUG NUTS

I made alignment marks on each lug nut using white correction fluid, which can be found anywhere office supplies are sold. Now, with a quick look, I can tell if any of the lug nuts have backed off and loosened.

Dean Cowdin, Murray, Utah

KINGPIN NOODLE

We have a fifth-wheel and are always worried about someone hitting the kingpin while we're parked. We've tried many protective devices, but nothing really worked well. One day, while heading to the beach, I noticed that my son's swim noodle was a perfect fit on the kingpin. They are inexpensive, come in bright colors and work just fine.

Dan Pederson, Fargo, North Dakota

EXTEND YOUR STEP

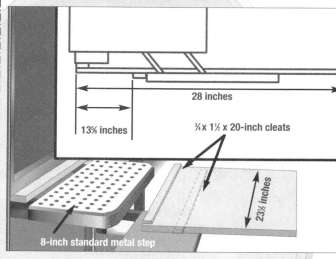

28 inches

13⅝ inches

¾ x 1½ x 20-inch cleats

23½ inches

8-inch standard metal step

My wife has very bad arthritis and needed a larger area to step on when entering or leaving our RV. I made this step extension that works beautifully. It is very easy and fast to attach or remove. It slides over the bottom step and is held in place by its own weight. It does not slip in any way and is strong enough to support a heavier person.

Cut the extension step from ¾-inch plywood to the dimensions shown in the diagram. Although RV steps are fairly uniform, measure the inside opening of your RV steps to confirm the exact width. Mount two ¾ × 1½-inch cleats. Cover the top surface with weather-proof carpet and you're ready to slide the extension step into place. Once in place, pull out slightly so that the bottom cleat is snug against the back side of the step. The back (top) cleat rests against the bottom side of the frame to hold the step extension level. The size of both cleats can be adjusted to fit any RV.

George Bostwick, Hood River, Oregon

CHIP AND THEFT RELIEF

The paint on the bottom of our LP-gas cylinders and their mounting plate was always getting chipped. After repainting the surfaces repeatedly, I took a scrap piece of heavy rubber pickup bedliner and cut it to fit the rack that houses the cylinders on the A-frame of my trailer. I also drilled a hole in the hold-down assembly, so I can now lock it to the mounting hardware.

A.P. Moreau Jr., Benbrook, Texas

FLASHLIGHT HOLSTER

Every RVer needs a flashlight on-board, and most have them. But how many owners have quick access to these useful tools? To make sure my 4D-cell Maglite is always handy, I built a nice-looking "holster" that's attached to the wall. The flashlight holder was made using ½-inch-thick oak plywood and stained to match the wood in our rig. If you want the holder to have a more finished look, you can have the wood edge banded. Measurements of the holder will be dependent on the size of flashlight you plan on using.

ED BERGMAN, PRESCOTT, ARIZONA

LP-GAS CYLINDER LOCK

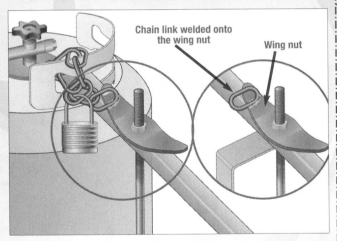

Chain link welded onto the wing nut

Wing nut

Like many trailer owners who reside in snow country, I prefer to store my rig during the winter in a facility with a more temperate climate, many miles from my home. Having heard of cases where the LP-gas cylinders have been stolen from stored trailers, I decided to make things as difficult as possible for would-be thieves. I had a chain link welded to the end of the big wing nut that secures the cylinders into position on the trailer A-frame. I then threaded a short length of chain through the link and the valve guard on the top of the cylinder and attached a padlock. The wing nut is now virtually impossible to turn. Make sure the other end of the long threaded rod is tack welded to the baseplate.

DIRK P. WOESTENBURG, CHESTER, CALIFORNIA

HIGH VISION

Ihave a Class C motorhome with a basement, which is great, but the coach windows are too high for the driver to use as an aid in maneuvering, especially when making turns. I solved the problem by using one of the wide-angle lenses that are normally attached to the rear windows of vans and motorhomes. I attached the lens to the front edge of the right-front coach window and now I can see the road to the right and tell when it is safe to proceed.

THOMAS R. CLEM SR., SILVER SPRING, MARYLAND

LADDER GRIP

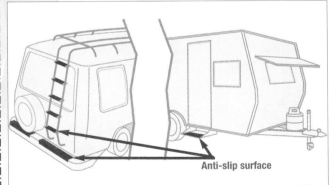

Anti-slip surface

Ilearned from experience when my foot slipped while climbing the outside ladder on my RV. It was wet, and I almost fell. Obviously, this can cause serious injury. I found an effective way to make my ladder safer. I use a product called Anti-Slip Surfacing, which is a long-wearing grip surface that has adhesive backing. The material can be cut into any size and it conforms to irregular surfaces; just peel off the backing and stick it on. It provides safe footing for my ladder, steps, a section of the rear bumper and on portions of the roof (do not use on rubber roofs). This stuff can be used just about any place where additional grip is needed.

RUTH L. COBES, ZEPHYR HILLS, FLORIDA

KIDDIE SAFETY

Ispent many a day trying to figure out how to build a safety rail on the two bunk beds for our small kids in our motorhome. The hardest part was figuring out how to make something safe that would require little or no alteration to the motorhome.

Finally, I discovered that a bed rail, something most people with little kids already own, could be modified to fit on the bunk beds in the coach. The installation of the bed rails requires no alteration to the motorhome, and the rails still can be used on the beds at home.

I used Fisher-Price bed rails that have metal bars. I simply measured the total length needed for the bed rail to cover the opening in the bunk bed, and cut it to fit that opening. Once I cut the rails, I then used a short length of coated wire to bunch the excess fabric covering at one end of the bed rail.

Now when we go camping, we feel quite safe having our two small children use the bunks. We do not have to worry about having them roll out of bed in the middle of the night. If the kids need to get out of bed, it is easy for an adult to drop the rail down, as can be done with the Fisher-Price model.

This has worked well for us. To make sure that the kids understand they are not to climb out of bed on their own, we constantly remind them of the dangers of falling out of the bunks.

KEVIN ARATA, FORT LEAVENWORTH, KANSAS

PIEZOELECTRIC LIGHTER

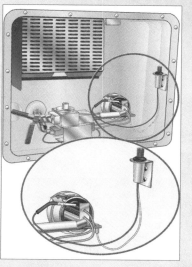

In order to eliminate the use of butane lighters or matches to light the water-heater pilot, I bought a piezoelectric lighter kit from Wal-Mart for $9.95 and installed it myself. I mounted the push-button assembly by using self-tapping screws (Pop rivets will also work) and attaching it approximately 3 inches down from the top, on the right side of the water-heater casing. Make sure the cover clears the button assembly before making the final attachment. I then loosened the pilot bracket and attached the white (ground) wire to the screw using an eye-type terminal; the other end of this wire was connected to the push-button assembly using a spade terminal.

Next, the screw at the top of the burner tube that holds the burner/pilot assembly was removed and a 2½-inch piece of galvanized plumber's tape was installed under the screw and tightened. The piezoelectric electrode bracket was attached to the plumber's tape (using two small nuts, bolts and washers), which was bent so that the electrode was within ⅛ to ⁷⁄₁₆ inch from the end of the pilot gas tube. The excess electrode wire was cut to fit. The black wire (positive) was pushed onto the end of the electrode and the plastic sleeve was installed next. This wire was then routed, away from heat sources, to the push-button assembly.

LARRY DRAWYOR, PRUDENVILLE, MICHIGAN

HOW TO BE WEB-FREE

*S*piders must love the odor of LP-gas; they always seem to build their webs in and around the RV flue and appliance burners, such as the refrigerator and water heater. Sometimes when you least expect it, the burners won't light.

My solution is very inexpensive. Just put some mothballs in an old sock, tie it closed, and place one in each compartment where an LP-gas appliance is located. It keeps the area spider- and, naturally, web-free.

RONALD ZINKL, KIRKWOOD, MISSOURI

BUZZ OFF

*O*n one occasion, we were camping in the Chilcotin area of British Columbia, Canada. The mosquitoes were so bad we couldn't comfortably sit outside. My friend said that if the wind came up to 5 mph or so, the mosquitoes would go away. My wife suggested we put an electric fan (ours had a 12-inch diameter) on a chair about 8 feet from where we were sitting to blow them away. To our surprise, it worked and we could sit outside mosquito-free.

JIM ALLEN, DELTA, BRITISH COLUMBIA

MAT IT

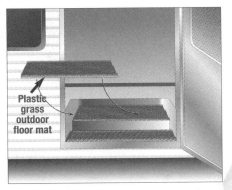

Plastic grass outdoor floor mat

I purchased a plastic grass outdoor floor mat that matched the RV's interior decor. The mat was cut in half and fitted on each step. They are very easy to shake clean or wash, and the rubber backing keeps the mat from slipping.

ARLENE CHIAROLANZIO, FLORHAM PARK, NEW JERSEY

GOOD REFLECTIONS

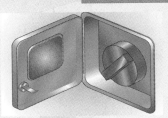

For added nighttime safety during a breakdown, attach a piece of reflector tape or a reflector with pressure-sensitive adhesive on the back to the inside of a fuel filler or power cord door. When pulled over, simply open the door and the oncoming vehicles will be able to safely see you from a good distance.

MARLON MILLER, YUTAN, NEBRASKA

JUST IN CASE

When my wife and I travel, we make sure that we carry copies of our medication schedules in case of emergencies.

Years ago, we prepared the format, and it contains names, addresses and telephone numbers (both ours and our home doctors'). The medication section is in columnar form, listing the medication name, strength, which days taken, usage per day and frequency. The schedule could be saved on a computer, but, in any event, must be promptly updated.

When the paramedics arrive, or when you find yourself in the emergency room, that is not the time to engage in a game of 20 questions!

JAMES KUCABA, ORANGE, CALIFORNIA

LOW-COST PROTECTION

A quick-and-easy way to protect your fifth-wheel from being stolen is to wrap and padlock a short piece of chain around the kingpin. It's not foolproof, but will make it harder for the thief to make a quick getaway.

WILLIAM WRIGHT, SANTA ROSA, CALIFORNIA

SAFE IS BETTER

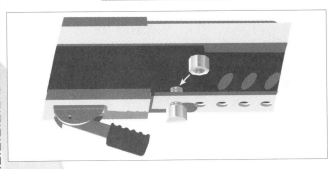

To prevent damage and/or injury from my awning's adjusting arm, I insert a $\frac{3}{16} \times \frac{3}{4}$-inch bolt with a wing nut in the next hole (after the handle), once the awning is out.

If a child or an inquisitive adult should pull the handle, the awning arm will drop only to the next hole and not all the way down, which might cause trouble. It is better to be safe than sorry, and it's very inexpensive for the peace of mind it brings.

RAYMOND PEETS, POUGHKEEPSIE, NEW YORK

RISE TO NEW HEIGHTS, SAFELY

Climbing up ladders installed on motorhomes is, at best, a chancy enterprise. With the addition of a little moisture from rain, dew or water from cleaning, the rear bumper can become hazardous when it is that final (or first) step. Placing a strip or two of adhesive nonskid tape beneath the ladder on the bumper makes for a great deal more safety.

DANIEL DOLAN JR., LAYTON, UTAH

SECURE CYLINDERS

When traveling, we keep the LP-gas cylinders and the gas regulator for our portable grill locked under the grill's cover. To protect them and the grill from damage, I slip the cylinders, with the regulator attached, into sleeves cut from an old sweatshirt. The cuff ends of the sleeves fit snugly around the cylinders and keep them from moving around under the grill's cover.

ARTHUR HOFF, NAUGATUCK, CONNECTICUT

SPARE THE ROD & SPOIL THE STORAGE

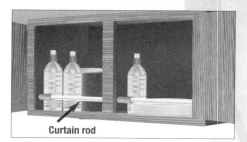

Curtain rod

We find that expandable curtain rods are perfect for holding items in space while on the road. Just push things as far back in the cupboard as they will go, position an expandable curtain rod inside the cupboard frame up against the items, and twist the rod to tighten it against the cupboard sides.

When settled at the campground, just loosen the rod and drop it down to the bottom of the cupboard.

DAVID MAULDIN, YARMOUTH, MAINE

SEE IT

This might be useful for those who have fifth-wheel trailers and use aftermarket hitch-pin stabilizer supports. Placing strips of reflective adhesive tape on the legs of the support greatly increases their nighttime visibility, and would help minimize running into the support by the vehicles of those who might choose to try and park under the fifth-wheel's front overhang.

DANIEL DOLAN, LAYTON, UTAH

SHELL WINDOW BASHING

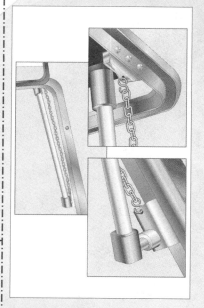

The second time I backed my tow vehicle into the garage — with the camper-shell's rear window in the up position — I bashed it good. This little encounter resulted in $250 damage to the window assembly. When relating the experience to my neighbor, I learned that he, too, had done the same thing, several times.

I discussed this with the man repairing my shell and was told that this type of collision is common. I fixed mine by drilling an ⅛-inch hole in both upper and lower gas-strut mounting brackets and connecting them with a light chain, purchased at a local hardware store. The chain is adjusted by removing the necessary number of links so that the door remains in the highest position without striking the garage structure. I used chains on both sides to equalize the stress on the door.

DIRK P. WOESTENBURG, CHESTER, CALIFORNIA

SIDE-VIEW LIGHTING

Side-view lighting is something every special-use vehicle should have, but is not on the menu from Detroit. I added right-side running lights to my pickup. Placed under the body at the passenger-side door, the light illuminates the road bed for anyone exiting, and solves the problem of "where is that wheel?" They are easily wired into the parking-light circuit, so no special switch is needed. To complete the solution of "where's that wheel," I installed a bike mirror onto the swing-away truck mirror bracket.

With this mirror aimed at the right rear wheel, and with the light for night vision, it is easy to stay out of trouble when making tight maneuvers on the "blind" side.

DON BURKLO, SOQUEL, CALIFORNIA

SIDE-VIEW ILLUMINATION

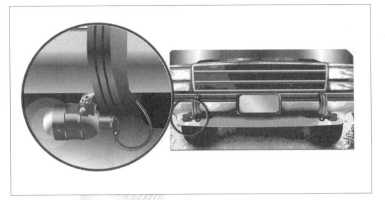

When maneuvering from a dark highway onto an even darker side road, I find it very difficult to see where to turn. My headlights do not illuminate the areas to the sides. I, therefore, would sometimes turn a little early or late and be forced to make a quick correction so as not to land in a ditch.

I decided to install high-intensity driving lights under the front bumper, one on each side, with the beam directed to the sides of the road. I mounted the pair of lights on the air dam just below the bumper. With each light I used a 2-inch angle bracket secured with two 3/16-inch Pop rivets. The wires from each lamp were routed through the tow-hook openings and along the junction of the bumper and the air dam, using 12-gauge stranded copper wire. One wire from each lamp was grounded to the frame at a convenient chassis point. The 12-volt DC lead was fed through an existing hole in the fender/wheel-well fairing, just in from of the left wheel, and terminated at an SPDT bat-handle switch installed on the turn-signal housing cover assembly. The 12-volt DC source wire, with inline fuse, was connected to the power-distribution panel on the right-side firewall. The bat-handle switch makes it easy to flip up or down as left or right turns are made.

There's enough room in the Snap-On directional cover cap to mount the switch. The wires were sheathed in spiral wire wrap and routed through the opening between the steering column and dash. Those who are electrically inclined could add a 12-volt DC red LED on the dash to remind them the lights are on. I purchased the switch and LED from RadioShack and the lights at Pep Boys; the lights cost $29 a set.

WARREN DAVIS, SCOTTSDALE, ARIZONA

REPLACING STOVE-GRATE GROMMETS

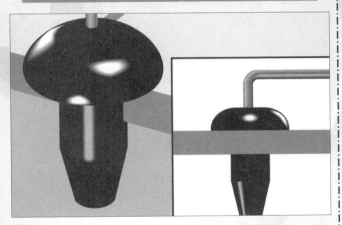

Some original-equipment stovetop grommets that hold the burner grates are not high enough and, due to the proximity of the cooking pans to the burners, allow the burners to overheat and cause the valves to stick open. We solved the problem by asking for discarded rubber air-valve-stem bottoms at our local tire store. The store manager was glad to give them to us. We then trimmed the sides to fit snugly in the holes in the rangetop. It is not necessary to trim the valve stems for length, as the long part will hang below the rangetop, where there is plenty of room. If you prefer new valve stems, they can be purchased at any auto-parts store.

PAUL AND JUNE BACHMAN, MINDEN, NEVADA

SWITCH COVER

Hook-and-loop

light fixture cover

After getting our new RV with a slideout, we noticed that the control switch was near a light switch. We were concerned that our grandchildren might accidentally use the wrong switch while turning the light on or off. To secure the slideout switch, I used a cover from a single-bulb, 12-volt DC light fixture and attached it to the wall with hook-and loop material. We applied the hook-and loop stick-back material to the cover and opposing spots on the wall. Not only does the look good, it's easy to do and gives me piece of mind.

ARLENE QUAKENLRISH, ALBANY, GEORGIA

SIGNAL SAFETY

In order to improve the safety of my motorhome while making wide turns or when switching lanes, I have made my front turn-signal lamps visible along the entire length of the rig. I added a waterproof aftermarket amber lamp assembly to the existing lens.

Simply remove the existing lens and secure the new "piggyback" unit to it. Place the new unit in the position you wish it to be, and mark on the old lens where the mounting holes of the new unit end up. Carefully drill these new mounting holes, and then fasten the two units together with appropriate-size bolts, nuts and washers. A spot of silicone sealer around the bolts should seal out any moisture.

Drill a 3/16-inch hole through the back of the old reflector, away from the bulb socket, and lengthen the wire from your new lamp and run it through the new hole. Then splice it to the existing wire, seal the hole and reinstall the old lens.

If your turn-signal lens does not provide a flat surface on the sides of the vehicle, just add the safety lamp to the side of the vehicle as close as possible to the existing lamps. Accessing the existing wiring should not be any more difficult than removing the stock lamp assembly and fishing the new conductor to the correct wire. In either case, don't forget to run a ground wire to the existing ground provision.

Frank Woythal, Andover, New York

STABLE LP-GAS

When we go camping, we usually carry an LP-gas barbecue grill, a, LP-gas cooker and an outside gas stove. We take three LP-gas cylinders, which I place in old milk crates. The cylinders fit snugly in the crates, making them easy to transport in the bed of our pickup. The crates also make the cylinders more stable when used on the ground close to the appliances. I remove the cylinders from the crates only to refill them. Milk crates can be purchased at most flea markets.

Gerald Cole, Temple, Georgia

YOU LIGHT UP MY LIFE

The steps on my new coach were, like everyone else's, black. At nighttime they proved very dangerous because they couldn't be seen. To solve this problem, I painted the front-edge abrasive strip white. The steps now look like they have a spotlight on them at night. People who have carpet-type covers over their steps can paint the exposed left and right step edges.

Donald Farrell, Canyon Lake, California

THEFT-DETERRENT GAME

Numerous magazines have bonafide advertisements in the back of each issue about becoming a locksmith. For $25 or less you can obtain lessons and a professional lock-pick tool with which, after a little practice, you can open most locked doors. Having our locked coach robbed, and later being informed by the police that the perpetrator merely picked the dead-bolt lock, I installed a dead-bolt scheme that will drive an amateur thief up the proverbial wall. Of course, you can never keep a professional from entering your RV or any other secured facility. The scenario is to install two additional dead-bolt locks, of different manufacturers, in conjunction with the existing factory-installed dead bolt.

Here's the strategy: Lock two of the dead-bolt locks on a random basis and leave the third one unlocked. In the sequence of picking the three dead bolts, one will always remain unknowingly locked. There are nine possible combinations, more than enough to frustrate any unwanted intruder. And additional serendipity is the psychological climate that is developed with the awesome display of door locks. Any perpetrator will definitely pass you by, looking for easier prey.

C.E. Caveness, Lakewood, California

STEPPING UP...AND DOWN

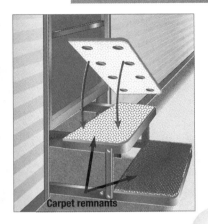
Carpet remnants

In order to eliminate slipping on our entry steps, and also to trap dust and mud, I designed simple removal step pads that are held in place with magnets. I purchased inexpensive carpet ends (or remnants) at a local carpet store. The cost is minimal and it is not difficult to find a color to match the rig's exterior. Then I purchased eight round magnets, ¼-inch thick and 1½ inches in diameter, for each step. After cutting the carpet to the exact measurement of the top surface of each step, I glued eight magnets to the underside of each newly cut step-pad. It's important to use waterproof adhesive; I used Goop.

To prevent the carpeting from unraveling, I applied (lightly) a flame from a propane torch to the edges. Once the adhesive hardens, the pads can be positioned on the steps. These pads provide a soft, cushioned, non-slip surface that will trap dirt and dust. When we hit the road, the pads are removed and stored just inside the door. When the pads become too soiled for long use, I take off the magnets and glue them to newly cut pads. The whole job costs around $12.
Dexter Blindbury, Chico, California

WARNING FLAGS

Many of us have Lynx Levelers for leveling our trailers. One of the sideline benefits is to use these "blocks" when I need roadside visibility protection in an emergency situation. I stack four (or more) behind my trailer and insert a small orange construction flag in the middle holes of the stacked levelers. The colors are highly visible and it is a stable platform. Any type of flag can be used, as long as it draws attention to the disabled vehicle. It doesn't take up any more room and we usually carry some small flags with us anyway.
Thomas Mucci, Elma, New York

SAFE IS GOOD

To keep children off our RV ladder, I cut a 28 × 30-inch piece of heavy-gauge vinyl and put snap fasteners on the top and bottom of each side. I then wrapped it around the ladder and snapped it together. There was little or no cost. The snaps are hooked in back, so the children cannot see them. The vinyl wrap has been on for a few years, and it works!
Lester Eisenbraun, Riverside, California

YOU WON'T GET A BANG OUT OF THIS

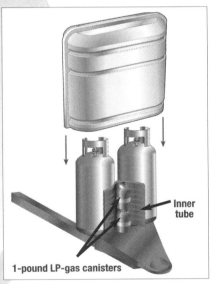
Inner tube
1-pound LP-gas canisters

RV owners should never grill or cook within an enclosed vehicle without proper ventilation. Yet it is quite common to see them unpack the picnic grill or stove from an enclosed storage area inside the RV. A safer place to store one or two of those 1-pound LP-gas cylinders is between the dual 30-pound LP-gas cylinders up front.

Obtain a discarded inner tube (ask at your local tire store) to cut and use as an insulator. Place one or two of the 1-pound LP-gas cylinders (OK to stack on the plastic cap) within the piece of inner tube and lower the LP-gas cylinders' cover. The cover will hold the extra LP-gas cylinders in place and the inner tube rubber will keep them from clanking against each other.
Vic Ferry, Waterford, Connecticut

APPLIANCES

A Bomb Shelter

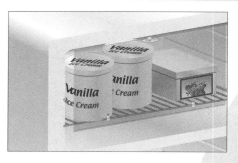

How many times after a day's drive do you open the freezer door, only to have your feet bombed by falling frozen food that's shifted?

To solve this problem and to save my feet, I attached a sheet of Plexiglas to the bottom shelf (rack) of the freezer, using two cable clamps that have the same inside diameter as the front bar on the shelf. These act as hinges to allow the Plexiglas to swing down.

The Plexiglas should be cut ⅛ inch short of touching the freezer top, and a twist-type latch placed so that the upper frame of the freezer acts as a stop for the latch. Don't cut the Plexiglas so it covers the entire front of the freezer. Allow space on the sides for cold air to circulate around items on the freezer door. The space below is left open for easy access to the ice-cube trays.

This installation does not waste any freezer space, as the freezer-door racks extend into the freezer area. The addition of this safety feature requires no holes or attachments to the freezer that could jeopardize its operation.

Fred Moldovan, Plantation, Florida

D E F R O S T I N G S E C R E T

Defrosting the freezer in our RV has never been high on our list of fun things to do. The ice at the back of the compartment has to be clobbered and pulverized into submission. But, the last time I defrosted the freezer, I dried out the compartment and taped a sheet of thin plastic across the rear, where the ice had formed. The plastic sheet was cut from a new, white trash bag. The frost and ice came back as it always has, but this time it formed on the plastic sheet instead of the freezer wall. Months later, when it was time to defrost again, I simply removed the frozen foods, pulled on the edge of the plastic sheet and all the ice and frost fell off. No pounding, no scraping, no kidding. Don't cover any of the fins; use the plastic on flat surfaces only.

Jim Cook, Livingston, Texas

Chill Out

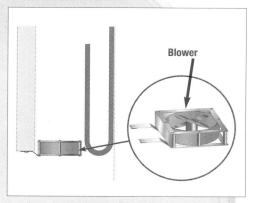

Blower

Those of us who travel extensively in our RVs have come to know that our refrigerators don't cool very well in extremely hot climates — usually due to lack of enough air moving past the outside cooling fins.

The solution? Simply mount any suitably sized computer blower that moves at least 100 cubic feet per minute (cfm) of air inside and above the lower exterior refrigerator compartment grille. Aim it upward toward the cooling fins, and plug it into a timer so you can set the on and off operating times. Be sure to attach a fan guard on each side of the blower. The blower can be mounted using very long screws attached to the corner mounting holes as support legs or mounted whatever way works for you.

Suitable and inexpensive ($5 to $20) blowers are made by various manufactures in a variety of voltages.

The 4-inch 65-cfm blowers sold by RadioShack and others are not suitable because they don't move enough air. Suitable 100-plus-cfm blowers are available from C&H Sales Company, 2176 E. Colorado Boulevard, Pasadena, California 91117; (800) 325-9465.

Robert Murphy, Washington, Utah

Editor's note: Do not attempt to fasten the fan to the back of the refrigerator. It can be done, but you are not going to know where it is safe. Dometic sells a fan kit for its refrigerator, which includes a diagram with a precise mounting location. It is activated by a temperature sensor mounted in the exhaust air stream.

H O W T O S U C K U P

An excellent way to clear your RV of all insects is to use a cordless vacuum cleaner, available anywhere small appliances are sold. Besides causing the insects to do a quick disappearing act, you avoid the messy spots that regular swatting leaves behind.

John Hash, Butte, Montana

GET IT HANDLED

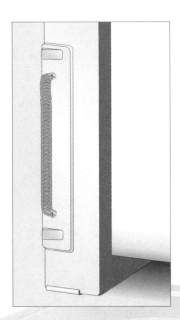

A quick fix for a broken spring in a Dometic refrigerator handle is to use an ⅛ × 2½-inch spring with loops on each end. These springs are available at local hardware stores and cost less than 50 cents each. The installation is easy; remove the handle screws and secure the spring. The refrigerator manufacturer sells only a complete handle assembly, which sells for approximately $15 at RV supply stores.

DALE R. REICH,
CEDARVILLE, MICHIGAN

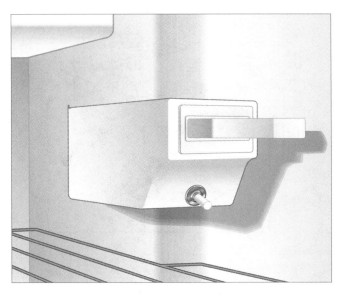

ON/OFF SWITCH FOR REFRIGERATOR LAMP

Upon returning home from camping trips, we usually remove the contents, defrost and clean the refrigerator. I didn't like the process of removing the refrigerator lamp and lens each time in order to leave the door open and not draw down the battery. There seemed to be no other way to de-energize the lamp without having to disconnect the battery.

Here's the fix: Purchase a small, single-pole toggle switch from RadioShack and install it on the lamp assembly. Take the hot wire (usually red) from the lamp socket and attach it to one side of the switch. Run a second wire from the other side of the switch back to the lamp socket. Now it's a simple process to flip the switch to turn the lamp off.

JAMES KEYLER, INDIANAPOLIS, INDIANA

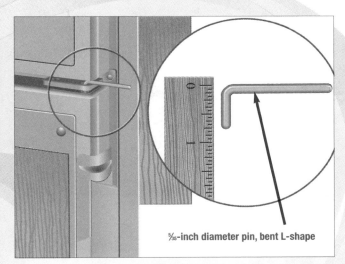

⁵⁄₃₅-inch diameter pin, bent L-shape

SIMPLE SAFETY LATCH

While my Dometic refrigerator is equipped with a safety latch in the handle, this latch failed on several occasions, making a real mess. I tried a couple of commercial latches from trailer-supply stores, but none would work in my situation because the refrigerator doors only extend about ¾-inch past the adjacent paneling. Since my refrigerator door can be set up to open and close from either side, I located a pin, about ³⁄₃₂-inch in diameter, bent it into an L-shape and fit it into the unused hinge mounting hole, extending into the hole in the door. The only disadvantage of this arrangement is that the freezer door must be opened first to remove the pin, but this is a small price to pay to insure that the door will remain closed while on the road.

GEORGE FORSELL, VENTURA, CALIFORNIA

PIE-PAN RECYCLING

*D*on't discard those round aluminum pie pans that come with a number of bakery items; use them as burner bibs. The ones that I use are 7¾ inches in diameter and have a 2-inch hole in the center. After making snips leaving ½- to ¾-inch flaps, I bend them back, enlarging the hole so that the pans fit around the burner. You may have to adjust the diameter of the pan, depending on your range. These pans make as good as, or even better, bibs than those available at the store.

CECIL SNYDER, TEMPLE TERRACE, FLORIDA

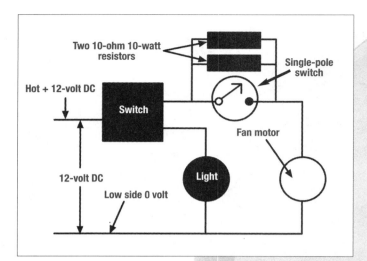

Two 10-ohm 10-watt resistors

Single-pole switch

Hot + 12-volt DC

Switch

Fan motor

Light

12-volt DC

Low side 0 volt

Tech-Tip Enhancement

Here's a great way to reduce the kitchen exhaust-fan noise. With the addition of a single-pole switch, you can have both high and low speeds. I purchased an appropriate switch, drilled a hole through the metal cover on the exhaust hood and installed the new switch. It also acts as a terminal block for the resistors.

KEN KLINGER, HACKETTSTOWN, NEW JERSEY

CLEANING, PROTECTING
TOOLS
DEVICES & GADGETS
LIVABILITY
SAFETY
APPLIANCES

MAINTENANCE

AUTOMOTIVE
IN CAMP
SYSTEMS
STORAGE
TOWING
ACCESSORIES
SANITATION
DOORS, HATCHES
& HANDLES

CLEAN WHEEL SKIDS

Over the years, I have had problems with the rear swivel wheel skids. There is so much dirt, sand and water thrown up into the bearings, it is a continuing problem keeping them clean and free. My solution was to install what I call a reverse flap.

It is made of light-gauge galvanized sheet metal, the type carried by hardware stores and furnace-repair places. I used two 4 × 6-inch pieces and shaped them myself. Although the metal is in the way when the wheel swivels 180 degrees, the metal just pushes out of the way and returns when the wheel swivels back.

B.C. McCrea, Port Angeles, Washington

A TEAR-RIFIC SOLUTION

Over the years I have been frustrated by what to do with annoying tears in tarps, car covers and awnings, among other things. I have come upon a great solution provided by our friends in the boating industry.

Buy a roll of 3-inch-wide by 15-foot long adhesive-backed Dacron sail repair tape. However, it is imperative that it be correctly applied.

First, measure the size of the tear and allow for an inch or so of overlap on each end. Then, cut the tape from the roll and, using your scissors, round off the ends. Next, expose the adhesive and place it over the tear. Finally, turn the item over and do the same to the other side.

I figure if it was designed to repair a sail used under adverse wind and water conditions, it will certainly hold up under RVing conditions.

David Jinks, Ventura, California

FREEING FREEZER FROST

We winter in Florida, where the humidity is high. Every time I open the freezer — frequently for ice cubes — it fills with humid air, which causes rapid frost build-up on all the inside surfaces. After about a month, the freezer compartment reduces in size by 20 to 30 percent. I have a quick-and-easy process for defrosting:

1. *Move the freezer contents to the refrigerator.*
2. *Turn off the refrigerator/freezer.*
3. *Lay a dry chamois cloth (the kind you use to wipe down your vehicle) flat in the bottom of the freezer compartment.*
4. *With the freezer door open, mount a small fan (6 inches or less) in the door opening and turn it on high. Use the door to hold the fan in position.*
5. *After the frost begins to melt, use a plastic spatula (metal can cause damage) to remove the frost. The drippings and chunks will be caught by the chamois. Use the spatula to remove the large chunks and slush from the upper shelves.*
6. *After most of the frost has been removed, take out the chamois and wring it out over the sink. Replace the chamois to catch the remainder of the drips.*
7. *Use the chamois or a sponge to remove food residue.*
8. *Wring out the chamois cloth and wipe down interior surfaces of the freezer, the exterior and door gaskets.*
9. *Return freezer foods from the refrigerator.*
10. *Turn on the refrigerator.*

Depending on the size of the freezer, the amount of frost, etc., the process should only take 20 to 30 minutes and the food does not have time to defrost.

Philip J. Harter, Colton, New York

DRAINING UNDER CONTROL

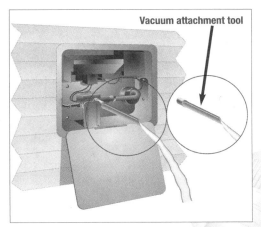

Vacuum attachment tool

We like to drain our hot-water tank often (it should be done at least once a year, according to the manufacturer, and even more often if equipped with an anode rod), but we don't like the water splashing all over the ground and onto the unit's components. I used to make a funnel out of a plastic milk carton or bleach container to direct the water. One day, while my wife was vacuuming, I got the idea to use the corner attachment to aid in the hot-water tank draining procedure. The round end of this long, plastic attachment (to connect to the vacuum hose) fits perfectly over the drain in the water heater. The attachment is installed after removing the plug. Some water will flow at first, but the greater flow will follow after opening the pressure-relief valve. This simple vacuuming tool allows us to direct the draining water to the ground without making a huge mess, and the attachment is always clean.

ROBERT CANO, SACRAMENTO, CALIFORNIA

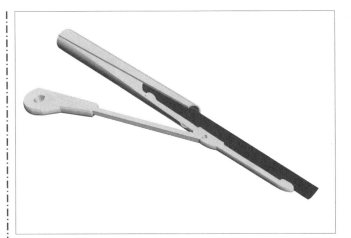

WELL, YOU CAN'T USE SUNTAN OIL!

Ultraviolet rays from the sun can rapidly deteriorate wind-shield-wiper blades, resulting in poor and unsafe vision when driving in the rain. This is especially true if the wiper blades are left unprotected when the motorhome is parked and/or in storage. A tidy, effective and inexpensive way to prolong the life of the blades is to cover them with the foam insulation that's made to insulate 1-inch water pipes.

These sections of round insulation are available in hardware stores and come partially slit lengthwise. Simply complete the lengthwise cut with a knife or scissors, cut a piece about 2 inches longer than the wiper blade, and slip it on.

As an added precaution during storage, I first wipe the blades down with a surface preservative designed for use with rubber, which means it contains no petroleum distillates.

When the blades look the least bit over the hill, even with improved preservative measures, they're cheap to replace, too. That's the safest course of action.

RICHARD RIVENES, PRESCOTT, ARIZONA

CLOSEUPS ◆ CLOSEUPS ◆ CLOSEUPS

FREE DISTILLED WATER

We have two deep-cycle batteries in our Airstream trailer and one in our tow vehicle, and they all need water now and then. We always use distilled water, but it's not always easy to find while on the road. For the last few years, I have been getting the water "free" from the tube that drains the condensation while the roof-mounted air conditioner is in use. This tube exits under the trailer so I just position a clean container so that the opening catches the dripping water. It actually fills rather quickly, and we never run out of water for our batteries.

THOMAS J. RONEY, GRAYLING, MICHIGAN

CLOSEUPS ◆ CLOSEUPS ◆ CLOSEUPS

EASY DEFROSTING

I hated defrosting my refrigerator because I had to take all the food out of the freezer and find a place to put everything and not let it spoil. One night I turned the control down to the least-cool setting. In the morning, the food in the freezer was still cold (even the ice cream). The ice had all fallen off, and I wiped the compartment up with a dry towel. I turned the control up, and I was back in business. Talk about easy! You could do this during the day instead of turning it down at night, if you prefer.

NANCY BECKMAN, SURPRISE, ARIZONA

PIVOT-PIN CLEAN UP

Regular maintenance of the fifth-wheel saddle is necessary for good operation. One place that needs to be serviced is where the 1½-inch-long pivot pin goes through the hole in the saddle. The pivot pin, according to the manufacturer, is impregnated with a lubricant to keep it moving freely and reduce rusting. If the hitch mostly remains outside in the truck, the metal inside the pivot-pin hole can rust.

This rust is difficult to clean with steel wool, or any light abrasive when done by hand. To get the rust out and clean the surface of the hole evenly and completely, I use a Lisle (brand) brake-cylinder hone no. 10000. It will adjust to 1½ inches and up to 2 inches for a little added pressure on the inside hole surface. Do not hone the inside surface of the pivot-pin hole more than just enough to get the rust off! You do not want to increase the clearance tolerance between the pivot pin and the inside of the hole. Just lightly clean away the surface rust using a light oil lube, such as WD-40 or TAL 5, on the surface being honed.

When clean and ready to reassemble, put a coating of grease on the pivot pin and in the pivot-pin hole. After reassembly, wipe away any excess grease to keep the area clean.

FRED HARRIMAN, ST. PETERSBURG, FLORIDA

ROOF BUFFING

Recently, while trying to clean the rubber roof on our fifth-wheel, we thought of a better way than getting down on our hands and knees to scrub the surface. We took a small floor buffer/scrubber up on the roof. We poured on the proper cleaning solution, turned on the machine and went to work. We started with a small area and worked our way from front to back, rinsing each section thoroughly. It worked better than we had thought. The roof is clean and our hands and knees do not hurt anymore. Always exercise caution when working on the roof; remember, it can get mighty slick up there.

JAMES AND PATRICIA RIEK, LANCASTER, WISCONSIN

FILLING BATTERY CELLS

In my motorhome, the 6-volt house batteries are on a slide-out tray. Unfortunately the tray will not slide out far enough to allow me to observe the cells in the rear-most battery without disconnecting the cables.

To easily service the cells, which I need to do, I purchased a small mirror on a telescoping wand and a syringe-style turkey baster (both available in hardware stores). The mirror allows me to observe the water level in each battery cell without disconnecting the cables. The baster allows me to fill all the cells, and greatly reduces spillage. This also works well for the chassis battery.

Keep the mirror and the baster in a small box near a jug of distilled water and you will be prepared to keep your batteries properly serviced with little effort.

RON THOMPSON, EPHRATA, WASHINGTON

CORROSION BUSTER

Recently, while cleaning the inside of the taillight lenses on my trailer, I noticed that corrosion was forming between the bulb base and socket. Direct-current connections plus moisture seem to add up to a green growth over time. I came up with a cleaning method that works most of the time, depending on conditions. Make sure there's no power to any of the fixtures. Spray the socket with Dow Bathroom Cleaner with Scrubbing Bubbles. Allow the cleaner to soak until it stops working (bubbles will subside). Rinse with plenty of clean water, and repeat the application of cleaner and rinsing again. A final rinse should be made with pure alcohol (gasline antifreeze works, too) to remove the water. The alcohol can be omitted if adequate air drying time is possible. The whole procedure works best if the socket is still damp.

PAUL J. WHITING, WALLED LAKE, MICHIGAN

TIRED OF SOGGY SOCKS

Tired of soggy socks when draining my trailer's six-gallon water heater, I assembled a very simple tank-draining device out of ¾-inch PVC pipe and fittings. Once I had all of the PVC pieces, the PVC cement, a tape measure, sandpaper and a saw, it only took about ten minutes to assemble the device .

You will want to make the overall length long enough to clear the sidewall of the trailer, and allow enough room to open and close the shut-off valve.

Close the hot-water faucets, remove the anode from the drain opening and quickly screw the device into place.

Place a bucket on the ground below the tank, and the water drains neatly into the bucket. When the bucket is full, close the valve, empty the bucket on your plants, then replace the bucket and finish draining the tank.

During this whole operation, make sure that the water heater is turned off.

JEFF ADAMS, SANTEE, CALIFORNIA

A SHOCKING SITUATION

*T*aking care of our vehicle batteries is something we all have to do and everybody knows how to service them, correct? Distilled water, gloves, eye protection, and so forth are involved in the maintenance of the batteries. But note where the batteries are located; usually in a very cramped area with thick wires preventing easy access. Unless your RV has a slideout tray, you may have to disconnect some or all of the wires and physically remove the batteries for maintenance.

This requires reaching into a very tight space with a wrench to loosen the battery posts' clamps. In the process of loosening these nuts, the servicer faces the very real hazard of creating a short circuit between the positive and negative posts. Although we're speaking of only 12 volts here, the short circuit can be hundreds of amps, enough to create a fantastic shower of sparks, enough to melt the wrench, and enough to make the rest of your day seem boring. This can be life-threatening, can cause a serious burn, or at the very least it could destroy your battery.

To minimize the chance of this occurring, wrap electrical tape around your wrench from one end to the other. Overlap the wraps to make sure the metal is completely covered. One full coverage of the wrench is usually sufficient.

DAN DOLAN, LAYTON, UTAH

BRIGHT BULBS

*R*V light bulbs often get old before their time, aggravated by infrequent use. A good tool for cleaning corroded light sockets is a wire brush made for cleaning gun barrels. A .30-caliber size is good for the larger tail/stop directional sockets. A .22-caliber size will handle the smaller side markers. The use of electrical contact cleaner (television tuner spray) will also help. When everything is working again, coat the contact surfaces with dielectric grease (comes in a little tube available at auto-parts and hardware stores). The grease will inhibit corrosion while passing the electrical current.

HERBERT A. SUTTON, TREASURE ISLAND, FLORIDA

TOOLS
DEVICES & GADGETS
LIVABILITY
SAFETY
APPLIANCES
MAINTENANCE

AUTOMOTIVE

IN CAMP
SYSTEMS
STORAGE
TOWING
ACCESSORIES
SANITATION
DOORS, HATCHES
& HANDLES
CLEANING, PROTECTING

DAYTIME RUNNING LIGHTS

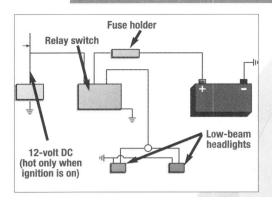

As a police officer, I believe that daytime running lights are useful. Only a few of the newer vehicles have daytime driving lights, and mine was not one of them. So I wired both of my vehicles to have automatic daytime running lights, which cost me only a couple of dollars. The system works with both quad and double headlight systems. All you need is a few feet of 14-gauge automotive wire, a fuse holder and fuse, one light relay and assorted wire connectors, all of which can be found in auto-parts stores or a RadioShack.

First, find a wire that is hot (12-volt DC positive) only when the ignition is on. Connect one end to that wire and the other end to the switch terminal on the relay. Second, tap off of the positive post of the battery (using an appropriate connector and the fuse holder) and attach that wire to the power terminal of the relay. Third, find the hot lead to one of the low-beam headlights and tap off of that wire and place the other end on the load terminal of the relay. When the key is on, the low beams will also be on. You still have to pull the headlight switch on for night driving so that the marker lights illuminate.
STEVEN R. SCOTT, SEEKONK, MASSACHUSETTS

DOUBLE YOUR PLEASURE

Years ago I chanced upon two older fellows who had found their early-model pickup had a crack in the distributor cap right across three consecutive plug wires. I used my knife to groove out the crack into a sort of "V" shape. Then I filled the void with a piece of chewing gum, which I melted with a match so that it ran smoothly into the groove. It sealed almost instantly, very firmly and their engine fired up on all cylinders. As we were in a very remote part of the Kootenays on a hunting trip, I'm sure the elderly hunters were pretty happy. I still carry a package of Wrigley's sticks to this day.
GLEN HAY, COQUITLAM, BRITISH COLUMBIA, CANADA

A GENERATOR TIP

Here's a tip for those who own an Onan AC Generator equipped with an oil filter. For ease of removal and installation, I do the following. Use a small piece of sandpaper to rough up the end of the filter and then smear a small amount of J-B Weld (Kwik Epoxy) on this roughed-up area.

Place a ¾-inch nut, centered on the filter end, into the epoxy. Let cure, and the filter will be easy to install and remove.
DARELE KENNEDY, HURRICANE, WEST VIRGINIA

BIG DRIP PAN

Periodic changing of fluid and filters will prolong the life of automatic transmissions. However, draining the fluid is usually messy, since most pans do not have drain plugs and the only way to remove the old fluid is to drop the pan. When the pan is broken loose from its seal, the fluid usually spills everywhere. Most drip pans found in auto-parts stores are too shallow to be effective in capturing the splashing fluid. To solve this problem, a simple, larger pan can be made from scrap ¼-inch plywood.

After cutting the appropriate size base, I tacked on 4-inch-tall sides. The wood joints were secured with wood glue. The interior of the wooden drip pan is lined with a sheet of clear plastic (available at garden and hardware stores). After changing the filter and fluid, the old fluid can then be poured into a container for proper disposal. I wipe off the liner with paper towels and save it for future use.
ARTHUR R. LEE, SANTA CRUZ, CALIFORNIA

FRONT-END PARANOIA

Last fall I purchased a new motorhome, and after driving it awhile, I was getting paranoid about having someone back into the front end of the coach. I've seen motorhomes with damaged front ends resulting from a traffic collision or hitting a deer, so I decided to find out about the possibility of having a custom bumper made for my coach.

I went to my local welder, and in about four hours he made the unit shown in the drawing from 1-inch-square steel tubing. He bent the tubing to the contour of the coach, and made custom brackets to fit existing bolt holes. Then I had the bumper custom-painted to match the coach, all for about $350. Considering the cost of repairing the front-end cap, I think the new bumper is cheap insurance.

GENE NELSON, MORA, MINNESOTA

DIESEL FILLER PIPE

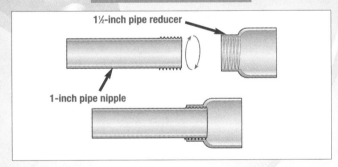

1½-inch pipe reducer

1-inch pipe nipple

Ford diesel-powered pickups have a small access hole on the fuel-filler tube. Many fuel stations only have large-diameter fuel-filler nozzles, which are used for 18-wheelers, on their diesel pumps. The accompanying illustration shows what I have designed and carry so I can use the larger nozzles when I run across them.

At your hardware store, buy a 1-inch pipe nipple and a 1½ inch pipe reducer, and screw the two together. The length of the nipple will depend on how far down your filler pipe is into the side of your vehicle.

ERNIE BREMER, LAKE CITY, OKLAHOMA

GOOD TO THE LAST DROP

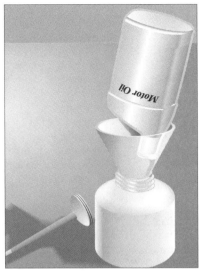

When adding oil to your engine, do not immediately discard the empty oil container. Instead, invert the container on a plastic funnel placed over your oil can and let it sit overnight. The remaining oil will drain down the walls of the container into your general-purpose oil can. A surprising amount of oil can be saved for future use.

ARTHUR LEE, SANTA CRUZ, CALIFORNIA

MAGIC NUMBERS

*H*aving trouble reading the numbers on your fan belt when it's time to replace it? Pour a small amount of automatic-transmission fluid (ATF) or power-steering fluid on the portion of the belt where you think the numbers are marked. Do not wipe off. The numbers will appear like magic. You'll no longer have to guess at the part numbers or try to measure the exact size of the belt, resulting in purchasing the wrong one and numerous runs to the auto parts store.

TED NOWELL, LONG BEACH, CALIFORNIA

KEEP THAT CAP

*T*o help you remember your fuel cap after you fuel up, place a piece of hook-and-loop fastener approximately 2 inches long on the inside of the fuel door or on the coach body, and the other part on the cap itself. When you remove the cap, stick the two surfaces together and you won't drive off and forget the cap. Works fine for me.

GERALD DOBIE, YUMA, ARIZONA

SAFE DIESEL SHUTDOWN

WESTBEND

Caterpillar and Cummins have strict guidelines for shutting down their expensive diesel engines. After running under a high load at road speeds, idle the engine for no less than three minutes before shutdown. Idling stabilizes the engine and normalizes the turbocharger's intercooler. Idle too long, and you wash lubrication from the cylinder walls; judging the proper time is therefore essential.

To observe the right time, we use a West Bend battery-operated kitchen timer (catalogue no. 4004). Just punch in three minutes on the timer and go about doing other tasks. When the timer runs out, it will beep until you shut it off. No more guessing. Need two minutes of warmup? Just set the timer!

The West Bend also looks good on the dash; it is white with HRS, MIN and SEC showing in the window. Timers can be purchased at any store selling kitchen utensils.
Robert Faulks, Apple Valley, California

OIL CATCHER SET-UP

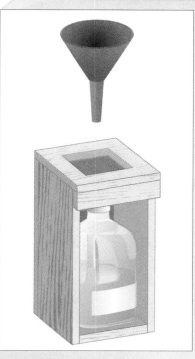

When changing motor oil, there is always the problem of properly disposing of the used oil. I like to put the oil into gallon milk jugs and transport them to the local discount auto store for disposal. Pouring the oil from the drain pan into the jug can be a tricky and messy task, especially if you are alone. To solve this problem, I constructed an open-front wood box that holds the milk jug and funnel snug and steady so that I can pour in the oil. To cap the filled jug, just lift the funnel and remove the jug. The box is now ready for the next jug.
David H. Schick, Lake Alfred, Florida

• CLOSEUPS • CLOSEUPS • CLOSEUPS •

HARD TO SEE

*A*s I've gotten older, in dim light it's become harder to find my transmission dipstick back in the dark recesses of my engine compartment. Even my oil dipstick seems to get lost in there. Once I get the dipstick out, there's the problem of finding the tube when I'm ready to replace it. My solution was to slip a piece of colored heat-shrink tubing over the end of the dipstick loop pull, making it easy to spot in low-light situations.

This solution will work for almost any dipstick that has a loop-type pull and virtually all tubes. It's easier and longer-lasting than painting them. Colored heat-shrink tubing is available in a variety of colors from RadioShack and most stores that sell electrical parts. Try to get heat-shrink that's close to the size of the dipstick handles and tube so it shrinks to a snug fit.
Tony Howard, Monroe, Washington

• CLOSEUPS • CLOSEUPS • CLOSEUPS •

HARD-LEARNED LESSON

*P*reparing for a trip to Alaska, we read numerous suggestions for protecting the front end of our diesel-pusher motorhome. We learned the hard way that you also have to protect the radiator in the rear.

A $3 piece of ¼-inch mesh wire screening to cover the bottom of the radiator in our coach would have prevented a rock from puncturing a hole in our radiator, which cost us $1,400. The screen can be held in place, secured to chassis components with screws and large fender washers or nylon wire ties as appropriate.

According to a number of mechanics we've talked to, this is a common occurrence for diesel pushers with rear or side radiators.
Robert Engelke, Upland, California

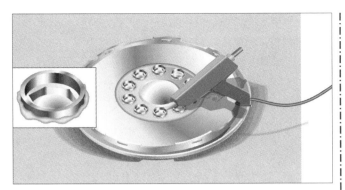

KEEP THOSE COVERS

After replacing a few lug-nut caps that fell out of my RV's stainless-steel wheel covers, I came up with a fool-proof way to retain those snap-in decorations.

Thoroughly clean and dry the back of the wheel cover, especially in the area of the tabs on the lug-nut covers. Flow a film of hot glue-gun adhesive over the tabs to permanently bond them in place.

I have not lost a single one since using this quick fix.
FRANK WOYTHAL, ANDOVER, NEW YORK

INSTANT CHROME

The plastic fixtures on my rig turn yellow and look old after about one year. Rather than discard them, I cover these fixtures with chrome detail tape that's available in auto-parts stores. All you have to do is cut the tape to fit, remove the backing and apply. The fixture will be better than new.
BRUCE J. MYERS, BEND, OREGON

NON-STICK DIRT

Getting tired of brake dust on your vehicle's chrome or aluminum wheels? I found an inexpensive solution. Remove the wheels and thoroughly clean them and the hub area. After everything is dry, apply a thin coat of non-stick cooking spray. Let the spray dry before reinstalling the wheels. The spray will withstand the high temperatures generated during braking. No more ugly mess!
ROBERT J. SMITH, ANTIGO, WISCONSIN

TWO LEAKY SITUATIONS

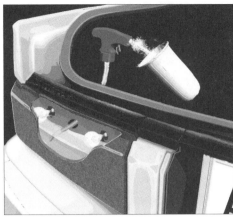

A neighbor said that the taillight was out in her dinghy vehicle, and I volunteered to check the bulb. When I looked through the red lens, I could see that the light assembly was half full of water. A leaking seal had allowed the water to enter the reflector chamber, shorting out the bulb.

Before I could change the bulb, it was necessary to rid the taillight assembly of the water. The assembly was held to the car by about eight screws from inside the trunk. Rather than take the taillight assembly apart, I borrowed one of my wife's spray-cleaner bottles. Removing the plastic pump and nozzle, I slipped the siphon-tube end down through the light-bulb socket hole and pumped the water out.

The bulb was then replaced and the light worked fine. To prevent a repeat of the problem, my neighbor will have the fixture seal changed.
ARTHUR LEE, SANTA CRUZ, CALIFORNIA

Editor's Note: Although it is always better to find and cure the source of this type of leak, if you can't, try drilling a tiny "weep" hole in the bottom edge of the lens.

After almost waterlogging my computer, GPS, inverter, carpet, dashboard and instruments in a downpour near St Joseph, Missouri, I spent the good days until spring cleaning and sealing the top of everything I could think of on my motorhome.

Summer travels that year didn't produce much rain, but in September I ran into a heavy rain in Montana and experienced more leaks.

It finally dawned on me that the front clearance lights might be the culprit. So I checked the sealant and it was good, but only on top — no sealant on the bottom. I removed, cleaned and resealed the lights and ran a bead around the outside of them. After coming through a huge storm in Wyoming this spring, there were no leaks.

I figured that the wind and water pressure at 55 to 60 mph was enough to force water "uphill" into the bottom of the lights. Evidently I was right because they don't leak any more — whether we're sitting or moving.
LUTHER STRUVE, POCATELLO, IDAHO

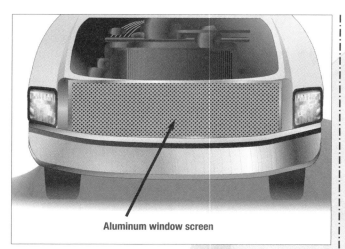

Aluminum window screen

SCREENING OUT BUGS

Last year, while we were traveling in Florida, I became concerned with the number of bugs that were filling up the radiator in my 1998 Dodge Ram Pickup. I was unable to find a satisfactory commercial bug screen. While visiting my brother, we found a 20 × 40-inch aluminum window screen (for homes) that fit perfectly in front of the radiator. All that's required for cleaning is to remove the screen and spray it down with a hose. Several sizes of window screen will work.
PETER N. GUZZETTA, MUSKEGO, WISCONSIN

STOP THAT LEAK

*W*hen an alarming spot of water and antifreeze appeared on my driveway every morning, I felt it was time to investigate. The radiator was full, but the plastic overflow reservoir was very low in fluid. When feeling the bottom of the reservoir, my fingers came away wet.

After draining the remaining fluid from the reservoir, I removed it for inspection. A small crack was visible near the bottom. Knowing that parts are costly, I decided to patch the reservoir. After cleaning the area of the crack, I laid a wide bead of epoxy glue over the crack. When this had dried, I smeared a heavy coating of nonhardening gasket seal over the epoxy. This was probably overkill, but I wanted to make sure there was no further leakage.

When the overflow tank was refilled, it confirmed that the repair was successful. After three months of driving, there has been no further leakage.
ARTHUR LEE, SANTA CRUZ, CALIFORNIA

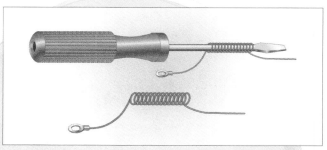

TIGHT WRAP

Here is a simple way to route wires neatly and leave enough wire for future repairs. Wrap the wire around a screwdriver or similar object tightly. When the wire is removed, it will resemble a coiled telephone cord. It will not dangle on objects, and many in inches of wire will be available when necessary.
JOE P. SIRECI, DREXEL HILL, PENNSYLVANIA

WHO YA CALLIN' A DIPSTICK?

*T*he dipsticks in two of my vehicles were extremely difficult to read when the motor oil was clean. To add contrast, I painted them. First, I cleaned the dipsticks by spraying them with starting fluid. Once clean, I sprayed them with 1,000-degree F heat-resistant paint. After several months, the paint is still sticking and the oil level is easily read.
BILL CHRISTENSEN, MONTESANO, WASHINGTON

SQUIRTING OIL FILTER

*T*hose of us who change our own oil know the frustrations of removing the filter and having the oil run down our arms. This is especially true when changing the filter when the engine is warm. I replace the pan plug after draining the oil and then with a sharp punch or ice pick, I make a small hole in the bottom of the filter and let the oil drain into the pan before removing.
DON SERVIS, WEED, CALIFORNIA

TAILLIGHT BRIGHTENER

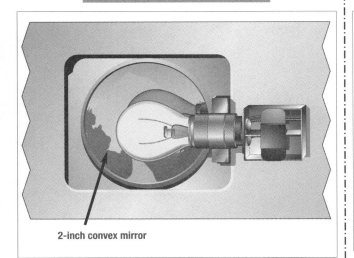

2-inch convex mirror

When the light from your taillight fixture starts to get dim, try mounting a 2-inch convex mirror behind the light bulb. The mirror I use is the same type designed to be placed on tow-vehicle sideview mirrors. This mirror reflects more light than aluminum foil. These 2-inch mirrors usually have self-sticking, two-sided tape on the backside and can be purchased at almost any RV supply store.

WILLIAM A. LIVINGSTON, FORT BRAGG, CALIFORNIA

WIPER BLOCK

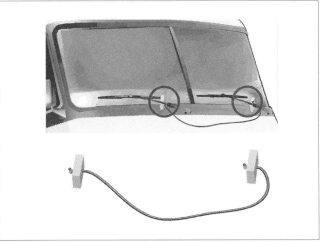

A vehicle's windshield-wiper blade's insert will become flattened or lose its shape when stored over a period of time, especially in hot weather. I found the blades to work better and last much longer when small blocks of wood are placed under the wiper arms to relieve the spring tension from the blades when the vehicle is not in use. A cord for easy handling and storage can connect the blocks. For my Ford E-350, I use 1 × 2-inch pieces of fir cut to about 3 inches long.

BILL BRYANT, MERRITT ISLAND, FLORIDA

DEVICES & GADGETS
LIVABILITY
SAFETY
APPLIANCES
MAINTENANCE
AUTOMOTIVE

IN CAMP

SYSTEMS
STORAGE
TOWING
ACCESSORIES
SANITATION
DOORS, HATCHES
& HANDLES
CLEANING, PROTECTING
TOOLS

A HANDY BOX

I made this handy box for carrying leveling boards and extra equipment or even firewood.

First I measured the width of the pickup bed and then measured the depth from the hitch to the rear of the pickup bed. I purchased a 1 × 6-inch exterior wood board and cut two pieces for the width and two pieces for the depth and fastened these together with deck screws.

I then cut two 3-inch triangles to fit two corners and installed them. I then purchased a piece of plastic lattice and cut it to fit the top. I framed the lattice with 1 × 2-inch wood, installed two hinges and a hasp to fasten the lid down.

In my case, I cut a "U" in the left rear side of the box for my electric cord and outlet. Paint the various parts before installing the assembly in the truck bed.

The kingpin easily clears the box as it slides into the hitch.
BOB ALEXANDER, INDIANOLA, IOWA

ASH SAVER

To keep hot coals and ashes from falling out of our grill while in use, during travel or in storage, I use a 16-inch oil drain pan to put an end to the problem.

I put the grill in the pan and spot-welded all three legs to the pan. Small holes could also be drilled in the pan and the legs wired in place.
GENE BOMKAMP, JANESVILLE, WISCONSIN

AWNING-SPRING ADJUSTMENT

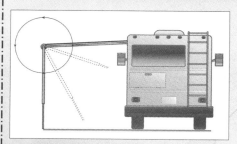

A simple way to tighten awning springs to snug the material can be done while in camp. Fully extend the awning. Remove the lower clamp on the awning leg and place it in the standing position. Take the front leg and lift toward the trailer, making a complete rotation back to the standing position. Repeat this procedure with the rear leg. I did this procedure with just one rotation on each leg and tightened the springs perfectly.
LEON TICE, SANTA BARBARA, CALIFORNIA

◆ CLOSEUPS ◆ CLOSEUPS ◆ CLOSEUPS ◆

A SIMPLE AWNING ADJUSTER

Each time we extend our exterior awning, we have to be sure that it is raised high enough to clear the entry door, and that it is pitched so rainwater will run off.

Once I found the correct height-adjusting hole in the awning arm that allowed for door clearance, I used a permanent-ink marker and drew an arrow on the inside of the support arm, pointing to the hole (mine was 10 holes from the bottom). I marked both arms at hole no. 10. No more counting. Now I just set one arm to the marked hole and the other two or three holes higher in order to clear the door and to create a pitch for rain runoff.
ARTHUR HOFF, NAUGATUCK, CONNECTICUT

◆ CLOSEUPS ◆ CLOSEUPS ◆ CLOSEUPS ◆

12-VOLT DC POWER SOURCE

If you plan on using a 12-volt DC submersible pump to transfer drinking water from a container to one's RV. For the power source, consider using a portable emergency battery. These routinely have a cigarette lighter plug as well as the jumper cables. Additional uses for this type of batt~~ could be remote operation of an air pump, television, 12-v~~ DC tools or even jump-starting a vehicle with a dead batter~~
DANIEL DOLAN, LAYTON, UTAH

An Illuminating Idea

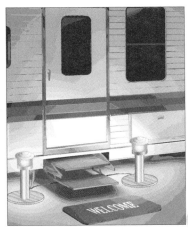

I wanted something quick and easy to use for lighting our motorhome's outside steps. While walking through a hardware store, I saw 12-volt DC light fixtures used to light up sidewalks and garden paths. I bought a pair and fashioned a base made of plywood for each one, large enough so that the lamps wouldn't easily tip over.

On our motorhome there is a switch by the entry door to turn on the basement-compartment lights. These lights can be individually turned off in each compartment, and I keep them turned off until I need them. I installed an outside receptacle right next to the steps and wired it to the basement-compartment light switch.

Now the lights are set up when we park, and when it gets dark we just flip the inside switch. Now we have entry lights that look nice, light the entry area and steps, but aren't high or bright enough to bother anyone.

RANDAL STRICKLIN, LIVINGSTON, TEXAS

A Clean Funnel

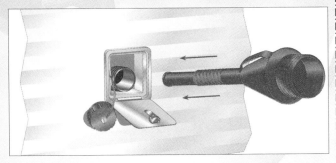

We spend a great amount of time in our fifth-wheel as dry campers. When it came time to add water from storage cans, we ran into some problems. The new water inlets have posed a challenge as they enter straight into the side of the trailer, causing wasted water.

I have found an easy, affordable solution — the Clean Funnel. It comes with a flexible spout that allows the easy entry into the water inlet of newer RVs. And it has a 1⅛-inch spout diameter, which allows for a quick flow of water into the tank. Additionally, these funnels come with screw-on caps on both ends to keep them clean for the next use.

JEFF WITTE, LAS CRUCES, NEW MEXICO

A Towel Dowel

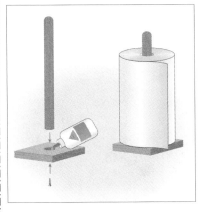

Instead of using regular paper napkins that constantly blow away in the wind, use a roll of paper towels at your picnic table. You can place them upright in a paper-towel holder easily assembled from a 6 × 6 × ¾-inch wood block (the base), with a 15-inch piece of old broomstick mounted to it.

Drill a hole the diameter of the broomstick, partway into the base, squirt in some wood glue and put in a wood screw from the bottom.

Remember to make the rod longer than the roll of paper towels, so the unit can be easily picked up.

RICH STILSON, HAMBURG, NEW YORK

◆ CLOSEUPS ◆ CLOSEUPS ◆ CLOSEUPS ◆

DIRT MITT

Rolling up the power cord and hose can sometimes be a real mess, especially if the site is on dirt and has become wet due to rain or spilled water. I use an oven mitten on one hand and feed the cable or hose through my fist. The dirt, gravel and water are cleaned away as the cable/hose is rolled into place for storage in my RV. When done, I shake out the mitt.
D.A. HENBEST, RIO RANCHO, NEW MEXICO

◆ CLOSEUPS ◆ CLOSEUPS ◆ CLOSEUPS ◆

BATHHOUSE BLUES

Tired of walking back from the bathhouse with wet towels and finding a place to hang them to dry? Use a chamois cloth, such as The Absorber (available at auto parts and RV shows). It absorbs water faster and you just ring it out and roll it back up into its handy container until next use. Also, replace the messy bar soap and wash cloth with liquid soap and a lathering puff. Makes those trips the showers, a hassle-free experience.
VICKI GORNY, STUART, FLORIDA

BE PET SMART

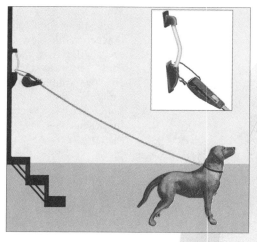

We travel with two small dogs, and after trying several ways to restrain them when we are out and about, I hit upon a very simple solution. Every recreational vehicle has an assist handle near the door. Take a spare nylon or plastic dog collar that has a snap buckle, and use it to attach an expandable leash to the handle. Then all you have to do is hook up your dog to the other end. Because of the height of the handle and the expandable nature of leashes, a dog doesn't get nearly as tangled as when on a normal tie-down. Because the leashes are always taut, dogs don't chew on them.

The length of the fully extended leash normally will not allow the dog to reach the road or the vehicles around us. If insects are not a problem, the RV door can be left open so the dogs can go in and out at will. They're now quiet around the motorhome; they don't annoy the neighbors; and they're safe.

This has proven to be a lot simpler than setting up elaborate miniature corrals, as many people do, or just letting our pets run free to harass the neighbors and be a danger to themselves. This may not work with large dogs, but it works very well for us.

CLAIRE RUSS, EDGEWATER, FLORIDA

BETTER FAUCET TEE

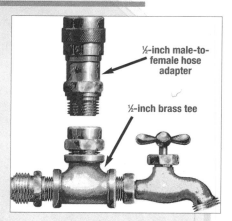

½-inch male-to-female hose adapter

½-inch brass tee

After having bent two commercial T-fittings used at campground water faucets to allow a second hose to be hooked up, I decided to assemble my own heavy-duty version. From a quality hardware store, I purchased a cast-brass ½-inch tee, a ½-inch male pipe-to-female hose adapter and a ½-inch male pipe-to-male hose adapter. Reuse the faucet from the old unit or purchase a new sill cock or boiler drain if you do not have an old one. Use pipe dope or Teflon tape when assembling the parts to prevent leaks. The cost, excluding the faucet, is about $10. Brass parts were used throughout to prevent rusting.

When staying in a campground with water on the site, I like to have the ability to connect a second hose to wash the truck, trailer or clean up around the RV.

PAUL J. WHITING, WALLED LAKE, MICHIGAN

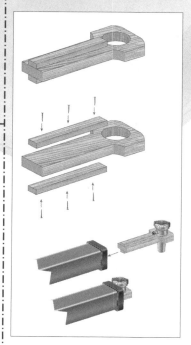

BUMPER FILTER HOLDER

Tired of seeing my water filter laying in the dirt and not wanting to drill into the side of our fifth-wheel in order to attach a mounting bracket, I made a hanger that fits into the end of my four-inch square bumper. All that is needed is a piece of 2 × 6-inch lumber about 20 inches long.

Cut a hole to fit the filter body in one end, and cut the board's other end to fit into the bumper opening. Add pieces top and bottom to make the board a snug fit in the bumper opening. Apply a coat of paint and the filter stays clean.

LESTER CHAN, VICTORIA, BRITISH COLUMBIA

CONFINE YOUR FILTER AND HOSE

I found an easy and permanent solution to containing the RV's water hose and filter. I used a clean 5-gallon bucket to hold the hose and filter when not in use. I cut a hole in the cover of the bucket to fit the bottom portion of the filter housing. After placing the filter housing in the opening, I sealed around it with silicone caulking to hold it in place. You should also drill a few holes around the sides of the bucket (near the top) to let moisture escape when the wet hoses are stored in the bucket. This will help the hoses dry and prevent mold from building up in the bucket while being stored.

This setup doesn't take up much space while traveling and when you get to your campsite, you just grab the bucket and you have everything ready to hook up your water.

KEN SUDDUTH, CATHAM, ILLINOIS

HANG OUT TO DRY

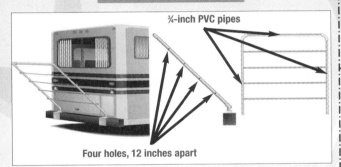

¾-inch PVC pipes

Four holes, 12 inches apart

We needed a place to hang our clothes to dry, without occupying a lot of space in camp. So we pieced together a break-down clothesline that attaches to the rear bumper of our trailer. I first cut three 5-foot-long sections of ¾-inch PVC conduit. Four holes, 12 inches apart, are drilled in two of the 5-foot sections of conduit. The three pieces of conduit are connected using two 90-degree elbows. The rope (you need around 25 feet) is strung through the holes in the two side pieces of conduit. The whole apparatus is attached to the bumper, using two handrail mounts designed for ¾-inch pipe and two 45-degree box connector elbows. The whole job can be accomplished in a few hours, and take down and set up requires only a few minutes. Make sure you leave a little slack in the rope so the conduit can be disconnected from the elbows. Now our clean clothes just blow in the wind, out of the way.

MICHAEL WILLARD, GREENFIELD CENTER, NEW YORK

DISH STOOL

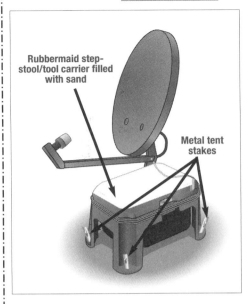

Rubbermaid step-stool/tool carrier filled with sand

Metal tent stakes

Here's an idea for those of you who don't want to mount your satellite dish to your RV roof. It's very simple. You take a Rubbermaid step-stool/tool carrier and fill it to the top with sand (it will be heavy, but not so heavy that you can't carry it).

Screw the dish onto the Rubbermaid, and then take four tent stakes (metal ones) and pound one through each leg of the stepstool and into the ground. The excess slack in the satellite wire can be wrapped around the container, or you can mount a coffee can on top of the Rubbermaid and wrap the wire on that. When it's time to move, take out the tent spikes, empty the sand and store the unit in your shower.

KRISTEN HENNUM, SEQUIM, WASHINGTON

COMPARTMENT LIGHTS

I have often found that while setting up camp after dark, I need a way to have a convenient light source, while still having both hands free. I found some porch/utility lights (each with their own on/off switch) at Wal-Mart for less than $6 each.

I wired them directly to the trailer battery using a 15-amp inline fuse, though they could probably be wired to any other convenient 12-volt source. I grounded the lights to the trailer frame and attached the lights to the compartment walls with double-sided tape.

Now, when I set up camp after dark, I have improved visibility and the use of both hands.

WARREN PETKOVSEK, LUMBERTON, TEXAS

DOUBLE YOUR PLEASURE!

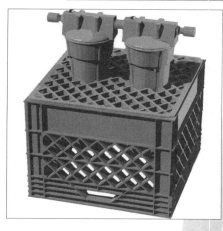

After trying some of the disposable RV water filters that are on the market and observing the replaceable cartridge types on other units, I decided to assemble my own version. I purchased two replaceable-cartridge filter assemblies, along with the necessary brass parts. I connected the two filter housings in series with a short nipple outlet-to-inlet. The open inlet end received a female hose-to-pipe thread fitting; the remaining outlet end received a pipe-thread-to-male-hose fitting. The fittings required adapters to match the diameters for size and to prevent leaks, and I used Teflon tape on all the threaded connections. All the fittings are brass to prevent rusting. Be careful not to overtighten the fittings into the plastic filter housings, which would strip the threads.

The first housing (coming from the water source) has a rust-and-sediment filter; the second contains a taste-and-odor element. From my experience, the woven rust-and-sediment element seems to provide better filtration than the paper element.

Two hoses are needed for the hookup: the regular long one, from the faucet, and a short one to the vehicle. The two filters are supported by inverting a plastic milk crate and cutting holes in the bottom to receive the filter housings. Be sure to sanitize the housings by rinsing with a bleach mixture, as you do with the rest of the water system, on initial use and at each filter change.

PAUL WHITING, WALLED LAKE, MICHIGAN

GIRL SCOUTING REVISITED

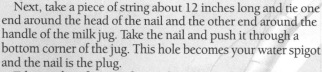

Milk jug

To save water when boondocking, I revert back to a handwashing station like the one I used when camping with my Girl Scout troop. All you need is an empty milk jug, a large nail, some light rope and an old nylon or net bag (like onions are stored in).

Tie a piece of the rope around the handle of the milk jug. This is used to tie the "handwasher" to your awning arm (or nearby tree branch), so make it a length that will give a comfortable height.

Next, take a piece of string about 12 inches long and tie one end around the head of the nail and the other end around the handle of the milk jug. Take the nail and push it through a bottom corner of the jug. This hole becomes your water spigot and the nail is the plug.

Take one leg of a pair of panty hose (or net bag) and place your bar of soap in the foot. Now tie the leg to the handle of the jug.

Now you are ready to fill the jug with water and tie it on your awning arm. When handwashing is needed, just pull the "plug" (nail) for a slow stream of water. Wet your hands and then soap them (right through the nylon) and rinse.

It is a very easy item to make and really conserves water when boondocking.

SUE McGARTLAND, STAFFORD, VIRGINIA

◆ CLOSEUPS ◆ CLOSEUPS ◆ CLOSEUPS ◆ CLOSEUPS ◆ CLOSEUPS ◆ CLOSEUPS ◆

DON'T BLOW IT

I spend the winters in southern Texas, in the Rio Grande Valley, and the wind never seems to stop. If the RV is pointed in the wrong direction, the wind wants (and usually succeeds) to blow out the water heater and/or the refrigerator pilot lights.

I found a 12-inch paint guide (they're sold anywhere that household paint is sold). It has a flat, thin blade with an attached handle. It is usually used while painting to keep you from slopping paint into unwanted areas. For our use, the blade was thin enough to fit into the opening between the water heater door/refrigerator vent door and the RV wall and not fall out. So when the RV was parked at the wrong angle (relative to the wind direction), the paint guide redirected the wind and kept the pilot lights from blowing out.

RICHARD PREVALLETT, LIVINGSTON, TEXAS

◆ CLOSEUPS ◆ CLOSEUPS ◆ CLOSEUPS ◆ CLOSEUPS ◆ CLOSEUPS ◆ CLOSEUPS ◆

Doggy Ramp

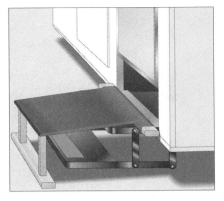

When we upgraded from a tent trailer to a motorhome, we found that our aging collie was unable to climb the steeper and higher entry steps. One trip of lifting her into the motorhome left us in need of a better way. The solution was to build a removable wood step that would not be as steep or slippery. I fastened 2 × 4-inch legs with a 2 × 4-inch base to a piece of ½-inch plywood using hinges. A piece of 1 × 2 was then fastened to the bottom rear edge to provide stability and to keep the unit from getting caught in the motorhome's steps if they were inadvertently retracted before the ramp was removed.

Indoor/outdoor carpet was stapled to the top of the plywood and around the back edge of the 1 × 2, which provides sure footing and prevents marring the sides of the motorhome. The legs fold over the top, at approximately 250 degrees, which permits storage in the flat area behind the passenger seat. A metal handle attached to the bottom of the front edge of the plywood makes for easier handling. The collie is no longer afraid to climb the steps, the schnauzer has an easier time and the larger area makes it easier for people to enter and exit, too.

RALPH FREDLUND, LAKEVILLE, MINNESOTA

F I R E   L O G S

When our family goes camping, everyone agrees that food tastes better over an open fire. We bring along our own fire-starter logs, which can be very easily made.

Save your empty paper-towel and toilet-paper cardboard rolls. Roll up old newspapers as tight as you can. Slide the rolled newspaper into the empty rolls. When starting your campfire, light the cardboard log and place it in the fire pit. It's easy to start and burns hot enough to ignite the rest of your wood. If you want to speed up the process, use lighter fluid on the logs. These fire-starters cost nothing, and they're fun for the kids to make.

DEAN CHRISTOFFEL, LE MARS, IOWA

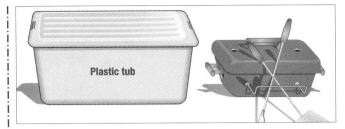

Plastic tub

Grill 'n Tub

Store your cooled-off outdoor grill and its accessories in a plastic tub with a snap-on lid. This makes it easy to carry everything needed around the campsite in one trip. But most importantly, it confines the dirt, grease and smell of the used grill to the inside of the plastic tub, not inside the RV storage compartment and its other contents. These plastic containers are very inexpensive and available at most discount stores.

ALLAN BLUESTONE, FOUNTAIN HILLS, ARIZONA

Hold It

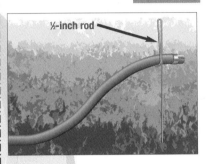

½-inch rod

I don't like to lay the end of my water hose on the ground when disconnecting and draining it. To help me, I bent a piece of ⅛-inch rod, which was purchased at a hardware store (stainless steel won't rust). Just stick the rod in the ground near the faucet and it's ready for use. I store it with the water hose.

ROY LARGE, LA PORTE, TEXAS

M A K E   A   T A B L E

Want a picnic table when there's none around? I have a good solution. If your RV has a table that's center-mounted on a length of pipe, buy another base (just like the one mounted on the floor of your RV) at an RV supply store. Mount it on a piece of ¾-inch plywood (I made mine 20 × 40 inches).

Take your table and pipe outside, mount it in the new base and you have your own picnic table.

CHARLIE MITCHELL, SURREY, BRITISH COLUMBIA

HEAVY LEGS

We use a portable sunshade while camping, but it cannot be set up in the wind. In order to make the sunshade more versatile, I devised a system to add enough weight to the four legs to keep the sunshade stable. The weights consist of four 1-liter soda bottles, four 12-inch sections of 1-inch plastic conduit pipe, four no. 2 screw-type eye hooks and half of a 60-pound bag of concrete mix.

I first cut a hole in the bottom of the liter bottle big enough to accommodate the 1-inch pipe (a hole saw works best). Measure the distance from the hole in the side of each leg used to attach the cover (with a hook). Drill a ¼-inch hole in the side of the bottle to match that measurement; cut off the tops of the bottles. Place the pipe inside the bottle and cover the bottom and side holes with duct tape to keep the concrete from flowing out. Pour the concrete mixture into the bottles, filling a quarter of the way at a time, tamping it to make sure the mixture is packed solid.

After the bottles are filled, remove the duct tape on the sides and screw in the eye hooks. Let the concrete set-up for 24 hours and cut the remaining plastic off. This makes an approximately 8-pound weight out of each bottle. In use, the legs of the sunshade fit into the pipes and the material attaches to the eye hooks. The pipes extend about 3 inches from the top, giving the user a handle to carry the weights. Now, the sunshade will stay in place, even in the wind.
STEVAN KELLY, SACRAMENTO, CALIFORNIA

LIGHTING THE WAY

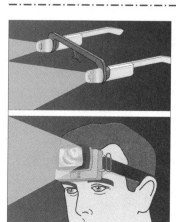

To help set up camp in the dark and leave your hands free, wear an eyeglass flashlight or a miner's headlamp as shown in the illustration. Both can be purchased from hardware or home center stores.
WILLIAM MCLAUGHLIN EAST PETERSBURG, PENNSYLVANIA

HI THERE!

Like many families who RV, when parked we like to display a sign with our family name and home state on it. We could never decide where to hang the sign, and once left it hanging on a tree three states away from home.

After walking around my trailer, I realized the perfect spot was to have an artistic friend paint our name and state right on the propane cover. It is always with us, and when parked at the site, all of our fellow RVers can see who we are and where we are from.
JOHN HETLYN, MAYBROOK, NEW YORK

HOOK & LINE

Before some of the clotheslines that are on the market came out, we came up with an idea for one to work on our fifth-wheel. We took a small piece of steel rod and bent a hook in one end and welded a small piece on the other end to form a tee. The rod was covered with plastic tubing and a clothesline cord was tied to the hook on the two pieces. The cord is just long enough to reach from one side of the fifth-wheel to the other. Tension holds the hooks on the side of the fifth-wheel. It takes up very little space when in storage and since the clothes are hung under the front section of the fifth-wheel, we don't have to worry about leaving the clothes on the line when we hook up or when it rains.
KATHERINE STEVENSON, CAMDEN, ARKANSAS

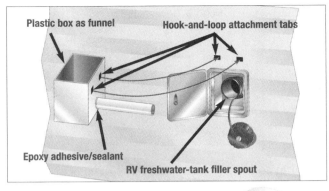

Plastic box as funnel

Hook-and-loop attachment tabs

Epoxy adhesive/sealant

RV freshwater-tank filler spout

IMPROVED FILLER SPOUT

Grab a small plastic box (approximately 4 × 5 × 7 inches), a 6-inch piece of plastic hose and some hook-and-loop tape and you have a simple solution for pouring water into your fresh-water tank's filler spout. Simply cut a hole, the same diameter as the outside of the plastic hose, near the bottom of the box, insert the hose and seal it in place with epoxy cement.

Attach the hook-and-loop tape near the top of the box (on the same sidewall where the plastic hose is), and on the sidewall of your RV above the filler spout. The hose will be inserted into the water-filler spout and the box will secure itself with the hook-and-loop tape to the side of the RV.

This is a quick simple method of adding water to your water tank.

DOUGLAS KOCH, MILWAUKEE, WISCONSIN

◆ CLOSEUPS ◆ CLOSEUPS ◆ CLOSEUPS ◆

HOT-WATER TANK TOOL

About two years ago I had the RV service department replace the anode rod in my water heater. I did not pay attention, and when I recently replaced the rod again, I found that there was a large accumulation of a white-paste-type of grit in the bottom of the tank. To help clean the tank during draining, I took a long piece (15 inches or so) of one strand out of Romex wire and put a curl on one end. You will have to experiment to get the curl right. While the water is draining out of the tank, I use the wire to scrape all of the contents out of the bottom of the tank. I occasionally put my finger in the hole to see if any grit remained near the outlet. Make sure you shut off the outside water faucet or turn off the demand pump before attempting to remove the anode rod. Failure to do so will leave you looking like a great speckled bird (trust me).

RICHARD PREVALLET, LIVINGSTON, TEXAS

QUICK CHECK FOR SHORE POWER

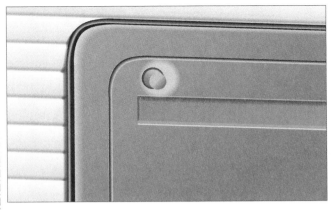

When connecting shore power to my trailer, it has been necessary to go inside the trailer and turn on a 120-volt AC device to determine that power is, in fact, available.

To alleviate this situation, I installed a small 120-volt AC neon indicator lamp on the refrigerator-vent door and wired it to the 120-volt AC outlet that is in the refrigerator compartment. I chose a green lamp (RadioShack no. 272-708).

Now it is a simple matter of just glancing at the indicator to determine that power is active into the RV. When it's necessary to remove the vent door, it is a simple process of reaching in and unplugging the indicator line, and then completely removing the door.

It is best to install the indicator lamp on the driver's side, since most campgrounds have their power terminals on that side. If your RV does not have the refrigerator on the driver's side, mount the indicator in another position on the driver's side.

JAMES KEYLER, INDIANAPOLIS, INDIANA

◆ CLOSEUPS ◆ CLOSEUPS ◆ CLOSEUPS ◆

HOT WATER ON TAP

When our kids were younger, we had a pop-up tent camper and went camping every weekend we could during the summer. Being normal, healthy kids, they caught frogs, played in the dirt and enjoyed the great outdoors. I was constantly heating water to wash someone or something until I remembered my airpot. I would heat water as soon as we set up camp and put it in the airpot. We'd have hot water for hours at the press of a button.

RITA DANIELS, SUNDANCE, WYOMING

ON THE LEVEL

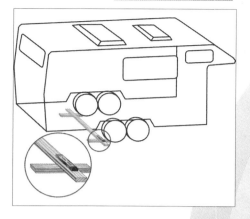

On almost any camping trip there are nuisances and problems that RVers deal with. With me it's always been leveling my travel trailer from side to side.

Now, however, I have a tried-and-true method of doing this without a jack. When I back into a campsite, I stop a few feet short of where I want to end up. Then, using a seven-foot straight-edge (a piece of board), with a level on top I lay this board straight across the ground where the tires will end up. Then I can see how many shims will be necessary to bring the leveling board and ultimately the tires up to level. Naturally the shims have to be long and wide enough to fully support the tires.

The bottom line here is to level the ground the tires will be sitting on, not the camper. In the event there is a rise in the center of the parking area due to tire wear, keep two short pieces of 2 × 4s handy to support each end of the straight edge.

All that's left to do is to back the trailer atop the shims.

Joseph Randazzo, Bridgetown, Missouri

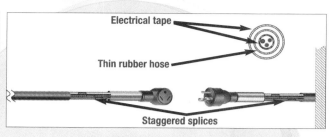

TAME THAT CORD

I had an uncooperative electrical cord that was stiff in cold weather. However, I did not have the physical structure and room in the trailer wall to support a plywood panel with an electrical plug installed as suggested by my friends. But I did have sufficient room between the wall and the drawers to accommodate a short stub of electric cord, which could be shoved back through the original opening in the trailer wall.

First, purchase heavy-duty male and female pigtails from a hardware or RV supply store. Make sure the plug amperage rating meets or exceeds the rating for your existing cord. Next, cut the electrical cord that comes through the wall of the trailer so that about 12 inches sticks out of the trailer. Install the male plug end. The splices are staggered for obvious safety reasons and convenience of working and appearance. Now, install the female pigtail to the severed portion of the power cord in the same staggered manner.

After double checking the color coding of the wires, I finished the project in layers. The first layer was a double wrap of electrical tape that was covered with a piece of thin rubber hose. The hose was then covered with another double layer of electrical tape.

Now, when we pull into our campsite, I pull out the short stub and install the rest of the power cord just like an extension cord.

Clifford Rodgers, Apple Valley, California

Editor's note: Make sure the power cord is disconnected before cutting it.

HOW NOT TO BE A NEEDLE IN A HAYSTACK!

We had a family camping weekend, where some people would be arriving at dusk or later and had some concern about locating us. To make it easy for the latecomers to locate us, I planned to have the trailer marker lights illuminated. This I accomplished by using a spare wiring socket (the tow vehicle) and connecting the no. 3 green marker wire to the no. 4 black battery wire with an 8-inch piece of wire. When the plug and socket were joined together, we had a standout trailer. The long piece of wire protrudes from the back of the cover when assembled, making a hook to hang it up for storage.

Ed Meuiner, Tecumseh, Ontario

SATELLITE SET-UP

I found an efficient way to set up my satellite dish with just one person and without having to run back and forth between the dish and inside the RV. I use a pair of wireless two-way radio headsets with one next to the speaker in our television; I wear the other one. I then adjust the dish while listening for the change in pitch. When I hear a high and constant pitch, I know I'm receiving a good signal. These headsets also come in handy when my wife helps guide our fifth-wheel into a parking spot.

Randall L. Larson, Everett, Washington

NOT JUST FOR AIR TRAVELERS

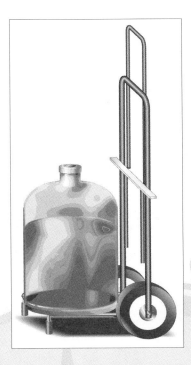

A fold-up, wheeled baggage carrier is a very handy piece of equipment for RVers to have. We use this mini hand truck to transport 5-gallon water containers from that far-off water tap. It makes a trip to the laundry a breeze, and can carry a large stack of firewood in one load. When we have an LP-gas cylinder refilled at the campground, we just wheel it to the office — no problem

These hand trucks come with a bungee cord for holding large objects, fold down to a very stowable size, are quite inexpensive and are available anywhere luggage is sold, including mass merchandisers.

MARY LOU KERCHNER, LIVINGSTON, TEXAS

LUCKY HORSESHOE

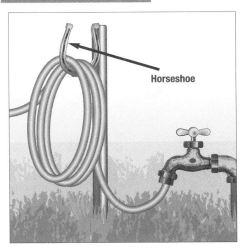

Horseshoe

To keep your water hose clean while in camp, we rigged up a hose holder using unique parts. We cut a 1-inch diameter pipe 40 inches long. Then we welded a horseshoe about 1 inch from one end of the pipe; the opposite end of the pipe was crimped to a point, and the while thing was painted to match the color of the RV. When setting up camp, we tap the pipe into the ground near the water source, connect the water hose to the trailer and loop the extra hose through the horseshoe. The other end of the hose is then hooked to the faucet. The hose stays clean and partially looped to make breaking camp easier.

SHIRLEY HAWKINS, WICHITA FALLS, TEXAS

MULTI-USE LEVELING BLOCKS

To make some leveling blocks useful in many different situations, get a length of 2 × 8-inch treated lumber, and a couple feet of ¾-inch PVC tubing. Cut the lumber into three pieces: 14 inches, 20 inches and 26 inches, for each number of blocks you want to make. Angle the edges up on all the edges. The three different sizes will form a pyramid shape. This is to make it easier to drive up on without having a high angle that would make the block slide out of place when trying to drive on it.

Make a stack of the three different sizes together, centering them on top of each other. Drill two 1-inch holes through all three leveling blocks, but do not drill all the way through the bottom one. This is because you don't want the pieces of tubing that will hold the stack together to fall through the bottom block when stacked.

Now cut two sets of the ¾-inch PVC tubing. One set will be a longer set to hold three blocks together, and the other set will be shorter to hold two blocks together. Make sure to cut the tubing just a little shorter than needed, so that when inserted in the holes they do not stick out of the top.

Repeat the procedure for each set of leveling blocks you wish to make. You should end up with a set for each tire you will need to support.

Now you have sets of leveling blocks that can be used individually or stacked together in combinations.

LAURIE WEST, SUGAR LAND, TEXAS

Editor's note: Be sure that the width of the boards you buy is wider than the footprint of the tire and that, in leveling, you support both tires on a set of duals. Tires hanging over the edges of leveling boards can become damaged, and one tire supporting the whole load on a dual set will likely be overloaded.

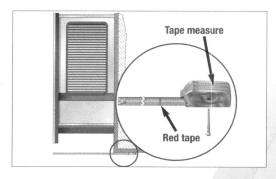

SLIDEOUT CLEARANCE

During the last year or so, I have seen many tips on slideout guides. Here's mine: I purchased an inexpensive plastic tape measure and removed the screw holding the two halves of the cover together. I drilled a hole through the screw holes and mounted the tape to be bottom edge of the trailer, under the slideout. I then placed a small piece of red tape on the minimum distance required to extend the room. There is nothing to store or try to locate when parking. Just pull out the tape and confirm there is enough room before extending the slideout.

BOB PORTO, GROVELAND, CALIFORNIA

OUTSIDE HANGERS

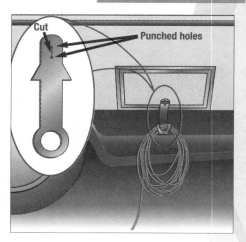

Ihave often wondered if there was a better way to store excess water hose and electrical cord while hooked up, rather than allowing it to coil on the ground where it is subject to dirt, mud and being stepped on and tripped over. I came up with a way to hang these items on the side of my rig using straps made from a tire inner tube (see sketch for actual shape). The water hose is suspended from the refrigerator vent lock and the power cord from the AC generator door lock. Make sure you do not block any vents when using this system.

NAT IRELAND, MARLOW, NEW HAMPSHIRE

POOP 'N SCOOP

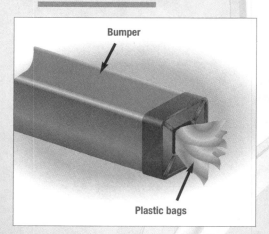

We have two dogs and my husband often takes them for strolls. He's always asking me for doggie bags that he can keep while on the walk. In looking for a method that would be handy for him, we bought a roll of produce bags from our local grocery store. We rolled out 20 or 30 bags and stuffed them into the back bumper of the trailer. The hole in the bumper plug serves as a dispenser. My husband now has his bags handy, the dogs are happy and so am I.

CHARLENE ROSS, STRATHMORE, ALBERTA CANADA

◆ CLOSEUPS ◆ CLOSEUPS ◆ CLOSEUPS ◆

SLIPPERY POWER CORD

*I*always had trouble getting the power-supply cord in and out of its small storage area. I discovered that applying vinyl and rubber protectant (the type for dashboards and tires) to the cord covering not only makes it easy to slide in and out of the storage area, but it also protects the cord from ultraviolet rays while camping.

EARL R. CREWS, ELIZABETHTOWN, KENTUCKY

◆ CLOSEUPS ◆ CLOSEUPS ◆ CLOSEUPS ◆

SUPER SCOOPER

*P*et owners get a bad rap because some irresponsible dog owners do not pick up after their pets. We have found very effective and economical "pooper scoopers." We keep the plastic bags that most retail stores provide for fruit and vegetables. Just slip your hand inside the bag, pick up the deposit, turn the bag inside out and tie. You are now ready to dispose of your dog's waste responsibly.

PAT PULLUM, ROGERS, ARKANSAS

RAIN, RAIN, GO AWAY

On a recent camping trip, we were watching cable television at the RV park when it started to rain and the TV picture shorted out. It turns out that water had leaked into the TV service connection. Wrapping the connection with electrical tape requires re-taping each time you set up at a new campsite. I solved this problem by using a spark-plug boot, which can easily be slid on and off the connection. It makes a tight, dry cover for cable or satellite hook ups.

FRED ROSL
VINELAND, NEW JERSEY

THREE FOR THE ROAD

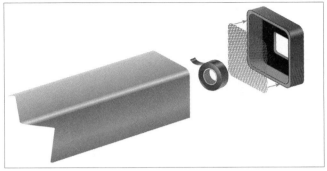

We have a seasonal site at our favorite campground. Last year a wren built a nest in the rear bumper of our fifth-wheel. We didn't have the heart to remove it until the end of the season, so it created quite a mess. To prevent this from happening again, we took a couple window-screen repair patches and taped them to the inside of the bumper caps (they could also be secured by a few globs of RTV silicone sealant), thus covering the little holes and preventing the birds from entering. No more nests; no more mess.

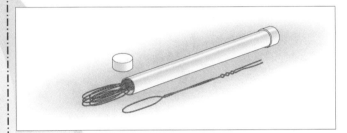

The plastic bag that contained our long campfire hot-dog forks was full of holes and falling apart. I bought a length of 2-inch PVC and two caps. PVC makes a perfect protective container for the forks and other long, skinny tools and hardware as well.

If you use a tote tank to empty your holding tanks during extended stays, you know how backbreaking it is to pull it to the dump station. To make the task easier, I bought a trailer dolly with inflated tires to pull it. Wow! What a difference! What used to be a backbreaking chore has now been made very easy.

BONNIE VALENTINE, PRESCOTT, WISCONSIN

PUMP IT UP

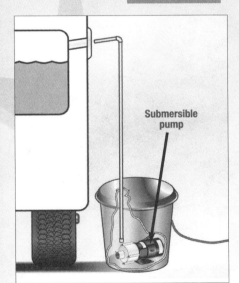

Submersible pump

Some water-fill access locations are as high as 4 feet above the ground, making it almost impossible to fill from a container larger than one gallon — when boondocking or camped in primitive places. Getting water into the supply tank can be made much easier by using a small submersible fountain pump. It can be powered by a small portable or on-board AC generator; the pump fits into the bucket. I use a 5- or 6-gallon bucket with a lid, the kind found in a bakery or supply store (keeps the bucket clean during storage). One end of the ⅜-inch clear plastic tubing is connected to the pump and the other is fitted with a PVC elbow and 6-inch tube. I can now haul 5 or 6 gallons of water at one time and don't have to strain my back filling the tank.

CHARLES D. BROWNE, LYNNWOOD, WASHINGTON

WATER-FILTER HOLDER

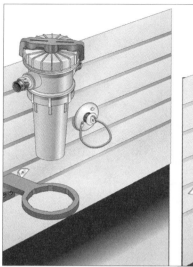

I use a "whole-house" water filter to help improve the quality of the water entering our rig. The filter works nicely, but I could not find a convenient place to put the filter when in use. I would lean it against the campground faucet or the tire of the rig, and when it rained the filter got dirty. Even the ants got all over it.

To fix this problem, I went to my neighborhood home-improvement center and purchased an extra filter wrench and a 65-cent drawer handle. The handle only came in black, so I painted it white to match the rig. I then mounted it to the side and bottom edge of the trailer, below the city water hookup. There is a wood beam under the skin in this location, so I had a strong mount. I gently heated the filter-wrench handle with a torch, bending it into a 90-degree angle.

The wrench is fitted into the drawer handle and the filter into the wrench. It holds the filter nicely off the ground and close to the trailer. When not in use, I put the wrench and filter in a storage compartment and the drawer handle rides nicely without sticking out far enough to pose any hazard to people walking by.

ROBERT TEED JR., NAPLES, FLORIDA

SMOKELESS CAMPFIRE

We found a way to make a campfire almost smokeless. We lay the bigger pieces of wood on the bottom, building up with smaller layers, and the kindling is put on the very top (yes, I know this seems strange). No need to add paper; just light a match and the fire will burn as long as you want and as long as the wood lasts. If retiring before the last layer is burned, just douse the fire with water and restart the next day using the same method. Now you can sit around the fire and not play musical chairs, running from the smoke.

NANCY BECKMAN, SURPRISE, ARIZONA

TUB FIRES

Campfires go hand-in-hand with camping, but it's not always easy to find places with safe pits to build the fire. One solution is to build a portable fire pit using an old truck wheel and the rescued inside tub of a retired automatic washing machine. The truck rim elevates and supports the tub, which keeps the fire contained and limits flying sparks. We use a Weber grill rack on top to cook our favorite foods. And the cover from the Weber grill fits perfectly over the tub so you can keep the wood dry before it's time to build the fire. The ashes are easy to dump and the truck wheel only gets warm. Although it's portable, it may be difficult to store in some rigs.

AGNES FIECKE, SILVER LAKE, MINNESOTA

Support Your Local Filter

We've been using a water filter with our motorhome for many years. I've come up with a very good way of supporting the filter assembly without using a strap or the hose itself. I bought an outdoor plant stand to serve as the filter holder. The top is open to clear the filter housing and hose connections, and the potted-plant hole holds the filter body perfectly. The stand can be placed on any kind of ground; in a sandy location, it can be pushed into the sand. The three legs make it very secure, and the weather will not hurt the stand. Plant stands are available almost anywhere and are very reasonably priced.

JAMAR HOWARD, GLEN DALE, WEST VIRGINIA

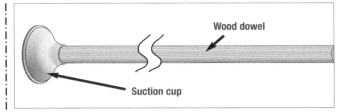

Wood dowel

Suction cup

Slideout-Room Feelers

A large number of RVs are equipped with one, two and even three slideouts. This feature requires an extra-wide campsite. When the campsite I'm assigned is marginal in width because of overhanging tree branches, bushes, hookups, etc., I use my homemade "feeler" system. I cut a wood dowel to match the width of the individual slideout. Then the dowel is fit into a suction cup. When backing into my campsite, I install the suction cups with the dowels on the corners of my slideouts, simulating the clearance I need. If the dowels clear all the obstacles, I park the rig and simply remove them. I can then open the slideouts with confidence that they will miss all obstacles. Total cost for this project is less than $10.

CRAIG E. WILSON, DIAMOND BAR, CALIFORNIA

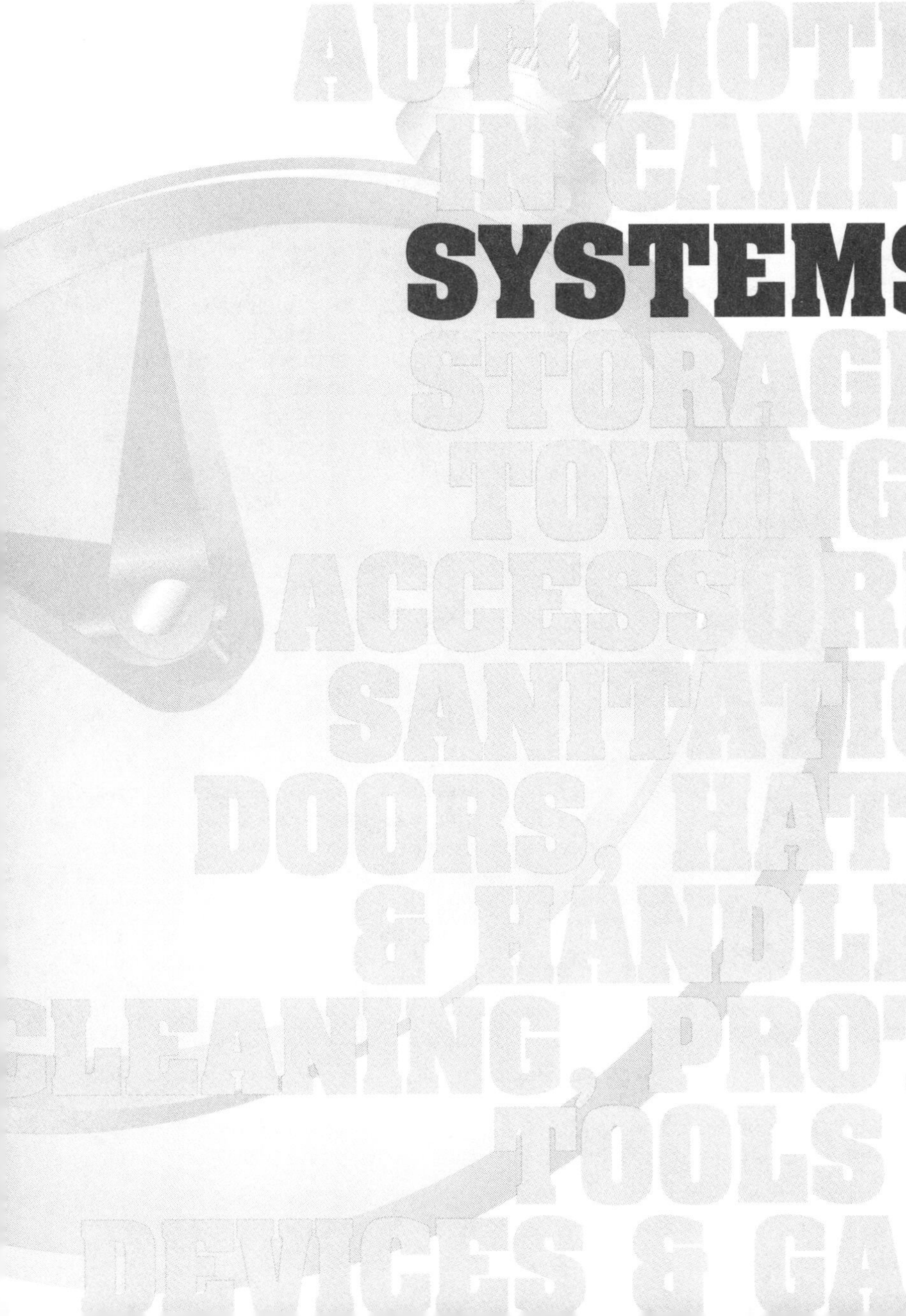

LIVABILITY
SAFETY
APPLIANCES
MAINTENANCE
AUTOMOTIVE
IN CAMP

SYSTEMS

STORAGE
TOWING
ACCESSORIES
SANITATION
DOORS, HATCHES
& HANDLES
CLEANING, PROTECTING
TOOLS
DEVICES & GADGETS

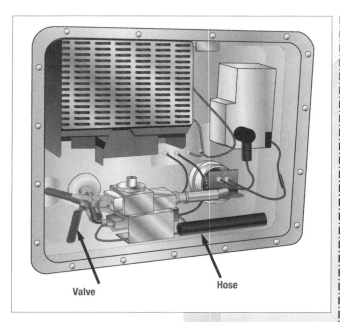

Valve   Hose

DRAIN-PLUG SOLUTION

Removing the drain plug from a water heater can be diffi-cult. From my favorite hardware store, I purchased an in-expensive drain valve that has a small lever and only requires a quarter-turn to open. I installed this drain in place of the plug. I had to temporarily remove the arm until the valve was posi-tioned just right and tightened. You cannot install this drain valve on water heaters equipped with anode rods. To be extra neat, I carry a short length of hose, which I slip over the end of the valve before opening, so the water can be directed with-out making a mess.

THOMAS KILBORN, PRESTON, WASHINGTON

ELECTRIC STEP CONTROL

The con-trol unit on our mo-torhome's electric step failed. I found that a new control unit would cost $250. Due to its age, I also would have to replace the motor ($100), so that the motor and the control unit would be compatible. A new complete step assembly would cost about $325, plus labor. Correcting the problem by purchasing a new step assembly seemed to be a no-brainer. But after giving it some thought, I decided on an alternative that has worked well for us.

I removed the control unit from the steps and wired the motor directly to a momentary-on-off/momentary-on reverse polarity toggle switch (from the hardware store), which I mounted in the motorhome's stairwell. Now, with a deft mo-tion of a foot or by hand from outside the coach, we can ex-tend or retract the step as we are opening or closing the door. We no longer have the automatic features of the original step, but my $15 manual-switch solution works great and saved us about $400.

DAVID MULCAHY, SAN DIEGO, CALIFORNIA

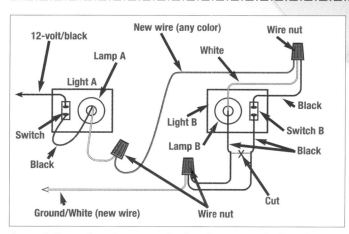

A ROMANTIC GLOW

Installing two 12-volt DC "aircraft-style" swivel lights with built-in switches above your dinette can provide the mood of the romantic glow of candles, but with the safety and convenience of electric lamps. Although dome lights might work, aircraft lights focus the beam of light onto the table better. The lights are installed and wired in series. To do this, you simply take the wire (usually the white) from the bulb in one fixture and connect it to the white wire from the bulb and the black wire from the switch in the other fixture. Cut the wire from the switch to the bulb (usually the black) and connect both ends to a new wire that is grounded. The black wire from the first fixture is routed to a source of 12-volt DC power. In use, the on/off switch is the one in the first fixture. With the other switch open, the lamps are in series and burn dimly for mood lighting. With the second fixture switch closed, the light is out but the other lamp burns brightly and provides extra light for the table. Besides being pleasant, soft lighting saves electrical power.

JOE BUTTERWORTH, SOQUEL, CALIFORNIA

ADD A WATER PUMP

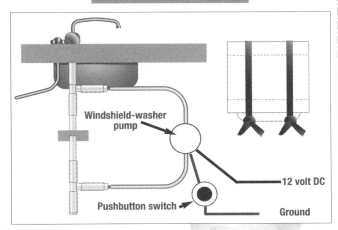

I am a full-time RVer and normally travel in a 32-foot trailer. In addition, several years ago I purchased a slide-in camper, with a crank-up top, to make some special trips and pull my boat.

I did not like the hand pump for the freshwater supply that came with the camper. I did not want, nor was there room, to add a commercially available electric pump and faucet, so I devised my own system.

I used a windshield-washer pump, which is mounted using a piece of preformed pipe insulation around the sink drainpipe. The pump is secured to the foam insulation with two plastic wire ties. This holds it in place and eliminates vibration and noise. Connect the pump wiring to the 12-volt DC truck battery and put a fuse in the positive wire. I mounted a pushbutton momentary switch in the front of the sink cabinet at a height which allows me to push it with my knee — a truly hands-free operation.

The plumbing involves cutting the water line coming from the freshwater tank and adding two ⅜-inch T-fittings, two ⅜- to ⅛-inch reducers and a check valve. Secure all connections with hose clamps. Adding the check valve allows you to continue to use the hand pump. If you think you will never want to use the hand pump, the check valve could be eliminated.

DONALD CRAIG, LIVINGSTON, TEXAS

GOODBYE TO CONDENSATION

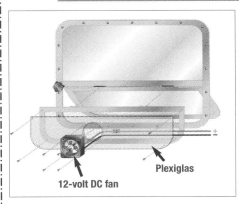

We full-time and spend time in cold areas. We were constantly dealing with excessive condensation forming in the morning. Leaving the windows open at night to relieve this situation doesn't fly in sub-freezing weather. Therefore, I came up with a great way to slowly replace the humid air overnight without leaving a window open, causing excessive drafts and furnace use.

I designed a system using a small, quiet 12-volt DC fan that will replace just enough air to keep the humidity down. The fan is used on computers and other electronic devices and is sold at RadioShack; a 3-inch model sells for $15 and the 1½-inch version is only $10. The fan is mounted in the bottom section that opens independently of the entire window.

To install, I popped off the window screen, traced its shape on a small piece of clear Plexiglas, as well as a circle in the center of the plastic the size of the fan blade. Any plastics shop will be glad to trace and cut a small piece like this for around $5. The fan is attached to the Plexiglas, which is then attached to the window screen using small screws, epoxy or silicone made to be used on plastics. The screen is popped back into place and the power leads are run to a 12-volt DC source and a switch is cut into the positive wire. Usually a nearby light fixture is a good source of power; 120-volt AC fans are also available.

The fan is turned on at night, or left on all of the time. It does not get hot or vibrate and makes virtually no noise; power usage is very slight. With the windows closed (except for the one with the fan) the air is slowly pulled through the cracks and small openings in the rig.

MARK DENSLEY, LONGWOOD, FLORIDA

SAVE THE MODULE

Have you ever forgotten to turn off the water heater in your RV and gone on down the road with the gas being continually blown out and relighting until the ignition module is damaged?

To act as a reminder to turn the switch off, I installed a light-emitting diode (LED) pilot light next to the switch. The LED, part no. 276-209, is available from RadioShack and costs about a dollar. It took me 15 minutes to install it. There is enough wire to allow you to remove the switch panel and to make the hook up. Drill a hole the diameter of the LED in the wood panel next to the switch to mount the LED.

BILL BORSTEL, SPRINGFIELD, LOUISIANA

FASTER (WATER) FILL UP

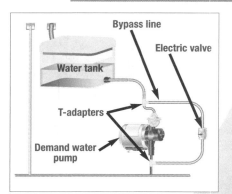

My potable water-fill pipe is very inconveniently positioned, so that the fill rate is very slow. To fix the problem, I added a bypass line (with a valve) around the existing water pump. When connected to the city-water hookup, I open the valve and the water is allowed to be routed to the tank. In case of an overfill, the water will be pushed out the overflow/vent tube. The valve is one that is used in sprinkler systems. Although it is rated to operate on 24 volts DC power, it seems to work nicely on the available 12 volts DC from my RV. Make sure the valve does not have an anti-siphon feature. The smallest valve I was able to find in my area was for ¾-inch pipe, and I used T-adapters to make the connections. Make sure you observe the direction of the water flow (indicated on the body of the valve) when making the installation. The electrical connection was made to the closest available 12-volt DC line and I used a fuse and switch. In practice, it now takes about 10 minutes to fill the tank.

A.T. MALUTA, REDONDO BEACH, CALIFORNIA

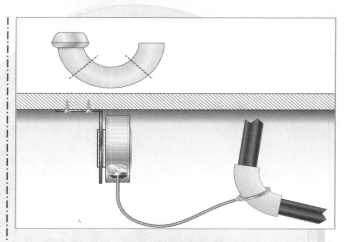

FAUCET RETAINER

I replaced the kitchen faucet with a pullout model, but the hose got in the way of other items in the space under the sink. I devised a way to manage the hose by removing the weight that helps pull the hose down when not in use. I purchased a key retriever (the kind you hook on your belt) and a plastic bell-end elbow (electrical department) at the local home center. I had a right-angle bracket and an O-ring, but these items can also be purchased at home centers.

I mounted the bracket between the stainless-steel sinks near the front and slipped the O-ring on the cut bell-end elbow. I then ran the faucet hose through the elbow and attached it to the faucet. The split ring on the retriever (used to hold the keys) was attached to the O-ring and the retriever body to the angle bracket using the existing belt clip. Now the hose is up and out of the way and moves in and out freely and is under control. The whole project costs less than $6.

MIKE MEIKLE, ROME, NEW YORK

◆ CLOSEUPS ◆ CLOSEUPS ◆ CLOSEUPS ◆

FORGET-ME-NOT

We were constantly forgetting to switch off the water heater in our motorhome. I intended to install a light that would indicate when the water heater was on, but the wiring was more complex than I wanted to handle.

The problem was solved for $2.96 by installing a battery-operated red safety strobe made by CMI Parts (P.O. Box 170, Deerfield, Illinois 60015, 847-735-8500), and sold at Home Depot and elsewhere. To have easy access to its on/off switch and to lessen the intensity of the flash, I installed it with a hook-and-loop fastener, with the light side toward the cabinet. Having the light mounted backward produces a nice halo effect.

Whenever we turn on the water heater, we switch on the strobe. We haven't forgotten to turn off the water heater since this installation.

ROBERT FALK, ATLANTA, GEORGIA

◆ CLOSEUPS ◆ CLOSEUPS ◆ CLOSEUPS ◆

FREEZING ANTIFREEZE

After the busy summer travel season, many of us have to winterize our rigs for the cold-weather season using RV antifreeze solution. Several years ago, we got a bad batch of RV antifreeze and it froze solid, cracking the toilet and necessitating an expensive repair. To avoid this from happening in the future, we always put the gallon of antifreeze in the freezer for 24 hours before using it. That way, when the mercury drops to minus 30 degrees F, we know our rig's plumbing is still safe.

ROY AND MARY HUDSON, WASHBURN, WISCONSIN

HELP WHEN IT'S NEEDED

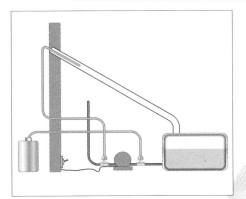

My wife and I have been campers for several years. Now that we are retired, we travel and camp for longer periods at a time. That leaves us with a freshwater-supply problem, as we aren't always lucky to get a site near a water faucet. I have severe arthritis in my knees and arms, which has made it very difficult to fill the freshwater tank with 5-gallon jugs.

I came up with an idea that cost less than $20. I already had a bypass valve (water heater) between the water pump and the freshwater tank for winterizing the system. I added another bypass on the outlet side of the water pump, then fashioned two 4-foot pieces of water hose with ½-inch male pipe thread hose connectors on one end.

Whenever I need water, I fill my 5-gallon jugs and run the hose from the inlet side of the water pump to the jug of water, and the hose from the outlet side of the pump to the freshwater fill pipe. I also added a 12-volt DC switch on the wall next to the pump. Then all I have to do is turn the two valves, flip the 12-volt DC wall switch and fill my tank.

CLIFFORD WAINMAN, GRIGGSVILLE, ILLINOIS

QUIET THAT PUMP

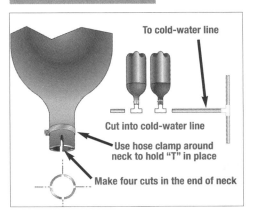

To cold-water line

Cut into cold-water line

Use hose clamp around neck to hold "T" in place

Make four cuts in the end of neck

If you are tired of hearing the water pump cycle every time you turn on the water faucet, add a 1-liter soft-drink bottle (or two bottles) to serve as a homemade accumulator tank. First, determine the water-line size and whether you want to use one or two bottles. Then round up the bottle(s), the appropriate size T-fittings (or elbow, depending on the type of installation) and hose clamps at your local RV or farm-supply store. You'll need a ¾-inch barb fitting to go into each bottle neck. Sand off the barbs until they just slip inside the bottle neck. Using a small saw, make four ⅜- to ½-inch-deep cuts in the end of each bottle neck. Install the T-fittings into the water line between the pump and faucets in any convenient place; I usually mount the bottle in a cabinet under a sink. Mount the bottles upside down (use silicone sealer on the barb fittings) so the water will drain out when you winterize. The bottles are very strong, and I have never had one break or leak.

VERLE R. GRITTMAN, SALINA, KANSAS

NO WATER SPILLS

No matter how careful you are while making plumbing repairs, some water always manages to spill out when the pipe fitting is unscrewed. Although the amount is usually less than a cupful, it always seems to go where it does the most damage and is hardest to clean up. Here's how to avoid this annoyance: After turning the water supply off, open the hot- and cold-water faucets that are furthest from the city-water inlet. With the water hose disconnected, depress the plastic pin in the center of the check valve in the city water fill. The water trapped in the pipes will flow to the ground, instead of soaking your bathroom towels. Close the faucets and go about your repair. This procedure will not drain the hot-water tank.

JOE BUTTERWORTH, SOQUEL, CALIFORNIA

FREQUENCY CHECK

Here's an easy way to check the line frequency of your auxiliary generator: Start the AC generator and allow it to warm up and stabilize. Next, put a glass of water in your microwave oven (to prevent damage) and set the heat control to its lowest setting. Set the timer for 60 seconds. Using a digital wrist watch, note when the seconds display reads zero. At this time, push the start button on the microwave and watch the seconds display on your watch. If the AC generator frequency is OK, the microwave will shut off at the same time your watch display shows zero again. If it runs past this, it's running too slowly; if it shuts off sooner, it's running too fast. The frequency is governed by the speed of the engine and should only be adjusted by an experienced technician.

ARTHUR W. WAGNER, KERRVILLE, TEXAS

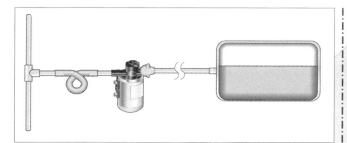

Quiet Water Pump

We are now traveling in our third fifth-wheel, and all of them have had water pumps that sounded like a machine gun going off every time we opened a faucet. The noise could be heard throughout our rigs. Considering the laws of physics as they relate to the transmission of sound waves, I tried the sponge-pad technique under the pump-mounting bracket. That helped a little, but there was still way too much noise — so back to the drawing board.

The trailer distributes water via a system of hard plastic tubing, so my technique was to try to dampen the sound before it got to the hard tubing. I achieved my goal by continuing the use of sponge pads and adding a coil of soft plastic water hose between the water-pump outlet and the fifth-wheel's water-distribution system. Now the running water makes more noise than the water pump. You'll need to make adjustments in the length of the water pump's inlet hose as necessary and re-attach the hoses to their respective positions.

CLIFFORD L. RODGERS, APPLE VALLEY, CALIFORNIA

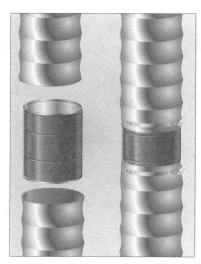

Experiencing Heat Loss?

If you are experiencing heat loss through your heating ducts, you might check for splices that, as in my case, were done with duct tape.

Now, I won't go anywhere without trusty old duct tape, but it may only work temporarily in taping heating ducts. Over time, the tape will dry out and release the connection.

I found a simple solution was to cut the ends out of a 13-ounce coffee can and use that as a splice. Secure it with hose clamps.

HAROLD COLEY, CLIFTON, COLORADO

Smarten Up Your Idiot Lights

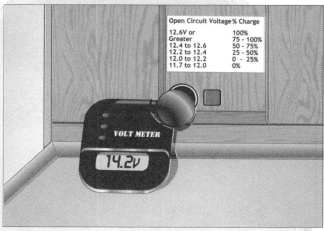

Open Circuit Voltage	% Charge
12.6V or Greater	100%
12.4 to 12.6	75 - 100%
12.2 to 12.4	50 - 75%
12.0 to 12.2	25 - 50%
11.7 to 12.0	0 - 25%
11.7 to 12.0	0%

Over the years I've experienced erroneous readings and frustration with the "idiot lights" installed in the monitor panels of my RV. I'm sure I'm not alone in this matter.

Voltage	% Charge
12.6 or greater	100
12.4-12.6	75-100
12.2-12.4	50-75
12.0-12.2	25-50
11.7-12.0	0-25
11.7 or less	0

Those battery indicator lights always displayed the percentage of charge well when it was less than 25 percent. To determine the true condition of my RV batteries, I installed a digital readout voltmeter.

Total cost for the project was about $25, with one hour to install.

I used a Road Pro digital voltmeter (available from almost any RV parts store) connected to a power accessory outlet (a.k.a. cigarette lighter) and a push-button switch (both available from hardware stores).

Installation procedure:

Determine the location and install the power accessory outlet.

Wire the groundside of the power accessory outlet to the negative terminal of the battery.

Install the momentary contact push-button switch.

Wire the ON side of the switch to the center post of the power-accessory outlet.

Wire the other side of the switch to the positive side of the battery. Because the digital voltmeter is normally off, there is no current draw on the battery. When you press the momentary switch, current will pass through the meter and give you a digital reading of the battery condition.

With the aid of this chart, you can tell the charge percent of the battery or batteries in use.

TOM WHITE, SAN JOSE, CALIFORNIA

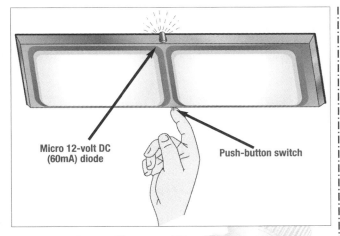

Micro 12-volt DC
(60mA) diode

Push-button switch

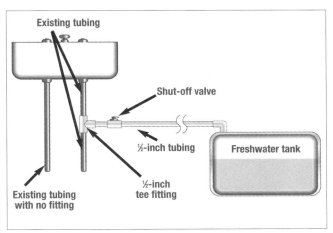

Existing tubing

Shut-off valve

½-inch tubing

Freshwater tank

½-inch
tee fitting

Existing tubing
with no fitting

VERY SMALL NIGHT LIGHT

To make a night light for the bathroom that does not consume much power — for camping in the boonies — I installed a RadioShack micro 12-volt DC (60 mA) diode in the ceiling light fixture. I wired it through a small push-button switch that's also mounted in the fixture. Simple, fast and cheap, and no more stubbed toes at night.
GARLAND E. WILSON, GRAFTON, VIRGINIA

◆ CLOSEUPS ◆ CLOSEUPS ◆ CLOSEUPS ◆

AWAKEN TO WARMTH

During cool weather, our furnace is activated automatically at a preset time and temperature. How? We installed a programmable thermostat. No more getting up out of a warm bed and shivering from the cold until the heat comes on. Our thermostat can be set to go on and off at any time of the day and at the desired temperature seven days a week. It is just a little larger than other thermostats, the cost was low — about $40 — considering the advantages and it's very easy to install. Check with the motorhome or furnace manufacturer as to compatibility before purchasing.
LOU BLUNDELL, LA LUZ, NEW MEXICO

◆ CLOSEUPS ◆ CLOSEUPS ◆ CLOSEUPS ◆

WASTING WATER

How much water do you waste while waiting for the hot water to arrive at the shower or sink faucet? This waste is especially critical when boondocking. There is a solution. Just run a length of ½-inch tubing from the hot-water tank to the top of your freshwater tank. Add a shut-off valve, and you're in business. You'll need ½-inch tubing of sufficient length to reach the freshwater tank from the faucet, a ½-inch tee fitting, one ½-inch shut-off valve, six hose clamps and a 1½-inch nipple. The nipple needs to be "welded" into the freshwater tank, which should be done by your dealer if you have no experience in such a process. When you want to shower or wash your hands, open the shut-off valve and let the water run until the tubing/hose gets hot. Shut off the valve before using the faucet.
NORM POZNER, ENGLEWOOD, COLORADO

SAFETY
APPLIANCES
MAINTENANCE
AUTOMOTIVE
IN-CAMP
SYSTEMS

STORAGE

TOWING
ACCESSORIES
SANITATION
DOORS, HATCHES
& HANDLES
CLEANING, PROTECTING
TOOLS
DEVICES & GADGETS
LIVABILITY

AN EXTRA SHELF

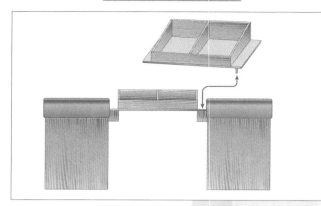

On a lengthy vacation in a small RV, there is always need for another shelf in a convenient location. Since there are only two of us when we travel, I use some of the space under the dinette table, against the wall. The shelf rests on the rails that provide support to the table when it is in the bed position.

A board was cut to fit the space between the seats. A back, a front and some sides were added to keep things from falling off. A center divider helps keep stored items from shifting around. A dowel was fitted to the bottom on the end, and a corresponding hole was drilled in the seat rail. This prevents sliding when on the road. The shelf assembly can be lifted out if the full dinette is needed. With the wood stained to match the rest of the interior, it looks like original equipment.
HERBERT SUTTON, SUN CITY, ARIZONA

CLEAR AND ACCESSIBLE STORAGE

We needed a place to put small items, such as glasses, books, etc., directly over the head of the bed. Since I had added an overhead storage row in this area years earlier, the solution was simple. (Many bedrooms have storage cabinets from the factory at the head of the bed). I made a module consisting of a small sheet of wall panel and then made compartment walls using thin strips of bas wood (which is found in hobby stores). I used a sheet of .09-inch-thick clear Plexiglas

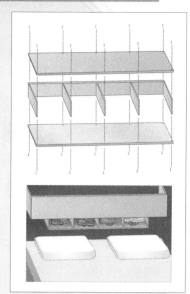

for the bottom surface, so we could see what was in each compartment located over our heads. The completed module was screwed to the bottom of the overhead storage box (or cabinets from the factory).
ROBERT MURPHY, WASHINGTON, UTAH

CORNER SHELVES

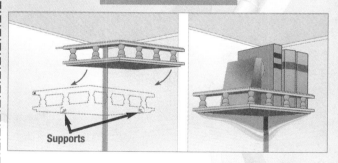

Supports

Installing corner shelves in otherwise wasted space makes a lot of sense for storage-hungry RVers. Here's a quick-and-easy way to add these useful corner shelves. I use Self Supports by Knape and Vogt that have a ¼-inch pin size and a screw hole on the other side of the angle. To install, I drill a hole slightly smaller than ¼-inch to assure a tight fit when inserting the pins. I position the supports so the angle is down to give the finished installation a cleaner appearance. I next lay the shelf on the supports and fasten with a screw up from the bottom. You can glue on some railing, and if you want to cover the small crack between the wall and the shelf, use gimp or fender welting.
PAT AND SYLVIA KELLY, KENT, WASHINGTON

BUILD IT

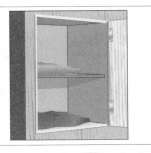

We have a closet in the rear bathroom of our fifth-wheel that only had a door in the front, making the back usable for semi-permanent storage only. After enduring this for more years than good sense should allow, we spent about two hours and $20 installing an alternative means of access. The answer — a wood-framed picture, hinged to make a door.

The project starts with checking the inside of the wall to identify an area with no pipes, wires, etc. Then the area for the door is measured, keeping in mind how it will look with the other room decor items. Cut out the opening and frame the opening vertically with 1 × 2-inch lumber. The 1 × 2-inch board is fastened inside the edges of the cut-out wall opening. Attach a pair of self-closing, flush-type hinges (hardware store item) to one side of a coordinating wooden picture frame that is slightly larger than the cutout. Attach the other side to the framing. Add a magnetic catch and the construction is done.

Hopefully, the frame included a good picture, but if not, replace it with whatever you prefer, which could even include the wood that was cut out to make the door.

Dorita Estes, Sarasota, Florida

FISHING-EQUIPMENT STORAGE

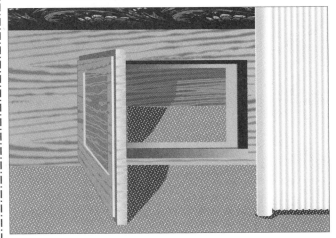

After looking in my motorhome for long storage spaces for my fishing equipment, I settled on the large area under the queen-size bed. There were three separate spaces: near the covered freshwater tank and two other separate walled areas that are accessed by lifting the mattress.

I cut an opening into the first space and installed a door with self-closing hinges. Directly in line with that door, I cut an opening into the second space. These partitions are used to give the bed's framework added rigidity, so cut only the plywood, not any wooden "ribs."

Now I can slide my rods, rod holders, rain gear and so forth out of the way. I don't have to wrestle with the mattress platform or try to use closets that are already crowded.

Frank Woythal, Andover, New York

A NOVEL WAY TO GAIN SPACE

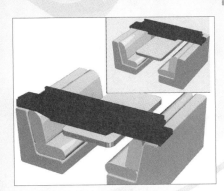

Because our motorhome had such a small food-preparation area, we thought long and hard about buying kitchen-countertop items. Of course, we could have tried sink covers, but my wife opted not to do that.

After our first summer of travel, I was still trying to figure out how to give her more food-prep space when finally, in exasperation, she said, "Why don't you just lay a board across the back of the dinette seats?" Bingo!

The accompanying illustrations show the solution. Originally I was going to remove/replace the dinette counter as we traveled. The cutouts in the back corners allow us to store it in the space between the shower stall and the bathroom-sink counter. Then my wife suggested just leaving it in place when we travel, since the only time we need four places at the table is when we have guests.

That led to a bowed-front design, giving us ample shoulder room at the table. I used ¾-inch plywood and covered it with plastic laminate on all sides. We banded all the edges. I attached two ½ × ½-inch cleats to hold the counter in place. The cleats are attached to the underside of the board, about 6 to 10 inches apart, to only one edge (depending on the layout of the motorhome). As you face the dinette, the cleats go on the edge resting on the back of the seat that is not against a wall. Space the cleats far enough apart to go over the dinette-seat back. I added a 1 × 2-inch horizontal piece of oak along the back edge, which eliminates any bouncing action. The piece looks good and gives us more than 6 linear feet of very useful counterspace.

Frank Brodsen, Springfield, Oregon

DRAWERS FOR YOUR DRAWERS

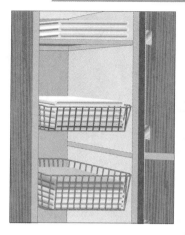

Our fifth-wheel came with lots of closet space, but no drawers for our clothes. We found some baskets at Wal-Mart that have a lip on both sides that fit into the closet in the bathroom. All I needed to do was to cut some boards to fit the space and the lips on the baskets. I routed the basket-side of each board for smoother sliding. Mounting was accomplished by pre-drilling holes and screwing the boards in place. We slide the baskets in and out as needed. Above the baskets I built a permanent shelf for towels, and left room at the bottom for a dirty clothes hamper.

BILL WATTS, LIVINGSTON, TEXAS

MORE STORAGE SPACE

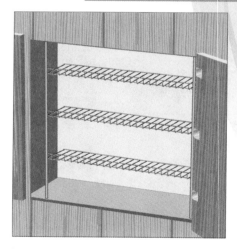

When we purchased our slideout-equipped motorhome, we didn't realize that there was not enough storage space for food supplies. We have a large floor-to-ceiling clothes closet and two shirt closets in the bedroom, plus an extra shirt closet in the hallway, with a drawer and cupboard space below. But there wasn't enough galley cabinet space.

Our solution? We visited a building-supply store and purchased plastic-coated wire shelving. I installed the shelving in the shirt closet with the shelves upside down, so the front edge prevents our supplies from sliding off. I also put small liquid items, such as sauces, ketchup, mustard, etc., in the bottom section of a 2-inch-deep plastic container, so they fit snugly and there is no chance of spillage. When I want one of those items, I just lift out the container. We keep the heavier canned goods on the bottom solid shelf and the lighter items on the top shelves. Works great!

ANNE FRANKLIN, ASHBURN, ONTARIO

EXTRA STORAGE

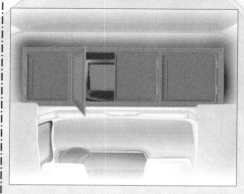

With two of us traveling in our motorhome, we needed storage space more than we needed the overhead bunk's extra sleeping area. My solution was to construct a cabinet in the unneeded bunk space. I included room for a television (on a slanting base) and a VCR. I used lightweight construction methods similar to those used in the rest of the motorhome.

The cabinets were built in three sections. The center section has the television and VCR; the other two sections fit along either side. Each section can be removed by loosening the one bolt on each side that holds the sections together. Dimensions vary, as each cabinet would have to be sized to the space available in your motorhome.

The space on top of the cupboard proved to be a handy place to store some items. The cabinet fits on the bed shelf in place of the mattress. Simply remove the mattress and store it at your home base. If additional storage is needed, the shelf unit could be pulled forward and items placed in back of the shelf unit. However, the rear-stored items would not be very accessible. The shelf-unit doors were constructed (or can be bought ready-made) to match the style of the existing motorhome-cabinet doors.

When we recently traded this motorhome, the dealer was so impressed with the shelf unit that he wanted us to leave it in place. He thought it would make the motorhome easier to sell!

ROY STOHLER, CONCORD, NEBRASKA

♦ CLOSEUPS ♦ CLOSEUPS ♦ CLOSEUPS ♦

FREEZER SPACE

To save space in our freezer compartment of the refrigerator, I put two ice-cube trays together (side-by-side), measured the length and width and cut a piece of $\frac{1}{16}$-inch clear plastic to cover both trays. I put both trays on the bottom of the freezer (freezes quicker here, also) and covered them with the plastic. Now I can stack items on top of the ice-cube trays. The plastic won't stick or freeze to the trays.

RICHARD ALLEN, WOODBURY, NEW JERSEY

EASIER PICKUP STORAGE

We got tired of climbing in and out of the back of our pickup truck to untangle the extension ladder and, often times, ourselves. By building a basement for the truck's bed, loose items are easy to retrieve.

I use the narrow side of the unit for the ladder, and the wider side for storage of a jack, sway bars, a tire inflator, tools, etc., in low-profile plastic crates (like the ones sodas come in). In order to easily retrieve the crates, I made a long-handled hook out of a piece of electrical conduit.

ROBERT GEIGER, MENA, ARKANSAS

FRONT STORAGE

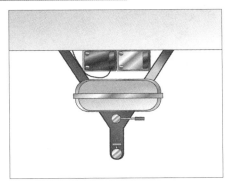

Most trailers have limited storage space that is easy to access from the outside. A lot of trailers only have one battery, but the rack behind the LP-gas cylinders holds two. For less than $10 you can purchase another battery box and hold-down strap, and use it to store extra tools, barbecue brushes and other small items that could use quick-and-easy access. You could also purchase a small toolbox of similar size and a hold-down strap for more organized storage.

JOSEF MEIER, AUSTIN, TEXAS

MORE HANG-UP SPACE

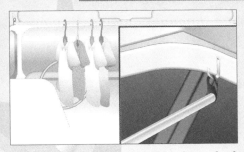

When guests stay in my Class C motorhome, I sometimes need additional hang-up space for their clothes. I came across this idea: I purchased a pack of wall hooks for hanging pictures. I screwed one to each side of the cabover cut-out and hung an expandable clothes rod between them. When in place, it's a handy extra clothes rod that can be easily removed for traveling.

JOE CAMPBELL, GOODWATER, ALABAMA

CLOSEUPS • CLOSEUPS • CLOSEUPS

QUARTER STORAGE

*E*mpty 35mm film containers and empty prescription pill containers are great for holding quarters needed for coin-operated laundries and newspaper and other vending machines. I mostly use the 2¾-inch prescription containers, which are a little bigger than the film canisters and thus hold more quarters.
MARILYN BURNETT, CHARDON, OHIO

OUTSIDE DRAWER

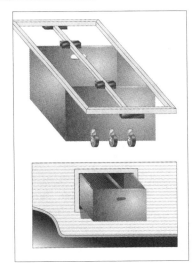

One of the outside storage doors on our fifth-wheel permits access to the area under a dinette bench seat. To use the entire space from the outside, I would need an arm 4 feet long. To solve this, I built a drawer that slides into and utilizes most of the space. The drawer is made of 1-inch white pine and has a smooth Masonite bottom. To make sure the drawer will slide easily on the carpet, I installed three wheels at the rear of the drawer to carry some of the weight. If your floor is below the bottom of the door opening, a spacer will be required. Countersunk flathead screws are used throughout and all wood edges are rounded.

I installed an old broom handle on the underside of the dinette seat frame as a track and to restrict the drawer from tipping down when pulled. Four large rubber feet are used to guide the drawer along the broom handle. The drawer works well and brings stored items out in the open for easy retrieval. I am now considering partitioning the space beside the drawer for additional long, narrow storage accessible from the inside.

FRED A. HIGGINS, ROYAL OAK, MICHIGAN

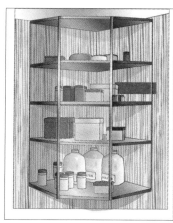

SAVING SPACE

Almost every RV has some square-corner wall areas that are wasted. Consider capturing some of this lost space by building and installing a lightweight corner shelf. My corner shelves are built from Plexiglas scraps and have no doors. These shelves fit in unused corners and can also be constructed of thin wood. Since they mount on two walls, they are very sturdy with little weight.

The corner shelf in the bath of our 25-foot trailer measures 11 × 13 × 21 inches high and holds 10 bath towels and washcloths. The larger shelf in our bedroom measures 12 × 12 × 36 inches and holds 50 pieces of underclothing. Nothing has ever fallen from these shelves, even when traveling thousands of miles. If desired, you can install doors or netting, but they are not necessary for cloth items.

DAN W. BRANDT, RICHMOND, CALIFORNIA

PLASTIC-BAG STORAGE

We like to reuse those plastic bags that come from the grocery store, to line our trash baskets in the motorhome, but storing them was always a problem. So, we took an empty tissue box (I like the small square ones) and placed it under the sink near the trash pail. Then we folded each plastic bag in thirds, lengthwise, then in thirds again. We continued by rolling up each bag into a little package and put it in the tissue box. You can store at least 50 at a time (because when you need one, you need one now!) in a small, neat convenient space — and they are not filled up with air and tangled under the sink.

DENISE PALMIERI, CINCINNATI, OHIO

SHOE FETISH

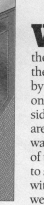

We don't normally wear shoes in our trailer, and the problem of where to put them when we enter was solved by adding a shoe shelf directly on the side of a cabinet just inside the entry door. The shelves are made from 0.09-inch-thick wall panel. Each shelf consists of two pieces of wall panel cut to size and held back-to-back with contact cement. To prevent wear, a vinyl placemat was cut to fit and glued to the top surface of each shelf using a few drops of rubber cement. Each shelf is held to the cabinet and trailer walls with suitable lengths of quarter-round and small wood screws. For stability on the unsupported shelf area, a length of ⅛ × ½-inch anodized aluminum strip was screwed to each shelf. The aluminum strip has a 90-degree bend at the bottom where a single screw holds it to the floor, and at the top where a single screw holds it to the bottom of the top shelf.

ROBERT AND SUZANNE MURPHY, WASHINGTON, UTAH

STORAGE, STORAGE

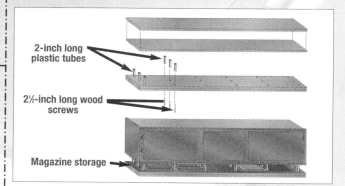

2-inch long plastic tubes

2½-inch long wood screws

Magazine storage

Since we live in a small travel trailer, finding enough space for things is always a problem. As magazines piled ever higher on every available flat surface, I needed to solve the problem quickly.

The solution became obvious when I looked at the overhead cabinet that spans the dinette area. I bought a sheet of wood paneling of suitable wood-grain pattern and cut out two large sheets the size of the overhead cabinet bottom. After laminating both sheets back-to-back with contact cement, I painted the edge and made 18 standoffs 2 inches long from a gray-color plastic tube. Next, I bought 18 2¾-inch-long wood screws and mounted the "magazine" rack to the bottom of the overhead cabinet, using the hollow standoffs as spacers.

ROBERT MURPHY, WASHINGTON, UTAH

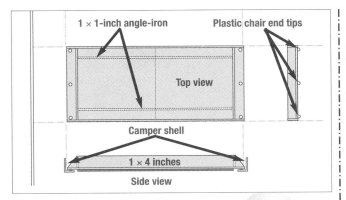

Top view

1 × 1-inch angle-iron   Plastic chair end tips

Camper shell

1 × 4 inches

Side view

SLIDING STORAGE

We tow a travel trailer with a pickup that has a camper shell over the truck bed. The truck bed is always covered from front to back and side to side with items needed for the trip. It is a job and a half to crawl into the truck to retrieve a needed item, and sometimes more than a little hazardous.

The solution I came up with was to install a sliding shelf where the camper shell meets the truck bed. This shelf is able to slide the entire length of the bed, from the cab to the tailgate. With the shelf next to the cab, we are able to reach through the sliding truck window and get items such as coats, hats and other things stored on the shelf. When the shelf is slid to the tailgate, all items are available even with the tailgate closed.

I built the base of the shelf in two pieces, which were put together with 1 × 1-inch angle-iron cut to the width of the bed. The angle-iron pieces were bolted to the shelf base. The reason for doing it this way was to accommodate the tight quarters; the shelf assembly would not go in as a one-piece unit. Later, the shelf was taken apart and reassembled inside the camper shell.

The next job was to place 1 × 4-inch pieces of wood around the outer edge of the shelf. I placed six plastic chair leg tips on the bottom side of the shelf (three on each side) so the shelf would slide easily. All pieces were put together with screws and were finished with several coats of varnish.
B.C. McCREA, PORT ANGELES, WASHINGTON

SIX-PACK STORAGE

Ioften use empty six-pack containers to store taller items in kitchen cabinets. They hold the items steady and the entire container can be easily removed and replaced. I suggest using the Löwenbräu beer six-pack container because it is probably the tallest carton made.
THOMAS MORAN, SANTA FE, NEW MEXICO

TAILGATE LOCKER

Painted hitch guide

Our small fifth-wheel has limited outside storage space; therefore, the area behind the hitch in the bed of the truck was ideal for adding a box. But most of the manufactured boxes open from the top, making it hard to reach the stored items when the trailer is hitched. My answer was to build a three-compartment box using 1 × 3-inch pine framing and ⅜-inch exterior plywood. Hand tools were used to complete the project, and the assembly is screwed and glued. The exterior enamel paint matches the truck, and the three doors are secured with the type of latch used on double-hung windows. Cam-locks were obtained from a locksmith and are keyed alike.

The middle compartment is cut low enough to let the hitch pin clear the structure, and I painted a guideline down the center to help align while hitching. The locker box is mounted forward, against the hitch assembly, and is held onto the truck bed by two pieces of 2 × 4-inch lumber that stand immediately ahead of the bed's stake pockets. Two screws go from inside the box into each 2 × 4. This holds the box in place, and, since the screws are internal, it would be hard to remove the box as long as it is locked.

I thought I might need to gasket the doors to seal against rain and dust, but the box has ridden successfully for about 50,000 miles and this has not been the case. The cost was about $100, and it took about one day to complete, including the time for planning.
THEODORE B. BROWN, JACKSON, NEW HAMPSHIRE

◆ CLOSEUPS ◆ CLOSEUPS ◆ CLOSEUPS ◆

STORAGE BAGS

*B*y *purchasing inexpensive clear sweater storage bags, I have solved a luggage storage problem in our travel trailer. The bags not only store neatly in any cabinet space, but they make getting dressed a breeze for the entire family. We fill each bag with the day's "to be worn" clothing. The other bags contain sleepwear, swimsuits and spare outfits. Once emptied and flattened, they take up barely any space. The bags also work great inside backpacks and suitcases.*
KAREN EBERT, PAWCATUCK, CONNECTICUT

◆ CLOSEUPS ◆ CLOSEUPS ◆ CLOSEUPS ◆

QUICK SHELF BRACKET

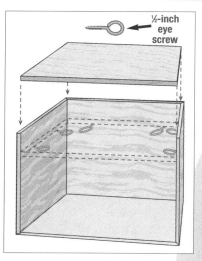

½-inch eye screw

A quick and easy way to add shelves in your storage compartments is to use brass eye screws as the mounting brackets. Measure the distance from the bottom of the cabinet to where the top of the shelf is going to be inserted; draw a line. Then install a ½-inch eye screw in each of the four corners. Cut a shelf to size and lay it on top of the eye screws. If the shelf turns out wobbly, just turn one or two of the eyelets until it becomes stabilized.

JIM SCHINSCHKE, LAKELAND, FLORIDA

SOME HANG-UPS ARE GOOD

For an orderly way to store small packets of sauces or snacks in your pantry area, get a piece of wood about 1 × 1½ inches by the height of your closet or pantry area. Paint it the same color as the closet interior, and fasten it to the side wall with screws. Place 2-inch finishing nails about 7 to 8 inches apart down the board. Keep a hole-punch, attached with string and fastened to a nail, to punch holes in the top edges of packages that don't come pre-punched for hanging on the store display. Use caution in making the holes so you don't puncture the main bag.

FRAN WARNER, MERRITT ISLAND, FLORIDA

TP HIDEAWAY

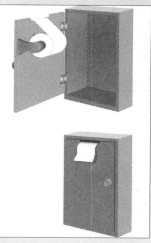

Most of us are constantly searching for ways to use space more efficiently and increase convenience. A particular inconvenience is the location of the toilet paper in our tiny bathroom. This was solved by mounting the holder inside the door of a nearby lavatory cabinet, toward the top of the door. A slot was then cut in the top of the door (the slot can also be cut through the door at different locations) and the paper fed so it can be accessed without opening the door. Reloading is very easy, and the cost of this project is negligible.

HARMON W. JOHNSON, SAN JOSE, CALIFORNIA

UNDER-TABLE STORAGE

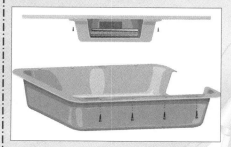

We needed more storage space near our dinette table in our motorhome. My husband purchased a kitty-litter box at the hardware store. He made a cutout in one end and mounted it, with eight screws through the rolled-over edge lip of the litter box, to the underside of the dinette table. This works great for storage of magazines and so forth while traveling, or for our laptop computer while in the campground.

MARILYN BURNETT, CHARDON, OHIO

◆ CLOSEUPS ◆ CLOSEUPS ◆ CLOSEUPS ◆ CLOSEUPS ◆ CLOSEUPS ◆

S T U F F   I T !

We like to recycle plastic grocery bags while traveling in our motorhome. To store the bags, we use a 1-gallon plastic milk jug. I cut a 3-inch hole in the side of the jug and stuff the empty bags into the jug. It is unbelievable the number of bags you can store! The milk jug is soft, can be stored in any corner, and will not scratch or dent the cabinets.
B.C. McCREA, PORT ANGELES, WASHINGTON

STORAGE FOR FIRST AND LAST

My LP-gas cylinder cover has a hinged lid, which I have found is a handy place to store items used when hooking up or unhooking. There is enough room for me to store the pipe used to tighten the chains, a cleaning rag and the name sign that I hang from my window cover.

These are the first and last items I use while setting up or breaking down camp, so I figure they should be stored in a convenient location.

LEONARD BLONDEALL, SKANDIA, MICHIGAN

UNIQUE AND WELCOME STORAGE

We are always looking for additional storage space or places to keep mail, magazines and other small items. One day I recalled how a piano bench had a great place to stow a variety of small things (music books) in the space under the seat. In our trailer we have a table and chairs and I thought the space under the chair seats would be a great place to stow a variety of small items. After removing the four screws that held each seat to the frame, I refastened the seat with two 1½-inch hinges and made a bottom out of ⅛-inch standard hardboard. I fastened the hardwood bottoms to each frame using a 1 × ½-inch wood strips on each side.

The entire project took less than two hours to complete (four chairs) and cost less than $20. The only tools were a saber saw, drill and screwdriver. You might call this our mini-desk drawers, and amazingly, this new storage space is already filled.

THOMAS BEAUCHAMP, PENSACOLA, FLORIDA

STORAGE RACK

We have two adjustable recliners, two folding plastic tables, and an aluminum cooking table and had no good way to store them in our pickup bed. The enclosed picture shows a rack I built to hold our tables and chairs.

I used ¾-inch outdoor plywood for the sides and end and ¼-inch plywood for the shelves. I didn't put a top on it because we have a tonneau cover on the pickup box. This box should be built to the size you need to fit your items.

GENE BOMKAMP, JANESVILLE, WISCONSIN

WHAT'S THE ANSWER?

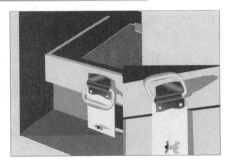

Basement-type motorhomes have a problem with the skinny, low-profile cross-chassis storage area that connects the deeper compartments on both sides of the motorhome. To keep chairs, small tables and other items from shifting in that area, a compartment box is the answer.

The bottom of the box is made of ⅜-inch plywood. The sides are made of 1 × 6-inch pine. (The dimensions of the box will depend on the size of the space in each individual motorhome.) The front tie-down is a piece of aluminum plate. It's fastened behind the pull handle and extends below the bottom front panel of the sliding box. The aluminum plate is secured to the deep compartment back wall with a wing nut and a ¼-inch carriage bolt.

Drill a hole in the back wall behind the spot where the aluminum plate comes to rest (make sure there are no holding tanks or other obstructions behind the area you plan to drill through). Insert the ¼-inch carriage bolt through the rear of the compartment so the bolt threads are facing into the compartment. Secure with a nut and washer.

Now, when you slide the new compartment box back in place, it is secured by a wing nut against the aluminum plate. The handle on the front makes it easy to pull out.

JIM COMPARONI, PALO ALTO, CALIFORNIA

UP WITH SHOES

To save space and keep the floor clear, we have taken shoe storage to new heights. Components include aluminum angle strips, plywood and (in our case) sheets of acrylic plastic for the shelves. The shelves rest on right-angle brackets that are Pop riveted to the aluminum uprights and wood strips on the plywood backer. For our six-shelf rack, we needed 12 right-angle brackets, 6 feet of aluminum angle stock, and a few scraps of plywood for the bottom and top pieces. It took about 90 minutes to get it all cut and assembled.
MARK KUYKENDALL, PRESCOTT, ARIZONA

UNIQUE STORAGE

Like other RVers, we try to maximize all the storage space in our fifth-wheel. Those shallow (or sloped) overhead cupboards in the bedroom became storage for our underwear and socks with the use of clear-plastic shoe-storage bags. I used the type that hang, which holds shoes in an upright position, and cut it into groups of four shoe slots per cupboard. Using large staples (or short screws), I attached them securely to the wall inside the cupboard. By using the clear shoe bag, I can see what is in them at a glance. This also frees up the shelf below the shoe pouches to store other items.
RITA DANIELS, SUNDANCE, WYOMING

USELESS ELEGANCE

Motorhomes of every type often share common flaws. Among these are interior cabinets with clear-glass doors, meant to give an elegant appearance, but often creating an impractical space where only decorations — or nice-looking items — can be placed, and nothing useful can be stored if you're concerned with aesthetics.

To reclaim this space, I created a cover-up for those doors using inexpensive materials. A piece of lightweight fabric of suitable color is cut approximately 4 inches longer than the height of the glass and about 1½ times the width. The extra length allows you to fold and hem the rough edges at the top and bottom.

Then a strip of hook-and-loop fastener is sewn to the top and bottom edges, gathering the material as the hook-and-loop fastener is attached. This creates a pleated panel for each "window," which then can be attached to the wood above and below the glass on the inside of the doors. Hook-and-loop fastener is sold with a self-adhesive backing, so the remaining half of each strip simply sticks to the inside of the door. This allows easy removal for laundering, if necessary, or even to change colors now and then.
NANCY BREMER, FALLSTON, MARYLAND

APPLIANCES
MAINTENANCE
AUTOMOTIVE
IN CAMP
SYSTEMS
STORAGE

TOWING

ACCESSORIES
SANITATION
DOORS, HATCHES
& HANDLES
CLEANING, PROTECTING
TOOLS
DEVICES & GADGETS
LIVABILITY
SAFETY

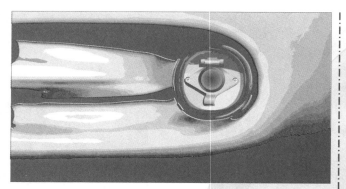

A BETTER WIRING METHOD

Instead of running my towed vehicle's wiring directly to a plug at the rear of my motorhome, I terminated the wiring at the grille area (of the towed vehicle) with a female connector identical to the one at the rear of my motorhome. I then made the connection by using a double male-ended jumper cable. This cable and the matching female connectors are available, as a kit, at Camping World and other RV-supply stores.

Using this method, I don't have to pull the unused wiring into a temporary storage area behind the grille each time I unhook the towed unit. Not having to open the hood each time I unhook is also an advantage. This method is a time-saver whether the tow bar stores on the back of the motorhome or on the front of the towed vehicle, or it comes off completely. The female plug for the towed vehicle can be installed in a number of locations — in the grille, or even better, in the bumper.

FRANK WOYTHAL, ANDOVER, NEW YORK

ANOTHER HITCH AID

Since we have an extended-cab pickup with tinted windows, I couldn't see well enough through the windows to back the hitch onto the pin on our fifth-wheel.

I placed a 2-inch reflector above the pin and turned on the pickup's cargo light. I lined up the reflector with the line of the divided glass rear window to hook up without problems. If your rear window is one-piece glass, put a short strip of tape in the middle.

OWENS KOLLAR, QUEEN CITY, MISSOURI

CATASTROPHE

*T*he electrically controlled slideout of my fifth-wheel is secured for travel by placing two metal poles between the inside wall of the slideout and the outside wall of the trailer.

These poles must be removed before the motorized slideout is opened. Failure to do so could result in serious and very expensive damage, including the strong possibility of puncturing the outer trailer wall.

To avoid catastrophe, I simply placed a "dot" of hook-and-loop fastener on the slideout switch and another on the rear of an index card. On the face of the card I wrote: "REMOVE POLES." The card is stuck to the face of the switch, completely covering the extend button.

RICHARD FIORUCCI, SHIRLEY, NEW YORK

ANOTHER SOLUTION TO AN OLD PROBLEM

*A*fter purchasing a saddle-type toolbox for my extended-cab pickup, I discovered, much to my dismay, that I could not see my fifth-wheel hitch from the driver's seat. This made it almost impossible to line up the hitch saddle slot with the trailer kingpin when hitching up.

I solved the problem by placing a couple of 1-inch-long pieces of black electrical tape exactly at the side-to-side center and at the back edge of the toolbox top cover. When hitching, I look in the rearview mirror and line up the black tape with the kingpin or with a point on the trailer directly above the kingpin (when I can no longer see the kingpin). Using the rearview mirror and the black tape to line up the centerline of the truck means that I should never miss the kingpin. I still find my wife irreplaceable in making sure that the kingpin clears the tailgate and is at the correct hitch height.

After I discovered that this worked so well, I masked out the area surrounding the tape, removed the tape, and used spray paint to put down a more permanent mark.

ART BROWN, AUBURN, WASHINGTON

ANOTHER LOCKING DEVICE

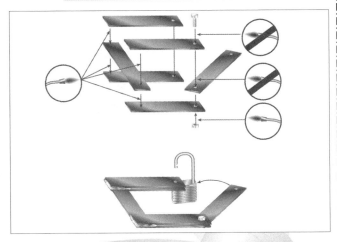

Illustrated is a locking device that I made to go around the hitch pin on our fifth-wheel. It is made from six pieces of steel, ⅛-inch thick and 5 inches long, and a bolt. There are two layers on the sides, one layer in the back and the locking piece in the front. Weld the sides and the back pieces together. Drill holes in each of the open legs of the device and the last piece of steel. Bolt the last piece of steel to one side of the opening, leaving it slightly loose to act as a hinge. Have the nut welded to the bolt, or a few seconds with a wrench will make the device useless. Lastly, place the device around the hitchpin and close it with a good, quality lock.

HAROLD OVESEN, WILTON, IDAHO

BASE RAIL PINS

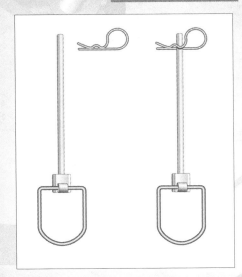

Pins holding a fifth-wheel to the base rails in the bed of the truck sometimes get stuck and can be difficult to remove.

Many farm supply stores have a longer pin with a swivel pull, making the disconnect easier. It might be necessary to grind down the pin collar on one side to insert it into the rail base.

CARMAN BRUMLEY, HUNTSVILLE, TEXAS

BACKING UP IS HARD TO DO

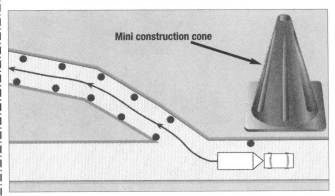

Mini construction cone

I pull a trailer. Because I travel alone, backing into a campsite, particularly one that has a bend in it, can sometimes be quite an adventure. I found an easy, inexpensive solution. I carry a dozen mini construction cones with me. Before backing into a site, I place a pair of cones where I want my trailer bumper to be (a cone at each corner). Then I place the rest of the cones in a double line along the length of the pad. When I back up, the orange cones are very visible in my outside rearview mirrors. As long I stay between the "runway" of cones, I know I won't be hitting any obstacles.

These cones are available at most mass-merchandise stores in the sporting-goods department. They are typically used as boundary markers for soccer games. They come in sets of four and sell for around $5. Buy the ones that have slits in their sides; if you accidentally run one over, they spring right back.

TIM STAATS, VENTURA, CALIFORNIA

BULL'S EYE

Like many other readers, I rigged up a mirror so I could see the alignment of the hitch ball on my tow vehicle and the coupler on my trailer, thereby making hooking up a one-person operation. The only problem I had was when the back end of my tow vehicle was in the shadows. This made it very difficult to distinguish the ball as I backed to the trailer.

I solved this problem by cutting a slot in a small piece of plywood that fits around the ball and painting it white. Now, as I get ready to hook up, I slide the plywood under the ball and it stands out like a bull's eye, even in the shadows.

C. HAROLD MATHEWS JR., HIGHLAND, CALIFORNIA

BALL-MOUNT HANDLE

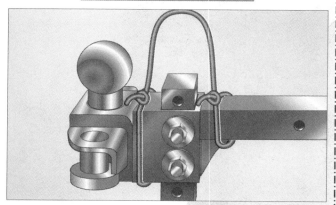

Ball mounts can often weigh more than 30 pounds and must be carried to be inserted into the receivers. Not only are they heavy and bulky, they are greasy. To make the handling task easier, cleaner and safer, I devised a cheap, simple system. Take a section of 12-2 electrical cable and attach it to the section of the ball mount where the head and shank are bolted together. This provides good balance. Secure the cable by knotting or twisting the ends. No more greasy hands or clothes and no awkward "arm's-length" carrying. The plastic insulation is gentle on the hands and, best of all, this "cable handle" can be left on permanently if it doesn't create any interference with the hookup. You might have to play around with positioning to come up with the best balance point for your ball mount.

STAN F. IMBODEN, LITITZ, PENNSYLVANIA

CLOTHESPIN TRICK

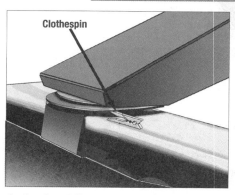

Clothespin

When I first bought my fifth-wheel trailer, I was constantly raising the front too high and jamming the kingpin into the hitch latch when hooking up. I glued a clothespin on the hitch saddle, so that it opens when the kingpin is in the right position to be seated properly in the latch. Now, when I hook up, I look at the clothespin. When it starts to close, the kingpin is at the correct height to latch up without interference and jamming. Any epoxy cement will work great, but make sure you clean the saddle surface with a solvent before gluing the clothespin.

JOE BARRETT, BOWLING GREEN, KENTUCKY

BATTERY SAVER

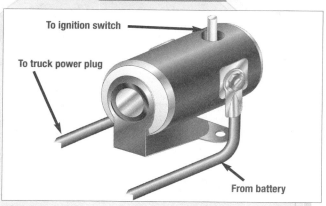

To ignition switch

To truck power plug

From battery

When traveling in my self-contained travel trailer, I often park at night without disconnecting from the tow vehicle. Since my vehicle has a charge circuit leading to the trailer, I felt it necessary to disconnect the electrical cord from the tow vehicle to prevent battery discharge. This was a nuisance and created the possibility that I might drive off without reconnecting it. I solved the problem by installing a high-amperage 12-volt DC relay in the charging line that closes only when the tow-vehicle ignition is on. Parts are readily available at auto- and boating-supply stores.

CARL GRAHAM, ANGIER, NORTH CAROLINA

CLEAN ELECTRICAL RECEPTACLE

Imount the fifth-wheel electrical receptacle in the left-rear stake pocket, just ahead of my pickup's tailgate. It's the best place I've found to mount this receptacle, and I have used this method since 1977 in five pickups. Not only is it convenient to use, but the wiring in the back of the receptacle is better protected. To mount this receptacle, remove the

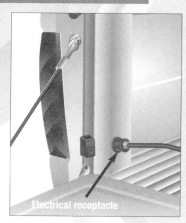

Electrical receptacle

taillight housing so that you can check for obstructions before drilling the hole. Once the "coast is clear," drill a ½-inch hole in the center spot you have chosen. Use a 2-inch knockout punch to make the hole large enough to mount the receptacle. (Your local electrician should have a knockout punch, or try using a good-quality hole saw.) Route the wires up through the stake pocket and attach to the receptacle. Drill four holes for the mounting screws.

REY PEDERSON, BAUDETTE, MINNESOTA

DOUBLE-DUTY TRUCK BED

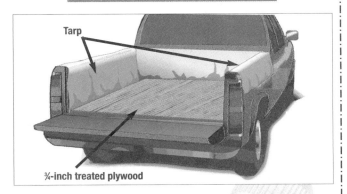

Tarp

¾-inch treated plywood

After having a fifth-wheel hitch installed, I found that the mounting rails in the truck bed interfered with sliding things in and out of the bed. To restore the truck's usefulness (for other things besides towing), I purchased a sheet of ¾-inch treated plywood and cut it to fit the truck bed. Needing to pick up loads of gravel and bark, I realized that the rails were going to be a problem while unloading and cleaning loose material out of the bed. My solution was to use an 8 × 12-foot tarp in the bed and then place the plywood on top of it. Being flat, the plywood made it easy to shovel the loose material out. When the plywood is clean, I pull it out and then remove the tarp, taking with it any left-over material. This leaves the truck bed and rails clean, ready for the next towing job.

When I put the tarp in the bed, I make sure it hangs over both sides and the front of the bed so that material doesn't get behind it.

JOSEPH DELEUW, PORT ORCHARD, WASHINGTON

FLAG HOLDER REVISITED

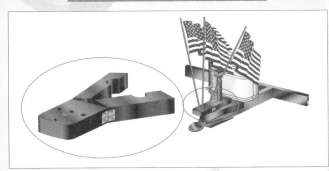

I'd like to share my flag holder so that travel trailers can fly Old Glory.

My flag holder is cut from a 2 × 4-inch piece of wood and held to the A-frame jack post using two ¼ × 2½-inch-long lag screws. Two small hinges are used to make the "arms" movable. The holes for the flags were drilled at a 20-degree angle; the holes should be sized for the individual flags used.

CHUCK LEWIS, ONEIDA, NEW YORK

IMPROVE YOUR STONE CONTROL

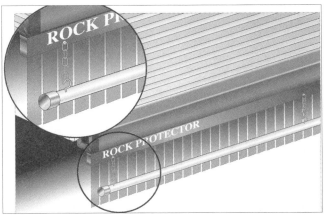

ROCK PROTECTOR

Ever notice how the stone guards at the back end of RVs are almost horizontal at highway speeds? This makes them less effective at what they were designed to do. To enable one to remain as vertical as possible, here is a simple fix. From the hardware store, purchase an 8-foot length of ½-inch iron pipe (copper is not heavy enough). Also purchase a few lengths of light chain about 9 inches long.

Attach one end of each chain to the pipe by drilling a hole through the pipe and attaching it with appropriate hardware. Drill these holes about one foot from each end. Attach the other end of the chain to the upper part of the stone protector, which will be either the steel channel or the solid plastic section that runs across the entire top of it.

You will find that this pipe hanging on the rear side of the stone protector will serve to keep it in place, thus doing a better job of protecting your towed vehicle.

PAUL POLETTO, SCOTIA, NEW YORK

◆ CLOSEUPS ◆ CLOSEUPS ◆ CLOSEUPS ◆

E A S Y   H O O K U P   O F   E Q U A L I Z E R - B A R   C H A I N S

W*hen hitching up, I use an easy-and-quick method to determine which link of the spring bar chains to use when attaching the bars to the brackets on my trailer's A-frame. I used a permanent felt-tip marker to color the proper link (blue or black works best). This way I don't have to count the links at all. In the early spring when I go on my first trip of the year, I don't have to ponder how many links I dropped during my last trip.*

RICHARD DIXON, SALISBURY, NORTH CAROLINA

◆ CLOSEUPS ◆ CLOSEUPS ◆ CLOSEUPS ◆

CONNECTOR COVER

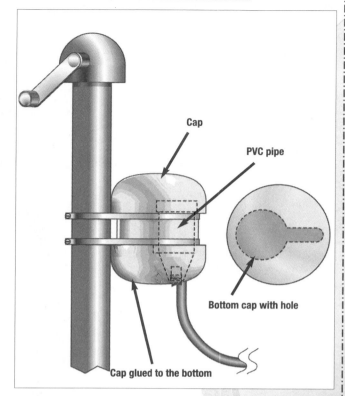

Cap

PVC pipe

Bottom cap with hole

Cap glued to the bottom

While looking for a way to store my trailer's electrical connector, I designed a PVC holder that attaches to the A-frame jack and keeps the connector clean and dry. The holder consists of two 4-inch PVC end-caps, joined by a short piece of PVC pipe and is attached to the jack post using two hose clamps.

To make the holder, first cut a piece of 4-inch PVC pipe long enough to hold the connector and allow an extra ½-inch of space. Glue one cap to the pipe. On one side of the remaining cap, cut a hole just large enough to pass the connector, but not the locking tab. On the other side, cut a hole 1/16-inch smaller than the diameter of the connector cable. Next, draw two lines joining the holes, keeping the width between the lines equal to the diameter of the smaller hole. Then cut along the lines with a coping saw. Finally, glue the remaining cap to the pipe and connect the pipe to the jack post with the opening face down. Make sure you can still turn the jack handle without interference.

To use the holder, rotate the connector so the locking tab aligns with the slot joining the two holes. Insert the connector into the larger hole until it clears the end-cap, then slide the cable into the slot toward the smaller hole. The holder shields the connector from rain and snow, but unlike a sealed container, it allows fresh air to dry any condensation that can lead to corroded terminals.

Paul J. Carreiro, Swansea, Massachusetts

DANGLING UMBILICAL CORD

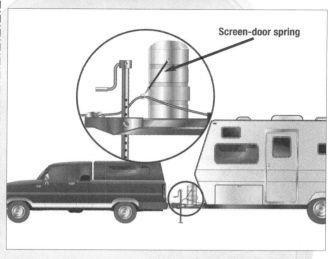

Screen-door spring

My electrical cord between the trailer and truck was hitting the ground when making tight left turns. Several times this caused the cord to unplug, damaging the cord and plug. I solved this problem by Pop riveting a hook onto the LP-gas-cylinder cover and putting a wire tie with screw eye on the electrical cord. I purchased a light-screen door spring from a local hardware store and attached it between the hook and screw eye. The cord now stays high and dry and has never caused a problem again.

B.C. McCrea, Port Angeles, Washington

HANDY MEASUREMENT

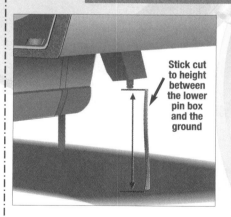

Stick cut to height between the lower pin box and the ground

I travel alone and am always looking for ways to make the fifth-wheel hitching process easier. Several years ago, a friend got me an old stick (any size will do), and I cut it to a length that represented the distance between the lower side of the pin box and the ground (clearance needed to hitch up). I just hold the stick near the pin box and use the landing jacks to raise the front. When the stick clears the pin box, the fifth-wheel is ready to be hitched. It hasn't failed me yet. I store the old stick in the pickup box and no one is likely to steal it.

Betty Callaway, Tigard, Oregon

EASY MIRROR ADJUSTMENT

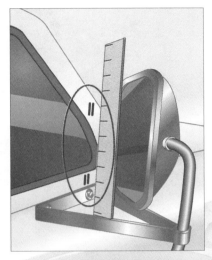

Here is an easy way to adjust your mirrors the way you want them. Take a straightedge and lay it across the surface of the mirror and slide it until it touches the body of the tow vehicle. Then place two marks; one where the straightedge lines up with the top of the mirror and one where it lines up at the bottom.

Do this on both sides of the vehicle when the mirrors are in the "in" and in the "out" positions. When this is done, all you have to do is to look across the mirror and line up with the marks on the vehicle and the mirror is adjusted.

I use a Magic Marker to make the marks as they will come off with mineral spirit. You might have to renew them now and then.

RICHARD WARD, SUN CITY, ARIZONA

GAUGE IT

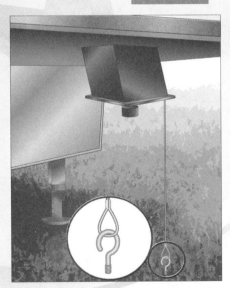

Every fifth-wheel comes with a "gauge" to determine how much the front of the trailer needs to be raised or lowered for easy hitching: your breakaway lanyard, which is always handy. In my case, an S-hook in the end loop not only gives me the right length but also provides a little weight to let it hang straight. When the end of the hook just touches the ground, I can back right in with no problem. When I'm done, I just toss the S-hook into the pin box.

JERRY HATCH, LIVINGSTON, TEXAS

HITCH ALIGNMENT

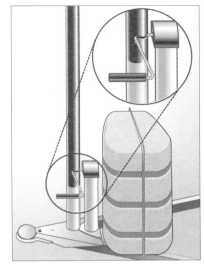

Here is an idea for aligning a pickup hitch with a trailer coupler. I've tried several methods, but this one works the best for me. It allows me to back up without turning around, I just look at the inside rearview mirror and align the turned-up handle of the rear window on my bed cap with the tube I mounted on the trailer's crank-handle mount.

I used a piece of 2-inch PVC tubing approximately 48 inches long and cut a slot in the side of the tube at the height of the crank handle. I marked the height of the crank handle and cut a ⅜-inch-wide slot about a quarter of the way through the diameter of the tube to allow the handle to enter. Using a round rasp or a rat-tail file, I filed a notch in the end of the slot to allow the handle to lock the tubing in place, so it would not fall off. To get better contrast against the white trailer, I painted the top section of the tube red.

Place the tube in front of the jack, slip the handle into the slot, press it down to lock it in place and it is ready to use. I stow it in the pickup when not in use.

A.P. MOREAU, BENBROOK, TEXAS

IT'S NO JOKE

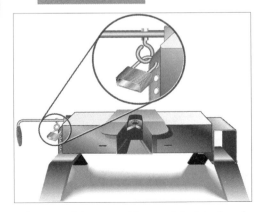

While you're parked in some areas, certain people think it is fun to release your fifth-wheel hitch, which will cause your trailer to tear up your truck bed and tailgate when you drive away. To stop this, I replaced the bolt in my fifth-wheel hitch with an eyebolt on the pull handle. I keep a padlock between the eyebolt and the adjustment bracket.

FRED WILSON, STOCKTON, CALIFORNIA

LIGHT UP THE CAMPSITE

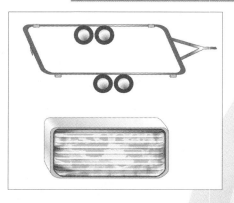

We find it very difficult backing our travel trailer into a campsite in the dark. Although my wife uses a flashlight to guide me, I still spend a great deal of time pulling forward and then reversing, trying to straighten out my combination, only to annoy my neighbors and find, in the morning, the RV is still way out of whack. To solve the problem, I purchased five clear automotive light fixtures from an auto-parts store. These are small inexpensive 12-volt DC fixtures with lenses similar to the outside porch light used on my trailer. I mounted the lights on the bottom of the trailer, with two on the street side, two on the curbside and one on the aft end. I then wired them in parallel with the power coming from the trailer's 12-volt DC fuse box and through a toggle switch that I mounted inside the trailer.

Now when we arrive at a campsite in the dark, my wife goes into the trailer and flips a switch. I can see the entire parking pad and back my trailer with ease. By running the power from the trailer's fuse box, I did not have to run another wire from my tow vehicle's back-up lights. I can also use the lights while camping, if needed.

R.D. PARPART II, HOBART, INDIANA

LOST PINS

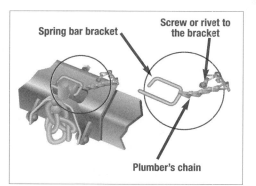

Spring bar bracket

Screw or rivet to the bracket

Plumber's chain

In more than 30 years of trailering, I have never lost a pin that is used to secure the spring-bar brackets. I simply slip a 6-inch-long piece of plumber's chain on the pin, drill a hole in the bracket and Pop rivet or screw the chain to the bracket. The weight and restraint of the chain will keep the pin from rotating or moving. It can't be lost and it will be right there to remind you to use it. All this for less than a buck's worth of material.

EDSON B. SNOW, POMPANO BEACH, FLORIDA

MIRROR, MIRROR

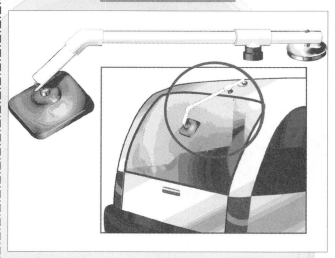

To make life easier while backing my Tahoe to hitch up the trailer, I fabricated a simple and inexpensive mirror system. It's easy to build and can be positioned on the roof of the vehicle in seconds. I used 1-inch PVC schedule-40 pipe, a T-fitting and a 90-degree elbow to make the arm. A mirror is attached to one end and a strong magnet to the other. A crutch tip, attached to the T-fitting, is used for stability and to prevent scratches to the vehicle's paint. The total cost was only $8.

BILL JANZING, GRAHAM, WASHINGTON

PULL THE FUSE — NOT YOUR HAIR!

When I traded my Saturn for a Malibu, I had to start pulling fuses prior to flat-towing. My wife had to keep looking at the chart to see which ones to pull, and after a short time, I lost the little fuse-puller. Pli-

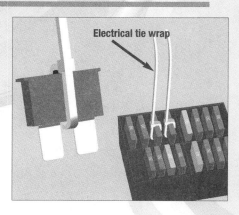

Electrical tie wrap

ers didn't work too well, and we still had to look at the chart.

I thought I'd try a small electrical tie wrap around the fuse for a puller, and it worked perfectly. Since I can leave it on the fuse, we just grab the tails, pull the fuses and drop them into the cup holder. To put the fuse back, the tail serves as a handle and makes it easy to re-insert. When the fuse cover is in place, the tails just fold down out of the way.

GEORGE ROEPE, EXTON, PENNSYLVANIA

ON THE LEVEL

To know where to position your trailer or fifth-wheel (up or down) prior to hookup, attach a small level within sight of your jack or leveling switch. Mount the level with a small screw, but only snug down so it can be moved back and forth.

When parking, raise the trailer so that the coupler clears the hitch ball or the kingpin clears the hitch saddle, then by moving the level assembly, center the bubble between the lines on the level before you pull the tow vehicle away from the trailer. Then level your rig in the usual way.

When you're ready to hookup and depart, simply raise or lower your trailer to center the bubble and you're ready to back up for a perfect hookup!

BUD REED, ENID, OKLAHOMA

PLUG SAFETY CATCH

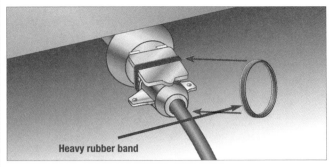

Heavy rubber band

Recently, while towing a 30-foot fifth-wheel trailer, I experienced a scary situation while traveling in traffic. Cars would pass on my left, blowing their horns and making gestures. Thankfully, I was finally able to make it through without a collision, but shortly after that I discovered that my brake control light was not lit, signaling a problem with the plug. Sure enough, the safety catch on the receptacle had opened and allowed the plug to jar loose. That left me without lights and trailer brakes. Looking back, this may have happened after passing over rough railroad tracks prior to entering the highway. A heavy rubber band solved the problem. By attaching the rubber band around the receptacle cap, the safety catch stays in place, securing the plug.

FRED E. ROSI, VINELAND, NEW JERSEY

STRINGS ARE ATTACHED

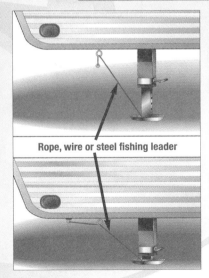

Rope, wire or steel fishing leader

Tired of dirtying you knees when lifting the leg extensions in your fifth-wheel trailer's landing jacks? I devised a way to make it easier. First, drill a hole under the fifth-wheel near each leg and install a screw eye. Next, tie a rope (or wire) to the pin at the base of the leg. The rope is put through the eye and terminates with a ring or magnet. I used a magnet to keep the ring from swinging. After pulling the pin while holding the extension in place, a simple pull on the rope raises the leg. Secure the pin and you're done. It worked best when using a spring-loaded leg-extension lock, rather than a pin and clip.

JASON ROSE, MIAMI, FLORIDA

WHAT A DRAG

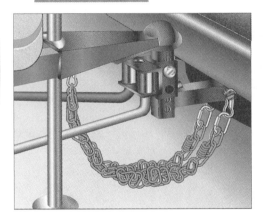

To keep my trailer's safety chain from dragging on the highway while traveling, I used a ⅜-inch-thick bungee cord. Secure one end of the bungee cord to the chain hook by bending the wire hook closed. Remove the other wire hook from the other end of the bungee cord. Interweave the bungee cord through every other link of the safety chain. Secure the end of the bungee cord to the trailer-hitch safety-chain attachment point by looping through, fold the end back upon itself and tie with wire. Do the same thing for the other chain. This method will allow the chains to extend and retract while making turns.

GARY NOKES, DEL RIO, TEXAS

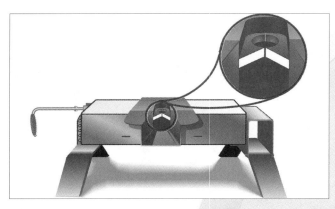

SEEING IS BELIEVING

To make it easier to see if your fifth-wheel hitch is in the locked position, paint the ends of the locking mechanism white. They will be highly visible, and there will never be a doubt about when the mechanism is in the proper position.
JACK FOX, CARTHAGE, TEXAS

◆ CLOSEUPS ◆ CLOSEUPS ◆ CLOSEUPS ◆

PREVENTING THE DROPS

If you want to prevent the front of your fifth-wheel from dropping onto the truck while hitching or unhitching (causing serious and expensive damage), follow these tips.

When hitching, make sure the trailer wheels are blocked. Back the truck toward the trailer, but stop when the hitch is about one foot from the kingpin. Attach the power connector (now is a good time to check the lights). Use the manual brake-control lever to lock the trailer brakes while you back the final one foot, until the hitch closes onto the kingpin. With the trailer brakes still locked, shift into low and slowly press the accelerator. The trailer should hold the truck, which will prove a solid connection. Raise the trailer jacks, remove the wheel blocks and you're on your way.

When unhitching, first block a trailer wheel. Lower the front jacks and release the hitch, while the trailer power cord is still connected. Apply the trailer brakes manually while pulling the truck forward about one foot. Apply the truck's parking brake and slowly release the manual lever on the brake controller, assuring the trailer doesn't roll. If all is well, unplug the trailer power connector and drive out from under the hitch. Now you may safely take care of your setup chores.
RONALD L. WHEELER, OCEANO, CALIFORNIA

◆ CLOSEUPS ◆ CLOSEUPS ◆ CLOSEUPS ◆

PARKING GUIDE

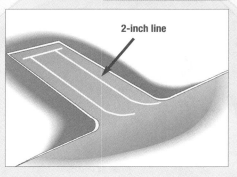

2-inch line

When parking my 30-foot fifth-wheel trailer beside my house, I rely on a system that works without a helper. The parking space is on a concrete pad and the eaves make for a very tight fit; maneuvering is very difficult without guidance. I fixed the problem by painting a 2-inch line on the concrete in the exact location of the arc that the RV's wheels will have to follow. The line starts at the point where I have to start the backing process and is painted so that the left wheels can be easily seen by the driver from his/her window or mirror. At the spot where the RV's wheels should be stopped, a short line is painted at a right angle, allowing the driver to know exactly where to stop.

To find the proper position, park the RV in the exact spot where you store it — with help, of course. Wash the concrete pad to remove all tire tracks and allow to dry. Mark the position of the wheels on the concrete. With help, slowly pull or drive the RV out of the storage space to the point where you start your backing process. Paint a 2-inch-wide line (or wider, if you wish) down the center of the tire track left on the concrete. At the point where you marked the wheel position, paint a right-angle line where the wheel should stop.

Using this method, I can back the trailer along within 12 inches of the house eaves, every time, without help. If you are not parking on pavement, you can use stakes driven into the ground, linked with rope.
HARVEY E. MARSHALL, ATASCADERO, CALIFORNIA

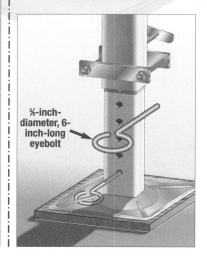

⅜-inch-diameter, 6-inch-long eyebolt

SAVE YOUR BACK

To make it easier to pull up the telescoping legs (landing gear) on the front of fifth-wheels, install a ⅜-inch-diameter, 6-inch-long eye-bolt through the lower pin hole on each leg. It gives you something to grab and easily hold.
JAY HARVEY, LOS ALAMITOS, CALIFORNIA

RIGHT ON TARGET

I believe I have discovered the ultimate method for aligning a fifth-wheel or trailer for less than $10 bucks. It allows the driver to back up and hit it right the first time, every time. The system uses a laser light mounted exactly in the middle and at the top of the tow vehicle's front window (many times a screw is already there). The laser shines out the rear window, onto the front of the trailer, where a washer that is glued in place is used as a target.

When backing up, the driver looks in the rear-view mirror, moving the steering wheel to keep the red dot in the middle of the washer (it may move vertically due to unlevel ground). You'll need a laser pointer that sells for around $7 in discount stores, a battery clip to hold the laser (available at RadioShack for $1) and a washer.

A Three-ring binder hole reinforcement can be glued to the rear window and the battery clip can be used to move the laser if the red dot is not shining through to the right spot on the trailer due to unleveled terrain.

DICK WILLIAMS, LONG BEACH, CALIFORNIA

VOILÁ — NO MESS

E very time I hook up our travel trailer, I seem to have a built-in magnet to collect grease on my clothes, hands or whatever. I solved this problem with some wax paper. Take a square of wax paper (12 inches), fold it in half, then in half again, so that you end up with a piece ¼ the size you started out with. Place the square of

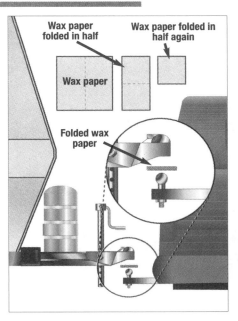

wax paper over the hitch ball and lower the trailer hitch over it, so that the wax paper goes up inside the hitch. There is enough lubricant in the wax paper to lube your hitch.

MARVIN ROSENBERGER JR., LOWELL, MICHIGAN

Editor's note: Make sure the coupler is securely locked to the ball.

SOMETIMES LIFE IS A DRAG

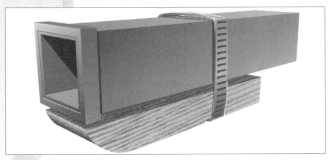

M y motorhome has fairly good clearance, but every once in a while the hitch receiver drags when going up a severely sloped driveway. So I cut a piece of oak the width of the receiver and about 8 inches long, cut a groove in it to receive a stainless-steel hose clamp, slightly beveled the rear edge and treated it with wood preservative. I clamped it onto the hitch receiver, so the wood drags instead of the steel receiver end. When it eventually wears away, it won't be hard or expensive to replace.

ROBERT FALK, ATLANTA, GEORGIA

MAINTENANCE
AUTOMOTIVE
IN CAMP
SYSTEMS
STORAGE
TOWING

ACCESSORIES

SANITATION
DOORS, HATCHES
& HANDLES
CLEANING, PROTECTING
TOOLS
DEVICES & GADGETS
LIVABILITY
SAFETY
APPLIANCES

BIKE RACK FOR CHAIRS

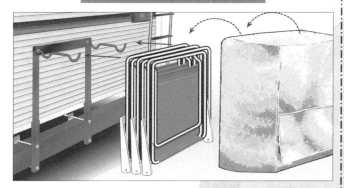

Finding a place to store outdoor chairs can be difficult in some rigs. We found that a standard bicycle rack installed on the rear bumper of our trailer will hold four chairs without modifications. These bike racks can be found in Camping World and other RV supply stores. While the bumper mount worked for our trailer, those rigs with hitches can use one of the many bicycle racks designed to be installed in 2-inch receivers.

A vinyl cover was made to protect the chairs from the elements. The cover was made with a flap that comes up from the bottom and is held with hook-and-loop material. Another flap hangs down to cover the open end and is also held with hook-and-loop material. Elastic is sewn around the bottom to assist in making it weathertight.

PAT AND SYLVIA KELLY, KENT, WASHINGTON

CAMPER STABILIZERS

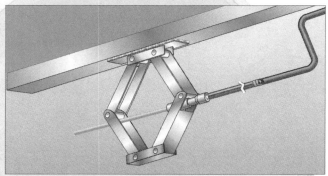

When we purchased our travel trailer, it did not have any stabilizers on it. I found an easy and inexpensive way to get and install the needed stabilizers. What really works well are the scissors-type car jacks. They are easy to find at your local auto junkyard. Turn the jacks upside down, place them 18 to 24 inches from the ends of the frame, extend to level and carry the weight of the rig. Your local welder can attach the jacks to the frame.

While at the junkyard, pick up a folding jack handle. Then purchase a ½-inch swivel extension and a ¾-inch socket to match the nut on the jack. Weld the ½-inch swivel to the folding jack handle and place the socket on the swivel. If you like, use a hand electric drill and socket to raise and lower your jacks.

DEAN CHRISTOFFEL, LEMARS, IOWA

BUMPER HEADS

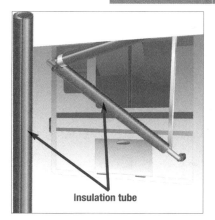

Insulation tube

When the awning is extended, the arms can become real head bangers, if one does not pay attention. I use removable foam sleeves that fit over the awning support arms on any RV. If you happen to hit your head after these foam sleeves are installed, you will not hurt yourself.

Just purchase 4-foot-long "hollow" insulation tubes from any hardware store, pool supply or discount center. These tubes are commonly used and are readily available. They cost $4 each. Split the center with a knife and then slip them over the supports. They are very light, stay on without straps and can be easily stored when not in use.

J. GERARD WEIPERT, PARADISE VALLEY, ARIZONA

CLOCKWORK

To save money, the manufacturers have the clock incorporated into the radios of our various vehicles, motorhomes included. This is very inconvenient, because the LED numbers are small and out of our line of sight as we drive down the road.

One of the answers to this problem is to buy an inexpensive battery-powered clock that fastens to your dash with hook-and-loop fastener. The clock comes with batteries that last for years. They are widely available at most hardware and discount stores.

ALLAN BENNETT, FOUNTAIN HILLS, ARIZONA

CLEVER CABLE CONNECTIONS

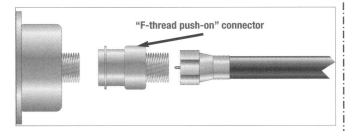

"F-thread push-on" connector

The connections for cable television in campgrounds are often corroded or have damaged threads, making hooking up somewhat more difficult. To make it a little easier, I purchased an F-thread push-on connector at the local electronics store and screwed it on the end of my TV cable. Now, when setting up, I just push the cable end onto the campground threaded fitting and sit back and enjoy watching television.

ARTHUR HOFF, NAUGATUCK, CONNECTICUT

DRYING RACK

Here's an idea for a drying rack. Attach one of your lightweight aluminum folding chairs to your rear ladder, using the ever-popular bungee cord. This gives you an extended drying rack for jeans, shirts, etc. without allowing them to brush against your motorhome.

MERIL TAYLOR, EMORY, TEXAS

◆ CLOSEUPS ◆ CLOSEUPS ◆ CLOSEUPS ◆

ARM EXTENSION

I have read about people who have problems adjusting the right-side mirror without a helper. I solved this problem using the rod for pulling out the awning to push or pull on the mirror. First, I loosen the nut that holds the mirror in position, then open the window and make the adjustments with the awning wand. When in position, I get out and tighten the mirror.

RON CRAIG, HIGH RIDGE, MISSOURI

GAIN SOME CLEARANCE

We spend our recreational time in the sun using our fifth-wheel and one-ton pickup. We take along our portable carport to shade the truck. Our carport is actually a tub-framed backyard gazebo. The trouble was that our gazebo was not tall enough to clear the cab of the truck. I went to the hardware store and got two 18-inch pieces of PVC pipe of a diameter just large enough for the gazebo legs to slide into.

I only needed to raise the front legs. To make the extensions, I drilled a hole in each piece of PVC, 6 inches from one end, to run the pins (bolts) through. The gazebo legs rest on the pins. The gazebo tie-down loops are still used, with the addition of a bungee cord, to anchor the gazebo in the ground. I used another ground stake to slip the extension over to keep it in a fixed position.

The carport is now 12 inches taller in the front and secures against gusty winds.

RAY JOYNER, CORVALLIS, OREGON

MORE VOLUME, LESS PRESSURE

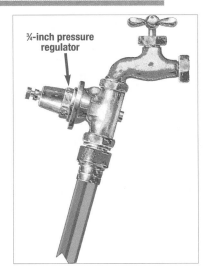

¾-inch pressure regulator

If you are dissatisfied with the low volume of water flow in your RV due to the restriction in the water regulator (¼-inch opening), try using a household type unit. I purchased a ¾-inch pressure regulator at a hardware store and put an adapter on each end to make it fit the water-hose-type inlet and outlet fittings. The regulator is preset for 50 psi, but there is an adjustment to reduce pressure to 45 psi (the desired pressure for RV water systems). This doubled the water flow in our rig.

TOM HARMS, SALEM, OREGON

EXTRA WATER

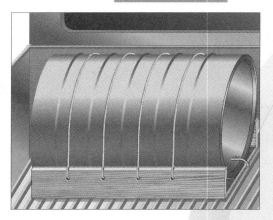

Idry camp most of the time, and the amount of water I can store is the only factor that limits my stay. Rather than shuttling 5-gallon plastic jugs to refill my 20-gallon water tank, I purchased a new 65-gallon spray tank from a farm-supply store, secured it to a wood base, so it wouldn't roll over, and added a cut-off valve at the lower-drain outlet. The tank fits crossways in the back of my Ford F-150 pickup and can easily be removed when empty. We usually drive to our destination with empty tanks, then fill up on water and gas at the last station before camp, because 65 gallons of water weighs about 500 pounds or so.

For refilling the trailer water tank, I have a dedicated garden hose that drains water from the 65-gallon nurse tank by gravity. The bottom of the truck bed is slightly higher that the filler on the trailer. I also insulated the tank with 6-inch-thick batts of fiberglass and covered it with black plastic for winter camping.

DENIS MCGRATH, FT. MORGAN, COLORADO

NO ARMREST?

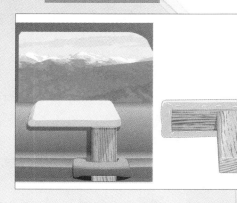

Lacking an armrest at a usable height on the driver's side door of our Class C, the only place to rest your left arm when driving with both hands on the wheel was on the windowsill. Because of the distance from the driver to the sill, this was nearly impossible and very tiring. The drawing shows an easily made armrest that can be adapted to a variety of vehicles.

The vertical post is a 7-inch-long piece of 2 × 4, sized to slide snugly into the existing door pull and reach the windowsill. The face of the 2 × 4 was sanded until a snug-sliding fit was obtained. A 3 × 9-inch piece of ½-inch plywood was used for the armrest itself.

For better comfort, the armrest was angled slightly toward the driver by beveling the end of the post and offsetting it toward the windowsill to ensure it rested solidly along the sill for support. Finally, the wood was sanded and sealed. My wife padded the armrest for comfort, using several layers of toweling covered with denim fabric stapled to the underside of the armrest. The armrest is easily installed or removed and is very comfortable.

J. ROBERT KELCHNER, MONTOUR FALLS, NEW YORK

LEVELING-BLOCK TRACTION

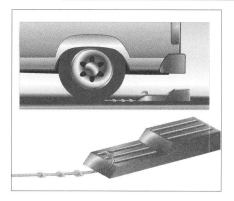

Our two-step plastic leveling block used to skid ahead of the tire when used on grass or gravel. My wife came up with the idea of using a rope to improve traction, so I modified the blocks and they work great. I drilled a hole in the lower end of the block and threaded a ½-inch rope up through the hole. A length of rope is allowed to dangle from the block and another knot is tied in the rope. Now the tire rolls up on the rope and holds the block from skidding.

PAUL HUSTON, ELKO, GEORGIA

◆ CLOSEUPS ◆ CLOSEUPS ◆ CLOSEUPS ◆

R A T ' S   N E S T W I R I N G

*W*ith the increasing number of connections to be made to an RV (cable or satellite television, phone, etc.), there always seems to be a "rat's nest" of wires to untangle when hooking up. I did away with the problem by laying the phone wire along the TV wire and wrapping the wires with spiral wrap tubing (available in hardware stores, RadioShack, etc.). This polyethylene tubing is able to withstand the elements and is stiff enough to keep the wires from forming another "rat's nest."

JAMES GODDETTE, VERGENNES, VERMONT

LEVELING-JACK PADS

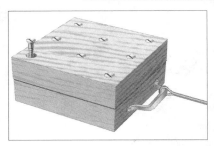

When making pads for use under your motorhome's leveling jacks, cut (or have the lumber yard cut) 12-inch sections of 2 × 12-inch wood (two pieces per jack). Screw the two pieces together so that the grain of each piece is running at right angles to the other. This will counteract the pressure from the jack and keep the wood from splitting. Attach a window handle to one edge, and tie a 3- or 4-foot length of brightly colored plastic (polypropylene) rope to the handle. The window handle will make it easy to carry the pads. The colored rope (left extended from beneath the vehicle) will help remind you that the pads are still on the ground and will keep you from having to crawl under the vehicle to retrieve them.

ALLAN BENNETT, FOUNTAIN HILLS, ARIZONA

PORTABLE SHOP BENCH

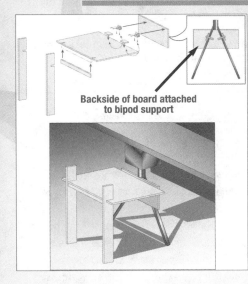

Backside of board attached to bipod support

By using the bipod support under the kingpin box of my fifth-wheel trailer, I've been able to construct a workbench. The arm swings behind the bipod to lock the framing in place. The bench surface is hinged to the back board and swings up for use or down for storage. The legs are notched to correspond with notches in the tabletop to avoid shifting.

The dimensions of the various parts will vary depending on how large a work surface you will want, the shape of your bipod, the height of the work surface you are comfortable with, etc. Use outdoor plywood, ¾-inch-thick, for a long-lasting, sturdy project.

The whole assembly folds flat for carrying in the bed of the truck.

MARK KUYKENDALL, PRESCOTT, ARIZONA

UNIQUE BATTERY BOX

The battery boxes that came on my new travel trailer had several undesirable characteristics. The access space made it difficult to check the batteries for state of charge and the water level because fabric straps and buckles are used to secure the covers. Also, these straps were not mechanically very sound. When one of these boxes fractured, I decided to search for an alternative. I found a plastic toolbox at a local hardware chain that is very rugged and is large enough to hold two batteries (Group 24). It has secure latches and provisions for a lock, and it mounts easily into the two existing angle brackets using four screws. And, it costs only a few dollars more than buying two of the same replacement battery boxes. Before going out to buy the toolbox, measure the mounting surface between the two angle-iron rails on the trailer's A-frame. Make sure there is adequate room for the cover to open. Also, the toolbox's internal measurement must be large enough to accommodate the height of the batteries and the connection posts.

JACK CASSON, CLAREMONT, CALIFORNIA

STEPPING STOOL

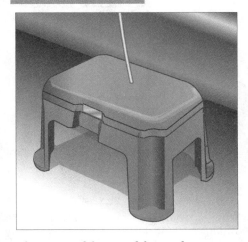

We pull a fifth-wheel trailer and are finding it increasingly difficult to get in and out of the truck due to bad knees. We needed something to step on while entering the cab, so we purchased a plastic kitchen stool. We drilled a hole in the center of the top of the stool, put a rope to the hole and tied a knot under the stool. We then put a loop in the other end of the rope for hooking over the door lick. This enables us to retrieve the stool after entering the truck without depending on someone else.

KATHERINE HILL, GOLIAD, TEXAS

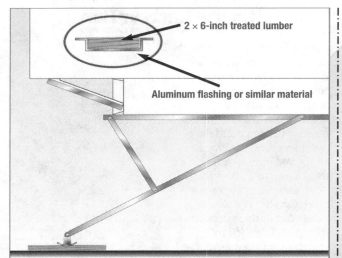

2 × 6-inch treated lumber

Aluminum flashing or similar material

STABILIZER-BOARD STORAGE

A convenient place to store your stabilizer boards is right where they are going to be used — near each stabilizer.

Construct each stabilizer board of 2 × 6-inch treated lumber about 12 inches long. Then, out of aluminum flashing material (or similar lightweight metal), bend to form a trough slightly larger than the dimensions of the stabilizer board. Fasten the trough underneath the trailer and fasten a piece of rope or window handle to the board edge (to assist in removing the board from the trough).

SAM SLEIGH, BROCKWAY, PENNSYLVANIA

SATELLITE SAWHORSE

A fter buying our satellite dish, I started to look for a platform on which to mount it. I remembered that our local hardware/home center store sold a metal sawhorse with legs that would retract for storage. I purchased one, and after drilling two ¼-inch holes, I was able to mount my dish to it.

Even without removing the dish, it makes a very compact unit to store when we travel. When we return home, I can remove the dish and use the sawhorse for home projects.

We have encountered winds of up to 40 mph and the dish has not moved.

AL LUTHER, MERRIN ISLAND, FLORIDA

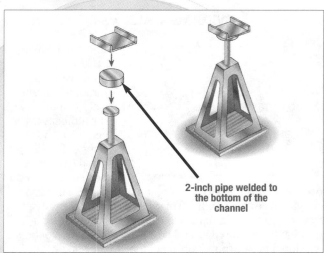

2-inch pipe welded to the bottom of the channel

STABILIZER JACKS

I feel I have improved on the way stabilizer jacks have been designed and used by devising a way that they can be used on places other than on the frame.

I had the channel, which is slightly wider than the trailer frame, cut into four-inch sections. My son-in-law then cut and welded a short section of two-inch pipe to the bottom of the channel to form a cup into which the top of the jack screw would fit.

This way you can use the jacks with the channel on the frame or without the channel elsewhere.

JAMES LLOYD, SAN DIEGO, CALIFORNIA

CLOSEUPS ◆ CLOSEUPS ◆ CLOSEUPS

B E T T E R B O A R D

*W*hen leveling our fifth-wheel, sometimes we need a little more elevation under the low side to get it right. I used ¾-inch plywood for blocking, but it gets broken up after a while and is messy. I bought a 12 × 16 × ⅜- inch-thick poly cutting board at a kitchen-supply store for $9.99; I then cut the board, making two 8 × 12-inch pieces (a band saw does a good job of cutting). The poly boards don't break and are easy to clean.

DAN HOLTERMAN, SALINA, KANSAS

AUTOMOTIVE

IN CAMP

SYSTEMS

STORAGE

TOWING

ACCESSORIES

SANITATION

DOORS, HATCHES & HANDLES

CLEANING, PROTECTING

TOOLS

DEVICES & GADGETS

LIVABILITY

SAFETY

APPLIANCES

MAINTENANCE

BLOCK PARTY

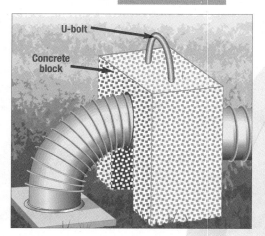

U-bolt

Concrete block

I made a special concrete block that's used to keep the sewer hose under control when hooked to the dump receptacle, and it is just about bulletproof. I started by making a mold from 1-inch-wide marine-grade plywood and a sheet of aluminum that was formed to make the bottom radius. The whole thing is held in place with straps and clamps. Once the mold is secured, I poured in the concrete and added a "handle" made from a brass-coated U-bolt. Fender washers are attached to the ends of the U-bolt using a nut on each side of each washer. This keeps the handle securely imbedded in the concrete. When the concrete is dry, the mold is disassembled and the block is ready for use. I painted the block with a bright color so that I would not leave it when breaking camp and to warn people who are walking by. I eventually remade the mold with marine-grade plywood with a Formica layer so I could make blocks for all the members in our club.

BERNARD GIANNELL JR., SACRAMENTO, CALIFORNIA

GET LOADED

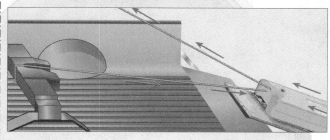

I have found a relatively easy way to load a full blue tank onto my pickup. I use a principle of physics I learned in high school. I tie a rope to an anchor (the fifth-wheel hitch), run it through an anchored pulley (the blue-tank handle) and then pull back toward the hitch. This method requires half the effort than a straight pull. Now it's easy for one person to pull a loaded 15-gallon blue tank up a ramp made from two boards.

ERNIE KLEVEN, LIVINGSTON, TEXAS

CLOSEUPS ◆ CLOSEUPS ◆ CLOSEUPS

HANDY TRICK

Save the small plastic bags used to pack groceries to put on your hands when handling sewer hoses. The bigger bags work well for your shoes when you need to work around the rig in the rain or in mud.
RICHARD PREVALLET, LIVINGSTON, TEXAS

CLOSEUPS ◆ CLOSEUPS ◆ CLOSEUPS

CLOSEUPS ◆ CLOSEUPS ◆ CLOSEUPS

AWFUL ODOR

I have read several descriptions of RVs producing an unpleasant odor from the toilet even though a good chemical was used in the holding tank. My wife and I found the "culprit." The odor was not coming from the black-water tank, but from a ridge in the throat of the toilet. We noticed a black fungus growing on this ledge while dumping the holding tank. We poured some chemical on our Johnny Mop and cleaned out the affected area. Now the odor is gone. Make sure you drill a hole in the handle of the brush and run a string through it that can be looped around your wrist. It would be very inconvenient if the brush was to be dropped into the holding tank.
VICTOR AND MARCELLA SCHWEIKERT,
NORTH FORK, CALIFORNIA

CLOSEUPS ◆ CLOSEUPS ◆ CLOSEUPS

CLOSEUPS ◆ CLOSEUPS ◆ CLOSEUPS

A SPARE HOSE
SAVES THE DAY

Did you ever find the apparatus at a dump station awkward to use? Particularly, the usually too-short hanging hose?

I solved the problem with a simple solution. From a scrap hose, I cut a 10-foot length and attached the male and female hose ends (available at the hardware store). Every station I have visited has a water spigot on or near the hanging hose pole that supplies the water. Attach your short hose section to this spigot and you can bypass having to use the dump station's short hose.
RONALD ZINKL, KIRKWOOD, MISSOURI

CLOSEUPS ◆ CLOSEUPS ◆ CLOSEUPS

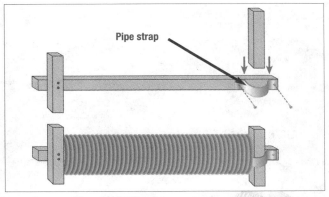

Pipe strap

COMPRESSED SEWER HOSE

Icarry an extra sewer hose besides the one in the bumper and it really can be a mess when stored in our tool compartment. I took a 1 × 1-inch pole (used to prop up tomatoes), cut to 24 inches long, and attached a 5-inch cross on one end. I then cut another 5-inch piece and attached a pipe strap to the other end. I slid the sewer hose over the pole and inserted the other 5-inch piece into the pipe strap so the 8-foot hose remains compressed to around 24 inches. Now it's easy to store in confined spaces.

JAMES (BILL) LATSHAW, LOOMIS, CALIFORNIA

CLEVER CLEAN-OUT HOSE

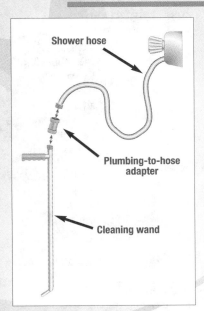

Shower hose

Plumbing-to-hose adapter

Cleaning wand

Using a wand that you place down the toilet throat is a neat way to clean out the black-water tank. The only problem is dragging a garden hose into the rig and hoping all connections are tight so that water doesn't spray all over. I solved this problem by purchasing a plumbing-to-hose adapter from a hardware store. When needed, I unscrew the shower head from the shower hose and hook the hose to the adapter; the wand is hooked to the other side of the adapter. The shower is positioned next to the toilet in my rig, so there is no problem with hose length. Using this method, the water controls are handy and you can even use hot water to flush the tank.

B.C. McCREA, PORT ANGELES, WASHINGTON

BUMPER STORAGE SOLUTION

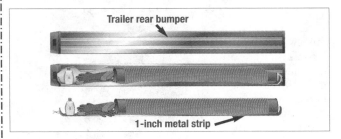

Trailer rear bumper

1-inch metal strip

The rear bumper on our trailer makes a dandy place to store the sewer hose and accessories, but access can sometimes be maddening, especially when the items end up in the center of the tube. To make access easier, I took a 1-inch metal strip long enough to cover the sewer hose, a pair of gloves and a bottle of liquid soap. Each end was bent up 1½ inches. One end is used to grab the sewer hose and the other has a cable tie attached. In use, we simply reach for the cable tie and pull the metal strip and out comes the soap, gloves and hose. The other side of the bumper is used to store the awing wand.

LARRY ST. GERMAIN, CUT OFF, LOUISIANA

MORE SEWER SUPPORT

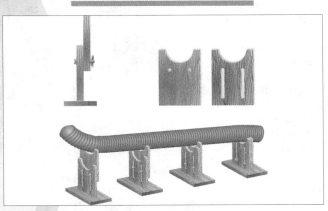

Over the years I have seen and tried many different types of sewer-hose supports. Therefore, I'll throw in my two-cents worth. I made mine out of a 6-foot-long 1 × 8-inch pine board. It's large enough to make four sets: one 10 inches high, one 8 inches high, one 6 inches high and one 4 inches high. This gives me enough versatility for most situations in camp. After making cuts to fit the radius of a PVC pipe cut in half, I slotted one side of the support and drilled two holes that line up with the slots in the other. The slotted side moves up and down depending on the exact slope needed, using 5/16 × 2-inch bolts, flat washers and wing nuts. A base is attached to the stationary half of each support.

ROBERT WALL, LIVINGSTON, TEXAS

ELBOW GREASE

I was never happy having to stow my sewer hose elbow inside one of my trailer compartments. Even though I rinsed it clean before putting it away, it just didn't seem very sanitary. I found a solution while browsing through my local RV dealer's plumbing parts area. An RV

RV toilet mounting flange

toilet mounting flange was purchased and mounted to the frame of my trailer, right next to my sewer dump outlet. A few washers were used behind the flange to shim it out a bit. Now, when I break camp, my sewer elbow screws into the flange and is ready for its next use.
JIM COPPINS, LAPEER, MICHIGAN

FANCY TOILET TOOL

After a few seasons of use, my toilet bowl (Thetford Aqua-Magic Galaxy/Starlight) would no longer hold water. It would leak out into the holding tank, leaving the bowl empty. I was envisioning an expensive toilet replacement. The cause of the problem was that partially flushed toilet paper had become lodged in the groove where the side-moving valve seats. I made a tool similar to the one my dealer used to fix the problem, which saved me a bundle.

The tool I made uses a 3/16-inch-diameter brass rod. With a hammer, I flat-

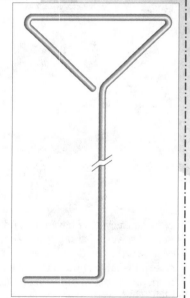

tened the "L" end of the rod into an oval shape and rounded the end so that there were no sharp edges to damage the rubber seal. To use, I step on the pedals and insert the "L" end of the tool into the curved valve seat and very gently move the tool around to dislodge any paper that has become trapped.
ALVIN WYLAND, WILLIAMSBURG, IOWA

DUMP-VALVE LEVERAGE

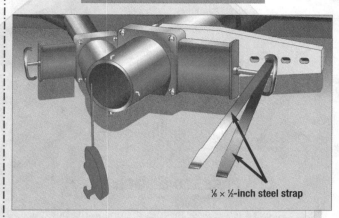

⅛ × ½-inch steel strap

Our dump valve from the black-water tank has become increasingly difficult to open. Some of this is caused by the tightness of the mating surfaces, but a lot is due to the awkward angle necessary to pull the handle. I've taken ¾-inch board, shaped it, screwed on a hose clamp and then attached it to the 3-inch black-water pipe behind the dump valve. Then, using two ⅛ × ½-inch steel traps and oval holes in the board as fulcrums, I can readily slide the valve open. It also works in reverse for closing. The T-handle of the slide gate is pinch point, so "handle" with care.
A.A. RAMIKUR, POINT COMFORT, TEXAS

TOILET TOOL INSURANCE

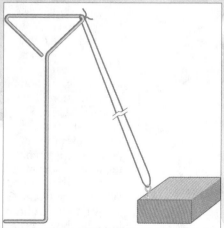

The 'Fancy Toilet Tool' I've seen in the past could use an improvement. What happens if you lose your grip on the tool while cleaning the seal groove? To prevent it from dropping into the holding tank, there should be a tether attached.

On mine, I closed and soldered the handle part (though you could just twist the metal together), and then attached a 2- to 3-foot piece of monofilament (fishing) line. The other end of the line is attached to a wooden block, shaped to fit between the toilet bowl and the pedals (to hold the pedals down and the drain open).
CHARLEY VAN DOREN, FT. WORTH, TEXAS

HOSE DRYER

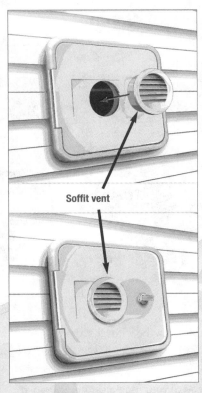

Soffit vent

Our RV Provides storage for the sewer hose in a compartment built into the side of the trailer, near the sewer outlet. This compartment has an access door similar to the ones used for the electrical and water hookups. I found that this compartment does not have very much ventilation through it. Thus, when a wet hose is put away for storage, after dumping, it never has a chance to dry out. My remedy was to purchase a soffit vent at local building-supply store. Using a hole saw, I cut an appropriate-size hole in the door. Once the hole is cut, the metal vent can be pushed in flush with the compartment door. To assure a tight fit, make sure the hole is as close as possible to the size of the vent.

The project is very inexpensive and takes only a short time to compete. I found that it does not take that much air to do the drying job.

BRUCE THOMAS, SPENCERPORT, NEW YORK

INSTANT HOSE HEATER

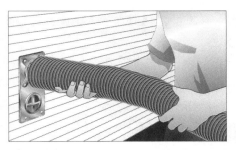

When you have to install a fitting (coupling or outlet adapter) to the end of a flexible sewer hose, it can be difficult. In cold weather, it can be next to impossible, since the plastic become less flexible and the opening smaller than the fitting. A simple solution is to turn on your furnace and use its exhaust heat to warm the hose. Just hold the end of the hose near the exhaust vent while warm air is blowing out. The heat makes the plastic soft again. If necessary, you can also lube the fitting with dish soap and insert it with ease.

DAVID W. SHULL, WEST COLUMBIA, SOUTH CAROLINA

◆ CLOSEUPS ◆ CLOSEUPS ◆ CLOSEUPS ◆

CLOSEUPS

S T A I N   B U S T E R S

You don't need an expensive new toilet with a spray attachment. You do need an old plastic squeeze bottle (a dishwashing detergent bottle is perfect). When you find that you need to spray water to help clean the bowl, apply a couple of squirts from the squeeze bottle. It doesn't add much volume to the blackwater holding tank, and it really gets the job done.
WILLIAM R. HINK, LAWRENCEVILLE, GEORGIA

CLOSEUPS

◆ CLOSEUPS ◆ CLOSEUPS ◆ CLOSEUPS ◆

KEEP THE SEWAGE IN THE SEWER

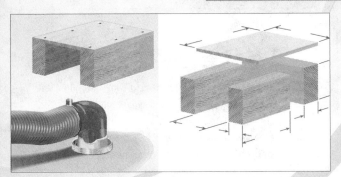

I have always had a problem when doing the sewer hookup with the standard red elbow, trying to keep the elbow from flying out of the campground-sewer opening under full-load dumping. I've seen more configurations to hold this baby in place than I care to count; even the threaded and pump-up-bladder elbows fail.

So I made a retainer in about one hour, using scrap 2 × 4s and plywood. Fully assembled, it is 3 inches thick, just right to rest on the flange and clear the top of the elbow. With the plywood securely screwed on top, I now have a flat surface that puts any hold-down weight directly on the elbow flange.

I had a cast-iron wheel, which I screwed to the top, and it was just enough weight to do the job. However, you could use anything that's handy, including a rock. I drilled two holes, installed a rope handle, spray-painted the unit, and that was that.

This thing works every time, even if the camp sewer pipe is tilted, has broken edges, is above or below ground level, threaded or not. It sure took care of my problem!

RON BAILEY, ST. CHARLES, MISSOURI

GET A HANDLE ON IT

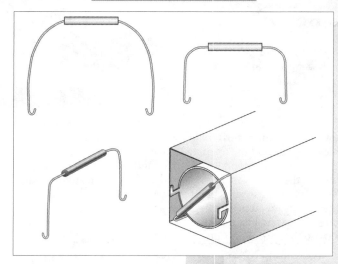

My sewer hose easily fits into the square bumper-storage tube, but the black plastic hose fitting on the end always gets stuck. I took the handle off a discarded 5-gallon plastic pail, cut some wire off each end and bent new hooks on the ends, which can catch the dog ears on the hose coupler. The handle stores in the hose-storage tube and makes it easy to pull out the stuck fitting and hose.
ROBERT FALK, ATLANTA, GEORGIA

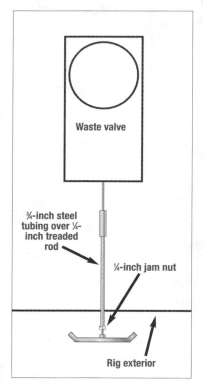

Waste valve

¾-inch steel tubing over ¼-inch treaded rod

¼-inch jam nut

Rig exterior

IMPROVE SLIDE-VALVE ACTION

Waste-valve actuator shafts are often extended for easy access using ¼-inch threaded rod. The rod can buckle if care is not taken when closing the valve. I fixed the problem by installing a piece of ⅜-inch steel brake line over the threaded rod and secured it using a jam nut on the outside end just behind the handle. This stiffens the actuator shaft and provides positive valve opening and closing.
GEORGE E. HUMPHRIES, WEST PALM BEACH, FLORIDA

SEWER-HOSE CADDY

The sewer-hose caddy provides protection from those annoying pinholes and makes storage easy, since you no longer have to battle the evil sewer-hose snake!

First, cut a section of ½-inch PVC pipe. The length of this pipe depends on the compressed length of sewer hose you intend to store on it (compress the hose like a Slinky and then measure). Next, using PVC cement, glue an unthreaded ½-inch PVC tee fitting to one end of the cut pipe; this will become the bottom.

Cut four 2½-inch sections from the leftover scrap of the ½-inch PVC pipe. Then, glue two of the 2½-inch sections into the ends of the tee fitting, and glue a ½-inch end cap over the other end of each section.

Now, on the opposite end of your long pipe, glue a ½-inch slide or union fitting that has external male threads on one end. Lastly, glue the last two sections of the previously cut 2½-inch PVC pipe into another tee fitting, this one with ½-inch female threads on the bottom of the tee. Glue two more end caps on the open ends.

Now slide the sewer hose over the long section of PVC pipe and hold in place by screwing the remaining tee onto the end of the long pipe. Allowing the compressed sewer hose to stand up until ready to store will allow most, if not all, the water to drain out.
RICHARD HARVEY JR., PERDIDO, FLORIDA

◆ CLOSEUPS ◆ CLOSEUPS ◆ CLOSEUPS ◆

IN THE BUCKET

*L*ooking for a convenient place to store my sewer hose and its accessories, I found that a 5-gallon bucket fits the bill nicely. I took a plastic 5-gallon bucket and drilled a few ½-inch holes in the bottom. I can coil up a 15-foot sewer hose around the inside of the pail with the adapters removed. The adapters are stored inside the middle of the coil, and the pail is stored in the truck bed. At camp, when the hose is in use, the pail is stored under the trailer.
KENNETH BISHOP, EDWARDSBURG, MICHIGAN

◆ CLOSEUPS ◆ CLOSEUPS ◆ CLOSEUPS ◆

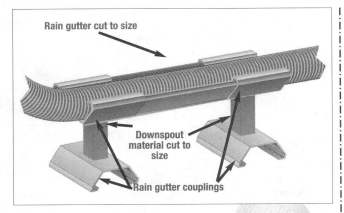

Rain gutter cut to size

Downspout material cut to size

Rain gutter couplings

GUTTER STANDS

A popular way to fabricate a sewer-hose support is to use sections of rain-gutter material. I have a very easy way to make stands for these supports. Simply snap together a gutter coupling and a short section of downspout material (cut to the appropriate size for your situation). Each stand should be cut to a different length so that the sewer-hose support will slope for proper drainage. This project requires no glue, nails or screws, and can be disassembled in minutes for storage.
FRED BROUSSARD, HOUSTON, TEXAS

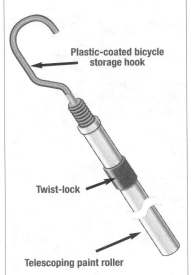

Plastic-coated bicycle storage hook

Twist-lock

Telescoping paint roller

LONGER ARMS

When the slideout of our fifth-wheel is extended, the gray-water dump-valve handle is unreachable without crawling under the structure. To ease the process, I took a Mr. Longarm (telescoping paint-roller handle with a twist-lock) and screwed a plastic-coated bicycle storage hook into the threaded end (where the paint roller would normally go). Now I can pull the handle open through the access panel without crawling under the slideout. I can close the handle by pushing with the top of the hook. The hook also comes in handy for retrieving items in the back of the basement or under the fifth-wheel.
BRUCE ROLFE, LIVINGSTON, TEXAS

CLOSEUPS • CLOSEUPS • CLOSEUPS •

TOILET-PAPER GURU

We have seen many fellow RVers with holding-tank problems. Some are due to not following the right procedure of letting the black-water tank fill before emptying and others are due to using the wrong type of toilet paper. After being in the toilet-paper manufacturing business for more than 30 years, I can tell you that all toilet paper is not the same. Toilet paper is made with different degrees of wet strength. Wet strength is the ability of the paper to hold together when wet. You need some, but too much is a problem in holding tanks. With too much, the paper will not break down, resulting in a plugged tank. Here's how to check for wet strength.

Put two sheets of paper in a large drinking glass that is half full of tap water. Place your hand over the top of the glass and shake it for a few seconds. If the paper is still in full sheets, or in a ball do not use it; that's the way it will stay in your holding tank. If the paper looks like lots of small fibers, it is OK to use and will break down properly inside your holding tank.
ROGER BALDWIN, GREEN BAY, WISCONSIN

CLOSEUPS • CLOSEUPS • CLOSEUPS •

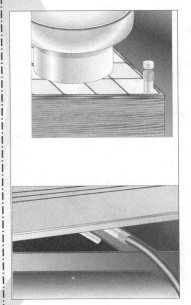

TO FLUSH OR NOT TO FLUSH

To flush the black-water tank without dragging a garden hose through the front door of our fifth-wheel, I installed a simple plumbing system to supply the flushing hose and wand. Using ¾-inch PVC pipe and assorted angles and elbows, I now have a part-time water-line feed going from just above the tank valves (under the chassis), up through a side storage compartment and ending up at the base of the toilet. This line has a fitting compatible to the female end of a garden hose. Now, I connect the water source to the fitting on the streetside of the rig, hook up the wand hose at the base of the toilet and have high-pressure water to flush the tank without all the mess. When not in use, I put a cap on the inside fitting just to avoid any "pranks" that may flood my home from the outside.
MARK KUYKENDALL, PRESCOTT, ARIZONA

MORE STORAGE

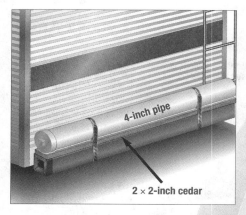

2 × 2-inch cedar

4-inch pipe

Most trailers have limited exterior or storage space. I was able to gain some very useful storage on my back bumper. I purchased a length of 4-inch plastic pipe and cut it to the length of my back bumper. I glued a screw-on clean-out plug, such as that used on a sewer line, on each end. I then formed two saddles out of 2 × 2-inch cedar blocks and mounted the pipe to the bumper using long hose clamps.

I have access to both ends of the pipe, which is ideal storage for fishing rods, an extra sewer hose, extension cords, rolled up rugs, etc.

B.C. McCrea, Port Angeles, Washington

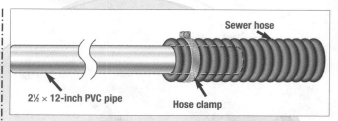

Sewer hose

2½ × 12-inch PVC pipe

Hose clamp

PIPE PLACEMENT

I think I've come up with a simple solution to all those drain-pipe-to-sewer-hose attachments, such as weight rings, screw-on adapters, clamp-on fittings, etc., that we all carry around with us. I took a 12-inch piece of 2½-inch PVC pipe and inserted it into one end of my drain hose and secured it with a hose clamp. Now, without any fuss, I just slip the PVC pipe into the park's drain pipe and I don't have to look around for the right attachment any longer. The PVC pipe is long enough to allow my hose to be removed easily and tight enough to stay in place when I dump my tanks.

Bill Wright, Santa Rosa, California

CLOSEUPS ◆ CLOSEUPS ◆ CLOSEUPS

POTTY TIME

*A*fter about two years of use, the commode in our travel trailer developed a crack in the top of the bowl, allowing leakage. The crack was beneath the seat, making the repair almost invisible. To avoid the expense and work of replacing the entire unit, I came up with a simple fix. The crack was mended with an ordinary soldering iron using a soldering tip to bond the plastic back together again. The commode is now restored to "good as new" condition.

Jack Fox, Carthage, Texas

CLOSEUPS ◆ CLOSEUPS ◆ CLOSEUPS

LOST YOUR HEAD?

*I*n our motorhome, the spray head on the Thetford toilet came off and went down into the black-water tank. I called several RV-supply places, and none of them had a replacement spray head — only a complete kit. I called Thetford, which also sells only a complete kit (about $40). I checked with Home Depot and found that it had a sink sprayer-and-hose kit that sold for about $11. It fit the hose that was already on the toilet, and it saved money and a lot of time because we did not have to remove the toilet to install the complete assembly.

Elbert Armstrong, Lompoc, California

CLOSEUPS ◆ CLOSEUPS ◆ CLOSEUPS ◆ CLOSEUPS ◆ CLOSEUPS ◆ CLOSEUPS

SEWER-SMELL SOLUTION

*W*e've found a no-cost way to keep the sewer smell out of our RV while traveling. When we get ready to go down the road, we put the plugs in our sink, lavatory and bathtub. When traveling over rough roads, long distance or on windy days, the water in the P-traps under the sinks and bathtub empties into the holding tank. This allows the "sewer" gas to backflow into the RV's interior. Placing the plugs in before you hit the road will stop the backflow and the smell.

Burch Ingram, Fritch, Texas

SUCCESS IS INDICATED

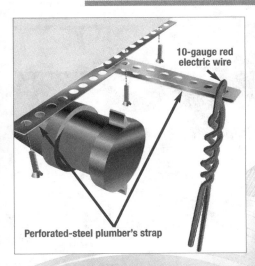

10-gauge red electric wire

Perforated-steel plumber's strap

On most motorhomes, it's difficult to line up the holding-tank dump valve with the dump station as you pull through. That is because of the lack of a reference point visible from the driver's seat. To solve this problem on my motorhome, I created a reference point using a short section of perforated-steel plumber's strap, 20 inches of 10-gauge red electric wire and two screws, all available from the local hardware store.

Here's the procedure: Bend the pipe strap into the shape shown in the drawing. Screw the strap under the motorhome with the bent area facing down. Seal the screw holes. Bend the bent area of the strap toward the outside, so that it sticks out 3 to 4 inches beyond the RV side wall. Double the red wire and loop it through the holes in the pipe strap so that it is hanging down. Adjust all measurements so that the red indicator wire is visible from the driver's seat.

Now, when you pull into a dump station and look in the driver's outside rearview mirror, you will see the red wire and know when you're in line with the drain.

B.J. MacPherson, Lacey, Washington

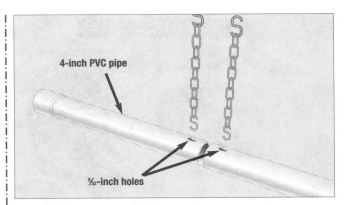

4-inch PVC pipe

5/32-inch holes

SEWER-HOSE SUSPENSION

We have found a very inexpensive, convenient and effective method of supporting our sewer hose. We bought a 10-foot-long piece of 4-inch PVC pipe for about $4. We cut it into one 4-foot and one 6-foot piece, and then drilled a 5/32-inch hole in both ends (at the cut) to accommodate an S-hook. A piece of small chain was attached to each S-hook and a second S-hook was affixed to the end of each chain.

We now insert our hose through the PVC pipe (putting the chain end of the PVC pipe near the rig). The 4-inch pipe will accommodate the 90-degree universal sewer adapter. We attach the sewer hose to the rig and use the chain up and under the rig to support the PVC pipe.

This keeps our hose straight and unkinked. We have two lengths for various needs, or we may attach the two lengths together again, as one end of the PVC pipe is larger and will allow the two sections to be reassembled to use as one long length.

John Hanson, South Hamilton, Massachusetts

◆ CLOSEUPS ◆ CLOSEUPS ◆ CLOSEUPS ◆

P-TRAP POWER FLUSH

We often park for several days without full hookups, so we limit our water use. That can result in a musty smell in the kitchen-sink drain. To eliminate these odors, we power-flush the drain pipes, using a garden hose with a spray nozzle. Just spray into the drain for 30 seconds to a minute. The pressure will flush out food particles caught in the lines. When doing this, open the cabinet below the sink and watch for leaks — should any of the connections come loose.

Coleen Sykora, Rapid City, South Dakota

◆ CLOSEUPS ◆ CLOSEUPS ◆ CLOSEUPS ◆

CLEAN YOUR PROBES

*A*fter several years of full-timing, our black-water-tank indicator probes were so fouled, the monitors read full even when empty. Our solution is to put about five bags of ice cubes down the toilet, along with about 10 gallons of water. We then drive down a rough road with a lot of sudden starts and stops, to really stir up the ice cubes. (Make sure that no one is on the road behind you.) This action causes the ice to scour the walls and probes better than anything we have found, and it works a lot better than just driving around the block. Check the monitor after dumping, and if more cleaning is needed, it is simple to do again. But one time worked very well for us.

Carl and Carol Wiesner, Livingston, Texas

SIMPLE SCENT SOLUTION

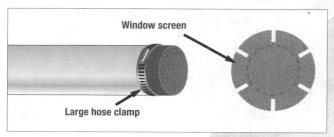

Window screen

Large hose clamp

On occasion, some campers have complained about stinky holding tanks. This has never been a problem for us. When we store our trailer, and after we have already dumped and flushed the tanks, I remove the cap from the drain line and open the valves to the gray- and black-water holding tanks. This leaves the tanks open to the atmosphere and permits them to dry and thus prevents bacteria buildup from a moist and closed condition.

To prevent the entry of insects and vermin, I use two layers of common window screen and secure it on the drainpipe with a large hose clamp.

WILL VANDERMEYDEN, SOUTH HOLLAND, ILLINOIS

SUPPORT YOUR LOCAL SEWER HOSE!

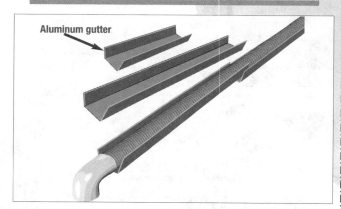

Aluminum gutter

Last summer, I replaced the rain gutters on my home. I was about to put the old lightweight aluminum gutters out as trash, when the idea that they would make great sewer-hose supports came to mind. Using a standard hacksaw, I cut them into four different lengths (for adaptability at different RV parks) and rounded the corners with tin snips. Holes were drilled on the ends, so that they could be fitted together and tied in place, if necessary.

The first length is tied to the sewer drain valve; the rest are supported by short pieces of old 2 × 4s, until the right pitch is acquired for the hose to drain into the sewer connection. Each section fits inside another for easy storage, and the wooden blocks lay inside the top gutter tray.

FRED ROSI, VINELAND, NEW JERSEY

THE SLIDEOUT VS. THE SEWER HOSE

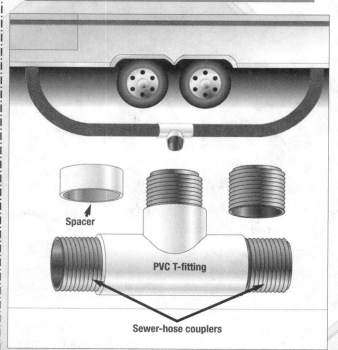

Spacer

PVC T-fitting

Sewer-hose couplers

On our fifth-wheel there are two sewer outlets located beneath and at opposite ends of the slideout.

Unless the slideout is in, they are very difficult to get to. To stop having to move the sewer hose back and forth, when parked for extended periods, I made a T-Connection for the hose.

I started with a 3-inch PVC T-fitting, a 6-inch length of 3-inch PVC pipe, some two-part epoxy cement and silicone sealer from a hardware store. Two sewer-hose couplers came from an RV supply center.

From the section of 3-inch PVC pipe I cut three 1⅜-inch spacers, made nice square cuts and cleaned off all burrs from the edges. Using silicone sealer, I inserted and cemented the spacers into the openings of the PVC T-fitting and made sure the spacers were bottomed out.

I cut the couplers, leaving a shoulder on the threaded end, and cleaned the surfaces of all burrs. After the silicone sealer cured, I smeared the epoxy cement mixture about ⅟₁₆ to ⅛ inch thick on the inner lip of the T-fitting, on the outer edges of the spacers, and pressed the shoulder ends of the couplings into the epoxy mixture. These pieces were clamped together for approximately 24 hours while the epoxy cured.

To make fittings, spacers and couplings easier, I placed them in the freezer for about 15 minutes just before getting started. This shrank them and made assembly easier.

After the epoxy cured, I filled any recessed areas on the outside of the coupling shoulder with silicone. Be sure to rinse well after use.

H. CATO LARSEN, COURTENAY, BRITISH COLUMBIA

SEWER-HOSE WEIGHT

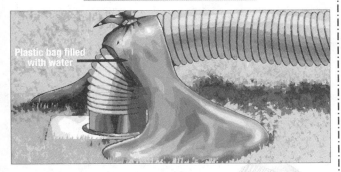

Plastic bag filled with water

Do you worry that the nasty end of the sewer hose will lift off the dump inlet at exactly the wrong time? To ease your fears, take a large plastic bag (about 24 × 30 inches) and fill it with one or two gallons of water. This will weigh 8 to 17 pounds. Securely tie off the bag as close to the water as possible. Drape the weighted bag over the sewer-hose end that's in the dump inlet with half the water on each side. The weighted bag will hold the fitting in place until that "critical" time has passed. When the operation is complete, pour out the water and save the bag until next time.

ROBERT LEGATE, SAN JOSE, CALIFORNIA

DUMP-VALVE LUBE

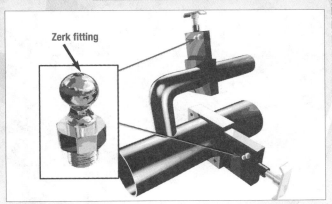

Zerk fitting

Over the years, my holding-tank dump valves were getting harder to open, and I had to find a solution. I decided that they needed some type of lubrication. With the valve closed, I drilled and tapped a hole in the upper corner of the valve and added a Zerk fitting (used to add grease to vehicle suspensions). Then I filled a small hand-operated grease gun with petroleum jelly and filled the area where the valve pulls back with the lubricant. When the valve is opened, a small amount of petroleum jelly comes out, but it can be wiped off with a tissue. My seals are now always moist, and the valves slide with unbelievable ease. The Zerk fittings and grease gun are available at almost all auto-parts stores.

B.C. McCREA, PORT ANGELES, WASHINGTON

WATER PASS-THROUGH

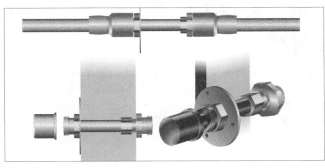

I was tired of pulling a water hose through my motorhome in order to use my toilet wand to flush the holding tank. To solve the problem, I purchased an RV water-inlet fitting with a check valve that ended with ½-inch female pipe threads; it's available at most RV parts stores. I then bought a brass ½-inch pipe-to-hose adapter. After drilling a 1-inch hole through the rig's side wall near the toilet, I joined the two pieces together with the inlet fitting on the outside. The length was just right to pass through the wall. After coating the outside flange with silicone sealer, I fastened it with two screws to the side wall. Then I sealed the inside fitting where it passes through the bathroom wall.

It is now time-saving and convenient to connect the wand and flush the tank after connecting the water hose on the outside. A water shutoff can be added if you don't already have one on the wand.

RUSSELL BANE, REDDING, CALIFORNIA

◆ CLOSEUPS ◆ CLOSEUPS ◆ CLOSEUPS ◆

TIP OF THE CENTURY

*S*ooner or later, everybody experiences a black-water tank that won't drain, even though you've done everything right. The usual solution is to break camp and drive around for a while and try again.

A self described "old oil-field worker" showed me a trick that has to be the tip of the century.

Make sure no one opens the toilet valve during this procedure. With the black and gray waterdrain valves closed, hold the end of the drain hose about waist high and fill it with water. Have someone open the black-water valve and raise the drain hose as high as possible. The water in the drain hose back-flushes into the tank. Quickly insert the drain hose into the drain and lower the hose. Usually, one try is all it takes.

PAUL PATTERSON, OKLAHOMA CITY, OKLAHOMA

SQUIRT-GUN FUN

If you don't have one of those fancy new toilets with a sprayer attachment, just buy a kid's squirt gun and holster it next to the john. Mine is one of the pump-up, air-pressure pistols, but any squirt gun will do. A few quick shots and you'll have a clean bowl. Plus, over time, as your marksmanship improves, you'll need fewer and fewer shots — and the volume of clean-up water you'll be adding to the holding tank will shrink accordingly.

MARK M. STEELE, LIVINGSTON, TEXAS

IN CAMP
SYSTEMS
STORAGE
TOWING
ACCESSORIES
SANITATION

DOORS, HATCHES & HANDLES

CLEANING, PROTECTING
TOOLS
DEVICES & GADGETS
LIVABILITY
SAFETY
APPLIANCES
MAINTENANCE
AUTOMOTIVE

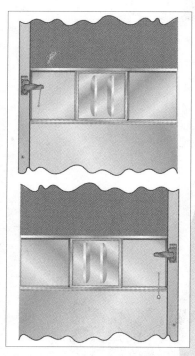

A Door Opener

I designed a way to open the screen door of our fifth-wheel from the inside, without having to slide open the plastic panel that accesses the door lever. This is especially handy when carrying something outside, as you don't have to reach back and up to close the sliding panel. All you'll need is a drill (with an ⅛-inch drill bit), an 8- to 10-inch piece of nylon cord and a miniblind pull.

Drill one hole through the end of the plastic door lever and another through the door directly below the lever, just below the opening for the sliding panel.

Knot the cord on one end, so the end of the cord will not pass through the hole in the door lever, and thread the cord through the end of the handle from the outside in. Then, from the outside, thread the cord through the hole in the door so that the cord will protrude on the inside of the door. Cut the cord to the desired length, slide the miniblind pull onto the cord and knot to secure.

Now you can operate the door lever from inside your rig by pulling the cord and not having to open and close the sliding panel.

Leon O'Hart, Bristol, Connecticut

A DOOR CLOSER

I have had cabinet doors come open on the road — and what a mess! I have tried several "solutions," none of which have been very satisfactory.

Then the answer presented itself in my kitchen at home. Since my grandchildren visit almost daily, we use child safety locks on the cabinets. I installed the safety locks on the cabinets of my fifth-wheel and have not had a problem since, and they are very cheap to purchase.

Don Johnson, Madison Heights, Virginia

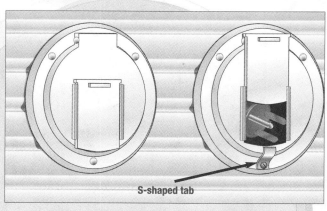

S-shaped tab

Better Late Than Never

After several incidents on the road, during which my electrical cord came out of the storage compartment, I found that the plastic catch on the cord's access-door was too weak to keep the door closed during more than normal road vibrations.

My fix was a small S-shaped tab, approximately ½ × ¾-inch made from 1/16-inch flat aluminum. This tab is secured under the bottom mount screw of the access-door assembly and is fashioned so that the small sliding flap will fit behind the tab when the door is in the closed position. This in no way interferes with the electrical cord or in the normal operation of the door.

William Jeffries, Camdenton, Missouri

Better Vent Screen

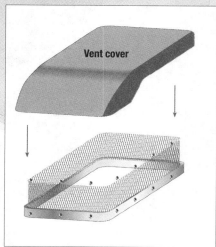

Vent cover

I have a very simple fix for an age-old problem: keeping the birds from nesting in the refrigerator vent. Replace the worthless screening in your vent with real screen wire, but instead of turning it down and crimping it over the top edge of the vent opening — as done at the factory — make the screen about 6 inches wider than the opening and secure to the lip at the top of the vent with self-tapping screws. Next, turn each side of the screen up so it sets against the bottom of the cap. That leaves no place for birds to build their nests and they will be happy to go somewhere else.

Lester Rose, Deming, New Mexico

MOON OVER MIAMI (AND ELSEWHERE)

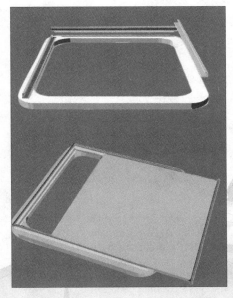

Are you tired of bright lights or the moon shining into your motorhome bedroom via the roof vent? Here is a removable, durable, opaque slide-in solution.

Materials needed (which are all available at your local hardware dealer): One 6-foot length of ⅛-inch aluminum cap molding, a small piece of ⅛-inch-thick rigid opaque sheeting (size to be determined by the size of your roof vent) and foam bonding tape to adhere the aluminum pieces to the trim retainer on the ceiling vent.

Step 1. Unscrew the trim piece from the ceiling vent and mark a square on the face, being careful not to cover any of the screw holes. Cut four pieces of the aluminum molding to match the dimensions you marked on the trim retainer.

Step 2. Adhere three cut pieces of the aluminum to the ceiling trim face.

Step 3. Cut the ⅛-inch slider material to size for the slide-in and fasten the remaining cut piece of aluminum to a side of the slide-in where it will remain permanently bonded.

Step 4. Insert the slide, and check for a good fit before the adhesive sets too well. Then leave undisturbed overnight.

Step 5. Install the completed unit on the ceiling of your motorhome, but make certain that the slide-in has sufficient room to be removed when desired.

DAN BRANDT, RICHMOND, CALIFORNIA

SCREEN-HOLE FIX

The best way to patch a hole in your screen is to apply Elmer's glue. I use a toothpick to apply the glue to the broken ends — a little dab will do. One of my repairs has lasted for 5 years. Long rips are best mended by gluing a short section at a time.

OPHA WATSON, TUCSON, ARIZONA

CABINET-DOOR IMPROVEMENTS

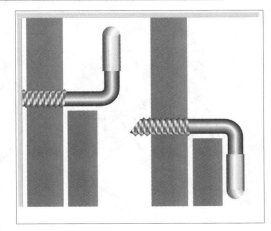

Ihad several problems with our motorhome's cabinet doors. Due to the size of the catches installed by the factory, the doors were hard to open. I removed the catches and replaced them with self-closing hinges purchased at the hardware store.

For doors that sometimes pop open when traveling, I screwed in a small brass 90-degree-bent hook by the corner of each door, opposite the hinge side. When driving, this hook is turned over the door edge; when parked, the hook is turned away from the door.

ERWIN NISTLER, MAPLE PLAIN, MINNESOTA

BUNGEE TO THE RESCUE

We upgraded our motorhome recently so we could have one of the popular slideout features in the main living area. When in the travel position, the rear of the slide blocks a floor-to-ceiling pantry cabinet. On our first trip, we found out the hard way that we had a problem. During movement of the coach, canned goods would fall out of the pantry cabinet. These items then blocked the slideout from moving outward when we got to our favorite camping site. We spent several hours retrieving the items in the very awkward space.

We prevented this from occurring again by utilizing bungee cords looped around cabinet door handles to ensure they don't open during vehicle movement. You also could use long hook-and-loop strips looped around the handles. Securing the cabinet doors before the slideout is brought in for travel is now one of our routine tasks before preparing our rig for any trip.

MIKE LABADIE, THORNTON, COLORADO

RANGE-EXHAUST OPENER

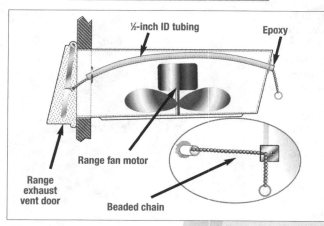

½-inch ID tubing

Epoxy

Range fan motor

Range exhaust vent door

Beaded chain

No one likes to go outside to open the range exhaust-vent door. Using simple parts, I devised a way to allow operation from inside the rig. I cut a piece of ⅛-inch inside-diameter (ID) tubing long enough to go from the front of the range fan/hood housing to the back. I then drilled a hole in the front of the range hood and secured the tubing using epoxy. I used a small metal tab and screw with a properly sized hole drilled in it to hold the back end of the tubing in the portion of the range hood that abuts the wall.

One end of a length of beaded chain was attached to the flapper door using a ring-type connector and screw. The chain is fed through the tubing and enough hangs out the front to place a ball on it. I then used a small L-shaped bracket with a notch cut in it to hold the chain when the door is closed (not in use). When the fan is on, the chain is relaxed and the flapper door is forced open. The entire project costs about $4.
DENNIS R. SWAIN, ARLINGTON, TEXAS

CUPBOARD LATCH

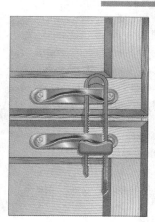

It only took one mishap in our brand-new fifth-wheel for us to learn how to load our cupboards and come up with a solution to eliminate the possibility of a cupboard door opening while en route. We went to the baby department of a variety store and purchased safety latches. As part of our last-minute check before heading out for a destination, we slide these latches through the handles of the cupboards and now we can breathe easier as we round the corners or hit bumps.
GENE AND PATTIE FERGUSON, WINSTON, OREGON

HOLD THAT TAB

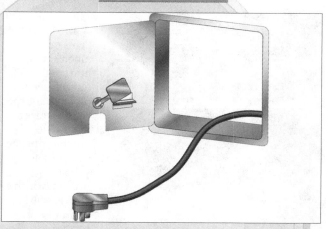

Quite often, that little tab that fills the space in the electrical-cord outlet door (and similar one in the water-hose connection) slips down just as you are about to close the door. To stop it from doing this, attach a piece of heavy-duty tape to the inside of the access door. I used 2-inch clear vinyl tape and folded it to create a "shelf" that flexes and allows the cover plate to swing up and rests on the tape.
VICTOR H. FERRY, WATERFORD, CONNECTICUT

SCREEN-DOOR CLOSER

You can make your own simple screen-door closer by purchasing a 13-inch screen-door spring, a ½-inch pipe support and four ¼-inch sheet-metal screws. Install the pipe support 6 to 8 inches from the hinge side of the screen door on the cross member. Affix the screen-door spring with one ¼-inch screw to the jam of the door. Pull the spring through the pipe support and then fasten the other end to the door jam. Quick and easy, and works every time.
JEFF SPANGENBERG, VALLEY SPRINGS, CALIFORNIA

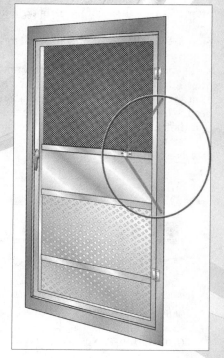

Roof-Vent Crank

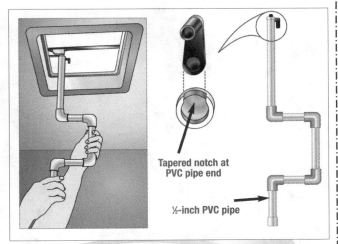

Tapered notch at PVC pipe end

½-inch PVC pipe

If you cannot reach those high-ceiling roof-vent handles, make a simple crank from ½-inch PVC rigid pipe to extend your reach. A notch cut in one side of the PVC pipe end allows the new extension crank to easily slip onto the vent handle shank. I cut the notch in the pipe on a tapered angle to keep the crank from slipping off the handle. Make sure the pipe and fittings are of the same type. The materials are available from local hardware stores and cost less than $5.
Marvin Wilber, Lupton, Michigan

Foil That Mouse

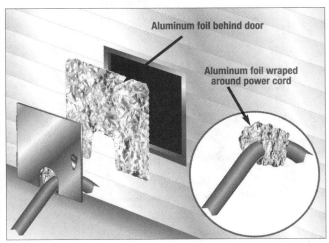

Aluminum foil behind door

Aluminum foil wraped around power cord

Mice are cute, but they are very destructive to an RV and its contents. We found out the hard way. To prevent these critters from destroying our rig, we wrapped a length of aluminum foil around the power cord and the adjacent areas of the utility door. We then tucked some aluminum foil behind the door, inside the opening. Our result: no more mice.
Timothy Hoffman, Middletown, Pennsylvania

Screen-Door Adjustment

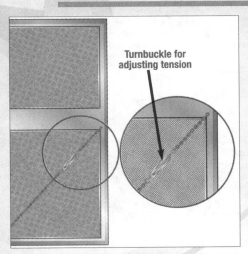

Turnbuckle for adjusting tension

I had a problem with the screen door on my motorhome dragging. My solution allows for adjustment even if the rig is not level. I purchased some light chain and a turnbuckle. The chain is cut and then the turnbuckle is installed between the two pieces of chain. The assembly is mounted diagonally on the lower half of the screen-door frame using the next longer size of screw. The tension can be adjusted by simply tightening or loosening the turnbuckle.
Doris Mullins, Montesano, Washington

Screen-Door Reinforcement

Here's another way to reinforce the screen door, preventing it from sagging. I Pop riveted a piece of aluminum expanded metal (available at most hardware stores or building-supply centers in a wide variety of patterns and colors) to my door after squaring it in the opening. This prevents children or pets from damaging the fragile lower screen material.
Marlan R. Miller, Yutan, Nebraska

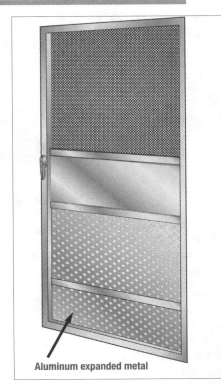

Aluminum expanded metal

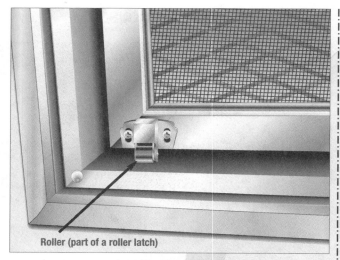

Roller (part of a roller latch)

SCREEN-DOOR FIX

A screen door that drags on the sill because of slope in the hinge is easily fixed by installing the roller portion of a roller latch at the bottom of the screen. Installation takes only minutes, and the latch also helps keep the screen from rattling on the road.

MALCOLM D. CAMPBELL, SAN DIEGO, CALIFORNIA

TOT LOCKS TO THE RESCUE

tot lok

A fter taking two trips in our new trailer and having the upper cabinet doors fly open, dumping much of the contents, I had to find a way to make sure it wouldn't happen again. At my local Ace Hardware store, I found a set of four child-proof cabinet locks. They are hidden on the inside of the cabinet and open with a magnet. The only time we use them is when we are on the road; otherwise the lock is left in the open position. The instructions on the package are quite clear and the installation went smoothly. The brand name is Tot Lok, and it works very well.

DON ZUBEK, MILWAUKEE, WISCONSIN

SLIDE-OUT SHELF

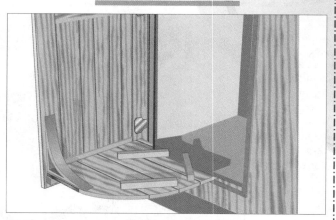

T he accompanying illustration shows a shelf, attached to the cabinet door, that I built under our RV galley to hold the wastebasket. The lower support is a 1 × 1-inch piece of hardwood secured to the door with construction adhesive and screws that must be long enough to go into the lower door frame, but not come through the other side. The right-angle bracket keeps the shelf level, and the strips on top of the piece of wood, which serves as the base, hold the wastebasket in place. This idea helps utilize our precious available space that's always in short supply.

FRANK WOYTHAL, ANDOVER, NEW YORK

WEED-WHACKER WONDER

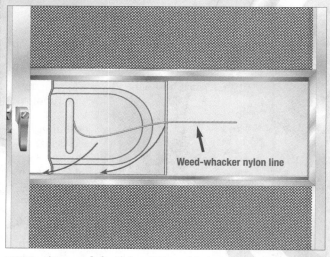

Weed-whacker nylon line

H ere's a quick fix if the sliding plastic cover on your screen door keeps popping out. After removing the cover, take a piece of weed-whacker nylon line and gently push it into the bottom track that the plastic cover slides into. Once the cover is back into the track, slide it back and forth a few times so that the nylon line seats. The nylon line will take up the gap and allow the sliding cover to move more freely.

TERRY FRITZ, LOCKPORT, NEW YORK

SMALL-CRITTER BARRIER

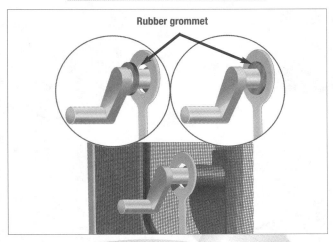

Rubber grommet

When looking for places where small bugs and mosquitoes might be able to enter my camper, I noticed some space between the crank and the roof-vent screening. Although small, it was, nevertheless, a possible entry point. To completely seal the opening, I used a rubber grommet with an inside diameter slightly smaller than the outside diameter of the crank mechanism. By sliding the grommet up close to the screen, so that it very lightly brushes the screen, I was able to completely seal the opening, yet not affect the operation of the vent crank mechanism.

BILL JONES, IRVINE, CALIFORNIA

UNWANTED VISITORS

Inoticed a small lizard had taken up residence in the cover port of my shore-power cable. To keep him and other creepy-crawly pests out, I cut a circle out of ½-inch-thick

½-inch-thick foam rubber

foam rubber. The circle should be slightly larger than the opening, with the inner hole (where the cord passes through) slightly smaller than the power cord. I sliced through the foam-rubber plug from the inner hole to one edge (to allow the plug to pass over and surround the power cord).

Now, after I hook up, I place the foam-rubber plug around the cord and slide it inside the cover port, making a tight seal to keep out unwanted visitors. I made a second plug the same size, with no hole in the middle, to place in the cover port when the cord is stowed. I used foam rubber, but a cheap sponge may work just as well.

B. D. HARDIMAN, HUBERT, NORTH CAROLINA

SUN BUSTER

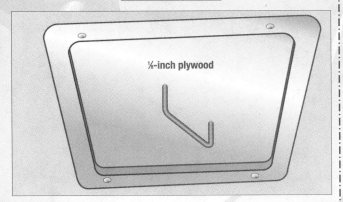

⅛-inch plywood

Our trailer has a roof vent above the bed. This is fine for ventilation on a warm evening, but not good for sleeping when the sun illuminates it in the early morning. Our solution is a panel made of ⅛-inch plywood. Since the vent frame has a slight taper, friction holds the panel in place very nicely. A small wood handle makes it easy to install and remove. The wood vent cover can be painted to match the interior colors.

BRUCE TRUDGEN, WILLIAMSBURG, MICHIGAN

TRIM AROUND THE RADIUS

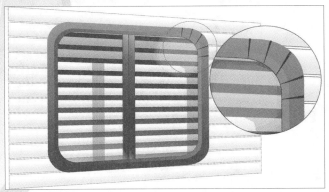

Ihave a trailer that used black vinyl trim in the strip of metal that surrounds the windows and exterior compartments. It seems like the sun shrinks this material making the trim pop out of the track, mostly around the radius. To solve the problem, I cut slits about halfway through the vinyl trim at the radius points. The cuts are made about an inch apart and the trim is placed back into the track. Now the trim stays put.

GLEN MUNNS, RENO, NEVADA

WINDOW PASS-THROUGH

*B*ecause I didn't want to drill a hole through my rig's side wall, I ran my satellite and phone wires through a slide-out window. To keep the resulting crack from letting in bugs or humid air and to keep the desired air inside, I simply cushioned the cords with a piece of cut-to-fit foam pipe wrap.

I nicked out a hole for the wires to pass through and trimmed both ends to make it seat better in the window channel. It should be installed seam-side down to prevent rainwater from pooling within the foam wrap.

Leftover wrap can be used as windshield-wiper cover while parked.

BRENDA BOYD, LIVINGSTON, TEXAS

SYSTEMS
STORAGE
TOWING
ACCESSORIES
SANITATION
DOORS, HATCHES
& HANDLES

CLEANING, PROTECTING

TOOLS
DEVICES & GADGETS
LIVABILITY
SAFETY
APPLIANCES
MAINTENANCE
AUTOMOTIVE
IN CAMP

ANOTHER PET-HAIR SOLUTION

To remove pet hair from our carpet in our travel trailer, we use a common window squeegee attached to a broom handle. To use, we simply pull the squeegee toward ourselves in short strokes and the pet hair will collect in one spot. The hair is then picked up and discarded.
BOB KRACIK, MAHOPAC, NEW YORK

BRUSH YOUR WINDSHIELD

One sure way to cut road film and grime from your windshield is regular toothpaste. It has just the right amount of fine abrasive and soap to do the job. Just be sure you have plenty of water to rinse it away. Your glass will sparkle.
DON NEWTON, ORLANDO, FLORIDA

A STICKY MESS

One of our favorite places to camp is the Adirondack Mountains. Thousands of acres of pine trees make a splendid place to spend your vacation. But with pine trees comes pine sap, and pine sap does not come off with soap and water.

I solved this problem by using rubbing alcohol instead of soap. Pour it on your hands, and rub until the pine-sap spots are removed. Rinse with clear water, and you're clean! This will also take the sap off your motorhome's vinyl flooring when it is tracked in.

Another means of removing pine sap and road tar from skin is vegetable shortening. Put some on the spot, rub with a paper towel, and it comes right off. The only problem with this method is you then have to use hot water and soap to get the shortening off.
SUSAN KRENICHYN, HERKIMER, NEW YORK

SPRAY IT DOWN

I have found an easy way to wash my righ in the cold winter months of while in campgrounds that do not allow washing — with only 2 gallons of water. I purchased a 2-gallon deck sprayer, the kind you use to apply wood preservative to decks. All you have to do is fill the tank with water, pump the handle to get the air pressure into it and use the attached hose to direct the water spray. After the initial rinsing I use a sponge to loosen the surface dirt and then rinse again. I use warm water, which helps prevent spotting. I also removed the fine-spray tip on the end of the nozzle to get a better stream of water. These spraying tanks are available at hardware stores for a little more than $20.
ANTHONY MINEO, WHIPPANY, NEW JERSEY

A STREAK-FREE WINDSHIELD

Cleaning the windshield on my motorhome was not easy and usually I ended up with a streaked windshield and a mess on the front end.

I solved this annoyance by purchasing a 2-gallon sprayer (the kind used for weed killers or insecticides) from a hardware store. I filled it with water and added a few drops of Jet Dri, an additive used in dishwashers to keep glassware streak-free.

After pre-wetting the windshield, I put a few drops of liquid car soap on my long-handled scrub brush and a spritz of the car soap on the glass, and I scrub it clean. At the same time, if needed, I do the rest of the front end. Next comes a quick rinse with the sprayer. The water runs off easily and smoothly and all is clear, with no mess running down the fiberglass.
BOB GEERS, CEDAR KEY, FLORIDA

CLEANING IN TIGHT SPACES

"Webster"

As the owner of a pickup truck with a fiberglass cap, it always bothered me not to be able to clean the windows between the truck and cap. One day I noticed my wife was using a cleaning tool called a "webster." It has a long handle with a soft, colorful bristle-type brush on the end of it. I found it works perfectly to dip in my bucket of wash water and clean the windows in this hard-to-reach area. Now my wife has a hard time finding the webster when it's dusting time, but it sure keeps my truck clean.

RICHARD TAWNEY, JACOBUS, PENNSYLVANIA

CLEAN AND SANITIZE

Spending our winters in the South where we keep our windows open, we get a lot of dust and sand on our blinds and window frames. Baby wipes clean these areas and leave them shiny and streak-free, as well as sanitized.

BEATRICE F. PALMROSE, LA FOLLETTE, TENNESSEE

BLACK-STREAK SOLUTION

My solution for removing black streaks: Mix one cup of Zip Wax and three cups of bleach in a 5-gallon bucket of water. Using a cotton mop and a step ladder, I swab the roof thoroughly about twice a year. Follow this by washing the sides with the same solution. Use this formula only for fiberglass or metal roofs. My 10-year-old fifth-wheel has minimal black streaks.

ROBERT WOODS, LAKE DALLAS, TEXAS

DUST SEAL

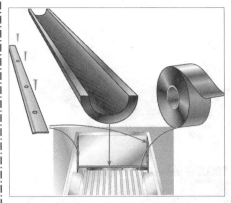

Everything stored in our pickup bed (which was capped with a fiberglass shell) was covered with dust when pulling our travel trailer. I installed a suitable seal made from a 5-foot piece of ¾-inch foam pipe insulation sold at a local hardware store. I cut the pipe in half and installed it in the bottom of the tailgate; the foam can be secured with duct tape or a metal strip with sheet-metal screws into the floor of the pickup bed. The sides of the tailgate can be sealed with vinyl door seal material, which can also be fastened to the side of the bed with sheet-metal screws in addition to the adhesive strip that is part of the seal. The whole project can be done for less than $10.

RON JORGENSON, CALLAWAY, NEBRASKA

FIGHTING MUSTY ODORS

Screen

Some time ago, my wife discovered that the under-bed storage area in our 21-foot trailer smelled a little musty. This particular model has exterior access doors on both sides. We decided that we needed to leave these doors open for a period of time to circulate fresh air, but we also needed to make sure that we didn't invite unwanted visitors to take up residence. (In our part of Texas, that could mean almost anything.) After some thought, we constructed screens to fit the dimensions of the access doors and secured them to the opening. The screen frames, made of wood, hold the door open and the weight of the compartment doors keeps the screens in place.

VALENTINE MAICKEL, SAN ANTONIO, TEXAS

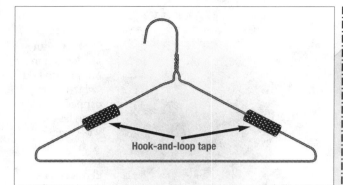

Hook-and-loop tape

CLEANING AND HANGING

To keep from lugging along a heavy bottle of laundry detergent on the way to the laundry room, I pre-measure what I will need and simply dump it on top of the dirty clothes inside the plastic bag. The laundry gets a pre-soak, and I have one less thing to pack back and forth.

Once the clothes are clean, I find that my blouses sometimes fall off the hanger inside the closet while on the road. To keep these blouses put, I wrap a 2-inch-long piece of hook-and-loop tape (the kind with a sticky back) lenghtwise around the top piece of the hanger. It doesn't matter which side of the hook-and-loop material you use, because they both work.
SUSANNE SMITH, SALMON, IDAHO

CLEAN BOWLS

To save time and water, I line my bowl with Saran Wrap before putting in food or heating in the microwave. After eating take the wrap off and the bowl is clean.
RICHARD PREVALLET, LIVINGSTON, TEXAS

BLACK STREAKS BE GONE

Black streaks are a common sight on fiberglass. To remove, take a wet sponge and sprinkle some Bon Ami cleanser on it. Rub it over the streaks until they are gone and rinse thoroughly with water. Bon Ami is recommended for fiberglass, so it would also be great for bathtubs, shower stalls and lavatories.
HARVEY R. KING, CLEVELAND, OKLAHOMA

MAXIMUM AIR — MINIMUM DIRT

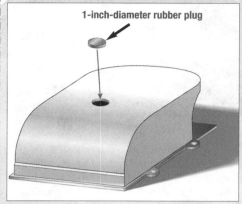

1-inch-diameter rubber plug

We have the Maxx Air covers over our RV's roof vents. To clean the original vent covers, I had to remove the Maxx Air covers, which was a lot of work. So I went to the hardware store and purchased some 1-inch-diameter rubber plugs. I cut a 1-inch hole in the Maxx Air, at the mold mark, and put in a rubber plug. Now, to clean the RV vent covers, all I do is remove the rubber plug and insert the hose nozzle and wash away! Be sure the vent cover is closed. The excess water runs out from under the Maxx Air cover.
CHARLES BENROTH, CASA GRANDE, ARIZONA

FROM THE WD-40 COMPANY

This tip was sent to 10-Minute Tech from the WD-40 Company. It recently completed its "Search For 2000 Uses" and were snowed under with more than 300,000 entries.

I have a 1984 travel trailer that had oxidation streaks covering the exterior surface. I tried numerous cleaners and methods and nothing worked. I was telling a friend about my frustration, and he replied with a chuckle, "Why don't you try WD-40 on it?" Upon arrival at home, I pulled out the can of WD-40, spread some on a rag and tried it on a section of the trailer...it looked new again.

I waited several days and a couple of good rainstorms, to see how the applied area was going to hold up and was amazed that it still looked like new. I then bought a gallon of this wonder liquid and did the whole trailer. I didn't even use a quarter of the can.
BRAD BOVA, MABLETON, GEORGIA

Editor's Note: For more RV-related uses of the product, visit the WD-40 Web site at wd40.com .

STORAGE COVERUP

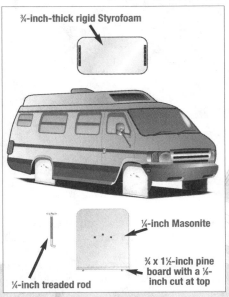

¾-inch-thick rigid Styrofoam

¼-inch Masonite

¾ x 1½-inch pine board with a ⅛-inch cut at top

¼-inch treaded rod

When I store my RV, I like to keep the windows and tires covered to prevent excess deterioration. The window covers are made from ¾-inch-thick rigid foam boards. I used newspaper for the patterns and cut the boards with a saber saw. I cut them large enough so that they wedge into the window frames. The windshield covers are held in place by the sun visors; matchbooks make good wedges. This may not work on all windows, but there are probably many other methods for securing the panels.

The wheel covers are made from ¼-inch-thick Masonite. The bottom strip is made from ¾ x 1½-inch pine board with an ⅛-inch cut at the top to accommodate the Masonite. Sheet-metal screws at the bottom keep the covers off the concrete slab. I use a ¼-inch threaded rod with wing nuts through the openings in the wheels to secure the covers. I drilled three holes in the covers so they can be secured regardless of the wheel position.

WILLIAM T. HORNADY, HAGERMAN, IDAHO

LIKE NEW AGAIN

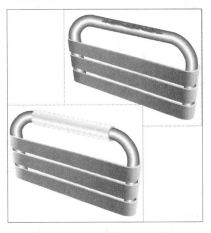

I hung one of my folding chairs upside-down on the back of my coach, where it was exposed to the weather, and the top bar rusted. To save the chair, I spent a dollar on one of those split plastic covers made for closet or shower rods and put it over the damaged area. These covers are easily cut with scissors and are usually available in white or coordinating colors.

JOE CAMPBELL, GOODWATER, ALABAMA

CLOSEUPS • CLOSEUPS • CLOSEUPS

NO SAND TRAP

We have our 30-foot travel trailer located on the shores of the Wisconsin River. As you can imagine, we track in quite a bit of sand. Our trailer has heating ducts in the floor, which become real sand traps. We prevent these ducts from filling with sand during the summer by attaching flexible magnetic sheets. This material is readily available from supply houses like McMaster-Carr Supply Company (your hardware dealer should have access to this catalog). It is very inexpensive and can be cut to size using scissors. We did our four ducts for $6.

BOB MIJOLEVIC, PARDEEVILLE, WISCONSIN

CLOSEUPS • CLOSEUPS • CLOSEUPS

CLEAN IS GOOD

My motorhome's sliding windows have holes in their channels to drain water outside that may accumulate during a heavy rain. The drainage seemed slow, so I purchased a can of compressed air that is used for cleaning computers (available at office-supply stores). I blew out the drain slots, both inside and outside, which also cleared debris out of the hidden channels and improved drainage immensely.

Be sure to wear safety glasses to avoid having dirt blown into your eyes by the compressed air.

JUNE DUTTON, ELGIN, ILLINOIS

CLOSEUPS • CLOSEUPS • CLOSEUPS

CLEAN IT

Regularly clean away road grime from your windshield-wiper blades with vinegar or rubbing alcohol. Apply with a soft cloth or paper towel and keep cleaning the length of the blade until no more dirt comes off. You'll notice the smooth difference during the next rain.

JAMES KUCABA, ORANGE, CALIFORNIA

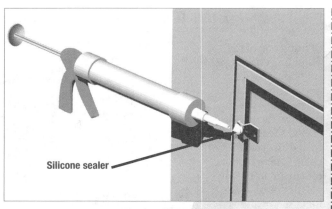

Silicone sealer

PREVENT SCARRING

To prevent scarring of the decals and/or walls of our motorhome when the basement-compartment doors are opened fully, we applied a small blob of clear silicone sealer to the tip of the door hardware that comes in contact with the wall. This forms a cushion between the hardware and the wall.
RALPH BEEGLE, MOBILE, ALABAMA

SINKING SOUR SMELLS

If you are having a problem with sour-smelling towels and washcloths in humid weather, try adding ⅛-cup of table salt into the rinse water when washing in the machine. Your laundry will smell sweet and clean.
JESSIE SEAVEY, SONORA, CALIFORNIA

IS THIS BUGGING YOU?

Is the front of your motorhome plastered with bug guts after a long trip? Here's a wonderful solution: Mix a cup of baking soda with enough water to create a creamy consistency. Using a soft brush, apply to the wet surface. Wow! Anything organic just dissolves away. I've used it for years on my cars and coach with no problems. (Note: Rewax the surface after using baking soda.)
RON WHITE, MUSKEGON, MICHIGAN

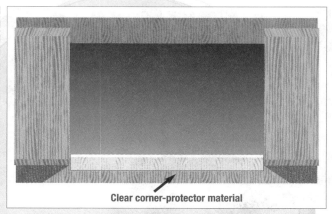

Clear corner-protector material

WOOD PROTECTOR

If your wood cabinetry is simulated-oak with solid hardwood doors, you may experience frazzling or nicking of the bottom edge of the opening.

To keep the cabinet framework looking new, I installed clear corner-protector material on all bottom edges of the door openings. These protectors usually come with peel-and-stick inside surfaces. No adjustment to the doors is necessary, and the clear plastic is barely noticeable with the doors shut. These protectors are available at hardware stores and home centers.
LAWRENCE WEILAND, HOISINGTON, KANSAS

KILLING BACTERIA

Over a period of time the constant reusing for a sponge or dishcloth contributes to the growth of germs and bacteria, causing odors, stains and mildew. To eliminate this unhealthy condition, moisten the sponge (or cloth) and place in the microwave. This cleans out the material internally and its surface fibers to degree the virtually eliminate the existence of any germs or bacteria. Here are the recommended microwave times:

1,000-watt unit	*55 seconds*
1,200-watt unit	*45 seconds*
1,500-watt unit	*36-seconds*

Note: *The microwave rating is on a label affixed to the door.*

When finished with this sanitizing process, let the sponge (or cloth) cool before using it.
C.E CAVENESS, LAKEWOOD, CALIFORNIA

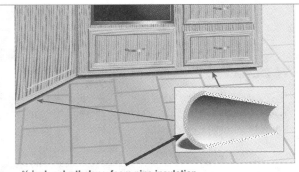

⅜-inch polyethelene-foam pipe insulation

SLIDEOUT SEALER

After our slideout is extended, I fill the gap between the slideout bottom and the floor inside with ⅜-inch polyethylene-foam pipe insulation, cut in half lengthwise. This keeps dust, dog hairs and other stuff from going under the unit, and it keeps cold air from coming in!

DON SPLAIN, LANCASTER, PENNSYLVANIA

STREAKS BE GONE

I have found that heavy-duty hand cleaner used by auto mechanics does a good job of removing unsightly black streaks from the metal and fiberglass side walls. It usually comes in a quart-size, wide-neck container; make sure it contains no abrasives. To make sure, dip your finger in the cleaner; if it feels like hand cream, you have the right stuff. I use the generic brand; it works fine and is less expensive. Using a slightly moistened car wax applicator — also found in auto-parts stores — apply the cleaner like wax. Most of the streaks will be removed with little effort. Use a soft cloth, and remove the cleaner while rubbing a little extra on the streaks that may remain. Make sure you rinse the applicator frequently and wring dry.

ROBERT C. VAN WYNGAARDEN, NORTHRIDGE, CALIFORNIA

PET HAIR BE GONE

Our vacuum cleaner does not pick up pet hair very well, so we use a damp cloth (an old sock on my hand works well) and sort of roll the hair along. When a bunch of hair is collected, we just throw it away.

WALT AND EVIE FILLMORE, HILLSDALE, WISCONSIN

GRUNGY GLASSES?

If your glassware gets to looking grungy, even after many washings on the road, and you long to see that fresh-from-the-dishwasher look again, here's what to do:

Make up a solution of a ¼ teaspoon dishwasher detergent in ½ cup of hot water, and sponge it onto your glassware. Let it stand a few minutes, rinse off and — voilá — like new! This strong detergent solution might bother those with sensitive skin, so the use of rubber gloves might be a good idea for this project.

CHANDLER JONES, RIO RANCHO, NEW MEXICO

OUT OF THE GUTTER

In order to minimize the ever-plaguing black steaks in the side of the RV, you should regularly clean the gutters, keeping them free of debris, dirt and mildew. Due to the narrowness and depth of the gutter, I usually wound up trying to do this with my bare fingers because none of my standard cleaning brushes would work very well. The other day, while gathering cleaning supplies for another wash, I noticed a combination snow brush/ice scraper with a broken scraper on the shelf. The brush was just narrow enough to fit in the gutter and the bristles were long enough to scrub down the gutter base.

I was a little uncomfortable with the protruding brass scraper blade running so close to my rubber roof, so using a coping saw, I cut off the scraper portion and the blunt end of the brush.

Cleaning the gutters is now as easy as hosing out the large debris, running the brush down the gutter with soapy water and rinsing out the loosened dirt. I recommend doing this before washing the side of the trailer due to the amount of dirt and grime you'll probably remove.

BRIAN BERCHTOLD, EGG HARBOR, NEW JERSEY

SCRATCH REPAIRS

I scratched and dinged the plastic coating in my pantry while installing new drawers. The wood stain used on the new drawers matched very well, so I applied a small amount to the scratches. The scratches disappeared like magic. We used the stain on the scratches and on all the woodwork throughout the trailer and it looks new. All you have to do is match the wood-stain color to your wood; put small amount on a clean rag and apply to the scratch. Wipe clean with a dry rag and you're done.

BURCH INGRAM, FRITCH, TEXAS

VENT-SCREEN PROTECTANT

W hen I contacted Fan-Tastic Vent for replacement screen for my power vent, a company representative gave me a helpful hint. After cleaning the screen, apply a thin coat of 303 Protectant before installing it. This will increase the time between cleaning and make the cleaning process easier. 303 Protectant is available from Camping World.

W.A. (PAT) CALL JR., SAN JOSE, CALIFORNIA

SMELLING NICE

P lug it in, plug it in. That's all you have to do with a Glade Plug In-type air freshener to keep the rig smelling nice. Plug the air freshener into any convenient 120-volt AC receptacle and the temperature inside your rig while in storage will usually be warm enough to activate the air freshener. When you use the rig and plug into campground hookups, the air freshener will work even better. In both cases, the smell is very nice. Glade Plug Ins are available at hardware and grocery stores.

LARRY BROTHERTON, WAYNESVILLE, MISSOURI

THE TOOTH FAIRY STRIKES AGAIN!

E ver try to clean a narrow groove with a toothpick, only to have it break off time and time again? I solved that problem with an inexpensive toothbrush that has three rows of bristles.

With a needle-nose pliers, pull out the two outside rows of bristles, leaving the middle row. You can leave this row as long as it came, or you can pull out as many tufts as necessary to get the job done.

DELORES PHILIPS, LA PINE, OREGON

SMELL, SMELL, GO AWAY

I learned long ago that if you are going to store a refrigerator, put coffee grounds in it. I have used this system many times, since my husband spent 20 years in the Army and we had to store refrigerators or freezers for long periods of time. I put about half cup of fresh coffee grounds in two clean margarine tubs and placed one in the freezer and one in the refrigerator. Works great. I did have one or two upset during moves, but the grounds clean up easily with a vacuum cleaner.

Here's another tip: To get rid of smoke smell from the inside of a vehicle, use a bar of Zest soap. We owned a car lot and when we traded for a car that smelled smoky, we placed a bar of Zest under the seat and it pretty well did the job. If the smell is really bad, you may need to scrape the outer edge of the soap to renew the aroma. You may have the aroma of Zest around for a while, but it disappears much faster than smoke.

JANICE M. PAUL, RED CLOUD, NEBRASKA

STORAGE
TOWING
ACCESSORIES
SANITATION
DOORS, HATCHES
& HANDLES
CLEANING & PROTECTING

TOOLS

DEVICES & GADGETS
LIVABILITY
SAFETY
APPLIANCES
MAINTENANCE
AUTOMOTIVE
IN CAMP
SYSTEMS

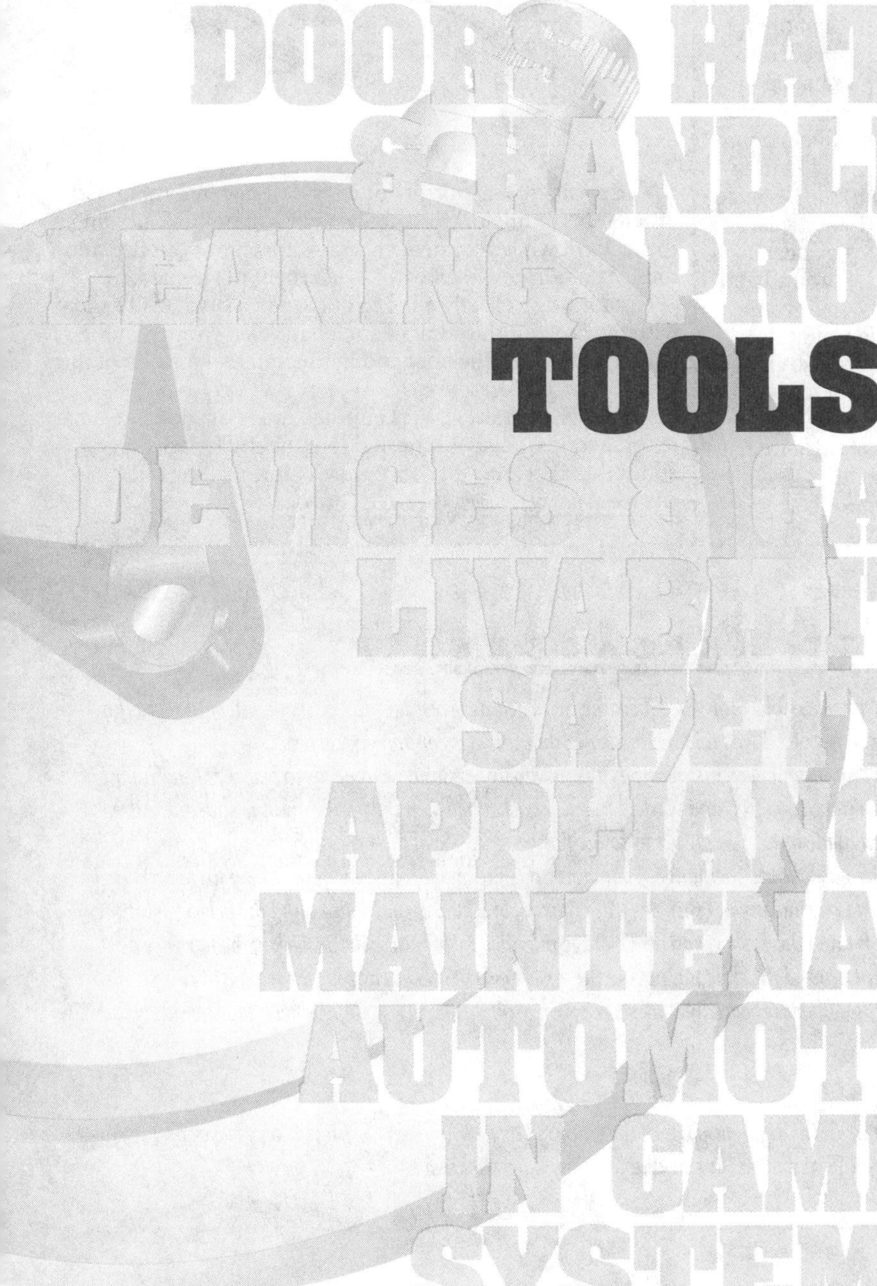

A Clever Solution

There are only so many tools that can be packed away in a motorhome. The other day, for the first time, I needed to change the oil and fuel filters on my AC generator. Because of the lack of clearance around and below the spin-on oil filter, the filter wrenches I had would not fit. I solved the problem by tightening a spare radiator-hose clamp around the filter. Then, by tapping the tightening screw on the clamp with a hammer and screwdriver (use of a designated steel punch or piece of steel rod would be a better idea than a screwdriver as a driver), I was able to loosen the filter.

FRANK GRISWOLD, MORGANTOWN, WEST VIRGINIA

Crank Be Gone

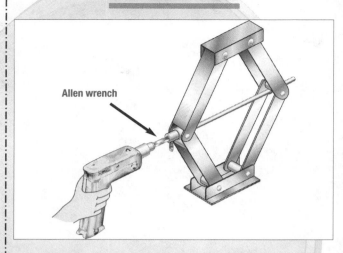

Allen wrench

Last year, during one of our trips, I discovered that I had left my crank for the stabilizer jacks at home. Cranking the jacks down was always a chore, requiring about five minutes of pain-in-the-back work to get them positioned.

Not knowing exactly what to do, I took a small drill I carry with me and put the straight end of an Allen wrench in the chuck and placed the bent end in the notched portion of the jack.

What used to take several minutes, was now done in a matter of seconds. I also discovered that the drill applied just about the right amount of pressure before stalling out.

GERALD WILLIAMS, BROWNS VALLEY, CALIFORNIA

◆ CLOSEUPS ◆ CLOSEUPS ◆ CLOSEUPS ◆ CLOSEUPS ◆ CLOSEUPS ◆ CLOSEUPS ◆

GASKET REPLACEMENT

The gasket that surrounds the slideout of our five-year-old fifth-wheel became detached as a result of the gasket's internal metal fasteners (which hold the gasket to the flange) rusting out. I was told by the dealer that this is a common occurrence.

As a do-it-yourselfer, I purchased a new gasket and commenced installation. It is easy to understand what needs to be done. After pulling out the old gasket, I cleaned the flange onto which the gasket fits, and worked the new gasket between the flange and the slideout. All this went pretty easily. The problem came when I tried to push the new gasket onto the flange. Because of the necessary tight fit, there seemed no way to gain the necessary leverage to work the gasket onto the flange. I could not push it on with just the force of my fingers. Then I struck on the idea of using a Roofing Pry Bar (used for removing old shingles from the roof of a house) and voilá! I had the perfect solution.

The flat end of the pry bar fit between the slideout and the gasket, and the leverage provided by the curve in the neck of the bar very neatly pried the gasket onto the flange. I then just went around the slideout, prying the gasket every 6 inches or so. This would, of course, also work to reseat a gasket which is coming loose, although if it repeatedly comes loose, you probably have rusted fasteners and should replace the whole thing.

CHRIS NORRIS, ANDOVER, NEW HAMPSHIRE

Editor's Note: This "Roofing Pry Bar" is also known (in different parts of the country) as a "Wonder Bar." It is a very clever and useful addition to your tool box, and can help with many different tasks. It's available at any hardware store.

◆ CLOSEUPS ◆ CLOSEUPS ◆ CLOSEUPS ◆ CLOSEUPS ◆ CLOSEUPS ◆ CLOSEUPS ◆

KEEP IT LEVEL

After I spent a season using leveling blocks and checking the motorhome's stance with a hand level, a friend suggested using a bubble level. I mounted one on a strip of aluminum, which I attached with three screws to the underside of the dash, next to the steering wheel. When I had leveled the vehicle correctly (using the refrigerator freezer-compartment floor as the reference point), I aligned the new bubble to match by slightly bending the aluminum strip and/or adjusting the screws.

Now after positioning the leveling blocks we think we'll need, I use the dash-mounted bubble level as reference. Circular levels are available at hardware and RV-supply stores.

JERRY CLOES, KIRKLAND, WASHINGTON

GET A GRIP ON IT

Many times, when attempting to remove a screw or a bolt, the screwdriver or wrench will slip, causing the screw/bolt head to be partially stripped.

Go to the auto-parts store and buy a small container of valve-grinding compound. Coat the head of the screw or bolt and the tip of the screwdriver or wrench with the compound, and the compound will allow your tool to get a good grip and save the job.

Valve-grinding compound (a.k.a. lapping compound) can be used in many situations, any time you need more grip — when using oil-filter wrenches, spanner wrenches, open-end wrenches, sockets — you name it!

EUGENE COWART, LANCASTER, CALIFORNIA

KNEEL AND STABILIZE

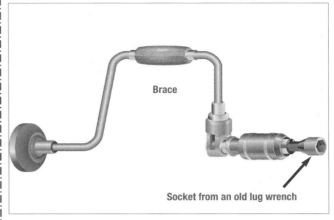

Brace

Socket from an old lug wrench

Although most of the stabilizer jacks on trailers have some type of handle for turning the screw for lowering or raising the mechanism, we found that an old bit brace is really comfortable to use. Once you locate a brace — I use one that belonged to my father — cut the appropriate-size socket off an old lug-nut wrench and install it in the end of the brace. The brace I have ratchets in both directions or can be locked in place. To save my knees, I cut a piece of carpet into a 12 × 12-inch section and use it to kneel on while working the stabilizer jacks.

CECIL K. FARNHAM, MELBOURNE, FLORIDA

LESS CRANKY

After having the axles "flipped" on my fifth-wheel trailer to make it tow level, I found that I had to either do a lot of cranking, use lots of blocks or do both to stabilize the trailer when parked. To solve the problem, I took two jackstands and put a 2 × 5⅝ × 9¼-inch block on

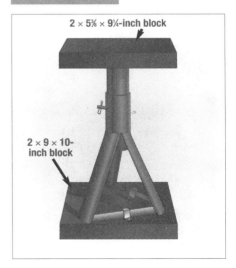

2 × 5⅝ × 9¼-inch block

2 × 9 × 10-inch block

top of each stand. Then I mounted a 2 × 9 × 10-inch block to the bottom of each stand. This gives me a lot of height and eliminates most of the cranking. Works great even if you have power-operated landing jacks.

MARVIN BRYANT, LITTLETON, COLORADO

STATIONARY BRAKE ACTIVATION

Push-button switch

Wires into #2 and #4

④ ③
⑥ ⑦ ⑤
② ①

7-way trailer connector

While doing my annual wheel-bearing maintenance, and the trailer is jacked up, I like to do a quick check to verify that the brakes are functioning properly. It is very inconvenient to run back and forth from the trailer axles to the brake controller — or to ask someone to help — so I have found that I can do the activation myself. I simply connect a push-button switch between the brake pin and the battery pin in the seven-way trailer connector. I use a remote starter switch, which is designed to crank the engine when setting valves, etc., with the leads extended so I can reach the switch while rotating the trailer wheels. This applies full power to the brake, but only while the button is pushed. Remote starter switches are inexpensive and available at any auto-parts store.

MARVIN BRYANT, LITTLETON, COLORADO

SPARE-TIRE ASSIST

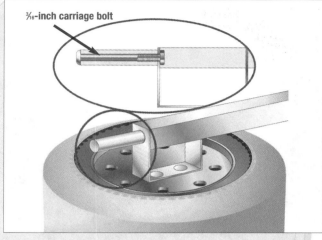

⅜-inch carriage bolt

I have a spare-tire carrier in the rear of my trailer, which has to be lowered and raised whenever I use the storage cabinet located behind it. Since I keep often-used items (sewer hose, water hose, etc.) in that cabinet, I'm in there a lot. It was necessary to raise or lower the spare by grabbing the tire. The tire was often dirty and sometimes wet, making the job a messy one.

I solved the problem by installing a lifting handle. On the top of the tire carrier was a ⅜-inch hole, so I purchased a ⅜-inch carriage bolt (about 5 inches long) and nut. I also purchased a piece of pipe 4 inches long. I put the bolt through the pipe and the hole in the carrier and screwed on the nut. Presto, a new lifting handle!

RICHARD WARD, SUN CITY, ARIZONA

◆ CLOSEUPS ◆ CLOSEUPS ◆ CLOSEUPS ◆ CLOSEUPS ◆ CLOSEUPS ◆ CLOSEUPS ◆

ROOFTOP SWIMMING POOL

*F*or more than 15 years, our two successive motorhomes have been protected by a cover when not in use. And for more than 15 years, each rainstorm leads to a rooftop "swimming pool" formed by the cover draping itself over the luggage rack.

Concerned with the weight of the water, stress on the expensive covers and prolonged moisture on the roof, I have tried many schemes to eliminate the problem. The first was an inflated rubber raft beneath the cover in the luggage rack. Next came a platform made from PVC pipe and Fome-Cor board resting on the luggage rack, all accompanied by numerous trips to the roof to scoop, bail or pump out the pooled water.

Finally, I found an inexpensive and simple solution! About 12 feet of ¾-inch plastic tubing (available at the local hardware store) does the trick. I use a flat rock to keep the tubing anchored at a low spot in the rooftop pool. The rock is heavy enough to keep the tubing in place, but not so heavy as to crush the tubing. The "drain" hangs down the side of the motorhome.

After a good rain, I simply begin water flow through the siphon with a little suction. I keep the hose end clean by covering it with a disposable latex glove. And I've found that, due to the length of the hose, I never get water in my mouth.

The result is an RV cover that dries easily and quickly in the sun and breeze!

DIANE PAULSEN, MEDFORD, OREGON

◆ CLOSEUPS ◆ CLOSEUPS ◆ CLOSEUPS ◆ CLOSEUPS ◆ CLOSEUPS ◆ CLOSEUPS ◆

No Back Strain

2-foot-long 1 × 2-inch wood

Heavy-duty tow vehicle, trailer or motorhome tires are a bear to lift while attempting to align the lugs with the rim holes when remounting the wheels. You can eliminate much of the back strain by using a 2-foot-long 1 × 2-inch piece of wood or even a long handle of the lug wrench as a lever. Center the lever on the ground in front of the axle, roll the wheel/tire on it, very close to the lug bolts, align the bolts with the holes and lift the lever. It really works!

VICTOR H. FERRY, WATERFORD, CONNECTICUT

Save Some Wear and Tear

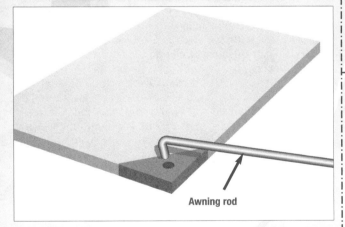

Awning rod

Instead of having to get on my knees and bend under the motorhome when placing or picking up the boards under the hydraulic jacks, I drilled a hole in the corner of each board. Each hole is just slightly larger than the diameter of the awning rod. I painted the corner of the board where the hole was drilled, so I would know to place that edge toward the outside of the rig. Now when it is time to pull them out, I simply insert the awning-rod end, pull and lift. This idea has saved wear and tear on my back and knees.

PHILLIP WISE, JOPLIN, MISSOURI

More Leverage

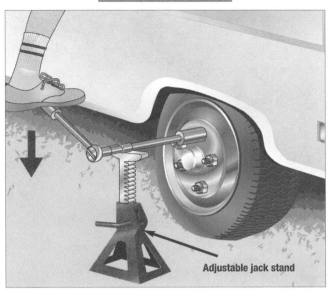

Adjustable jack stand

Trying to loosen lug nuts can sometimes be a real bear. We always carry a pair of adjustable jackstands in our 32-foot fifth-wheel as a support for a breaker bar, ratchet or X-type lug wrench. This gives us a stable support for loosening or tightening the lug nuts on the trailer or truck. This procedure will work great for motorhome lug nuts, which are usually very difficult to remove. Just raise or lower the jackstand height to accommodate the lug-nut location. As I've gotten older, the jackstand has helped with the use of leg power rather than arm/shoulder power, while providing the confidence of stability.

R.E. MAULSBY, ALPINE, TEXAS

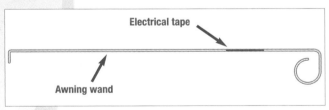

Electrical tape

Awning wand

Slideout Clearance Tool

The slideout in our fifth-wheel is great, but in the past, when we pulled into a site, we weren't always sure we would have enough room to bring it out due to obstructions, such as trees, electrical boxes, etc. To eliminate this problem, we took our awning wand (used to open the awning) and marked it with a short length of electrical tape indicating the minimum distance to extend the slide. The awning wand is kept in a handy location and is held against the slideout when needed.

CARL AND PAT PULLUM, ROGERS, ARKANSAS

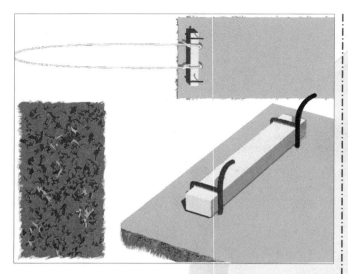

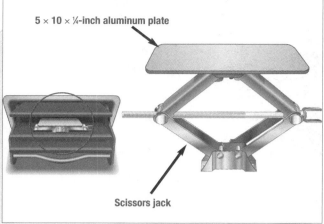

5 × 10 × ¼-inch aluminum plate

Scissors jack

SLIDEOUT ROOF CLEANER

To make a slide-out roof-cleaning tool that does not need a ladder to use, get a shag rug about 5 feet long. Cut the width slightly smaller than the width of the slide-out roof.

Attach a length of 1 × 2-inch wood to the bottom (non-shag) of the rug, using plastic tie straps. Fasten a long piece of cord or rope to the wood. Make the cord or rope at least 2½ times as long as the slide.

Have someone hold the rug, with the shag side down, near the top (side) of the slide-out while you throw the rope over the top of the slide. Then just pull across the roof.
CONRAD LIND, SPENCERPORT, NEW YORK

Editor's note: If you add a second piece of wood and a rope to the other end of the rug and wet the rug with soap and water, you and your helper could pull the rug back and forth in a scrubbing maneuver. Rinse with your garden hose.

STEP SAVER

I like the stability of a step saver, but dislike having to keep track of it. It is the type of thing that from time to time seems to get lost or left at the last park some 300 miles back down the road. I went to a local auto-salvage yard and acquired a small scissors jack that folds down to about 1½ inches. After I removed the swivel used to secure it to the car frame, I then cut a 5 × 10 × ¼-inch plate from a scrap piece of aluminum. After locating the center of the plate, I drilled a ⅜-inch hole, which I countersunk to accommodate a ⅜-inch tapered machine bolt.

I then cut a 1½-inch square from the ¼-inch-thick aluminum stock and placed it against the bracket that used to have the swivel, and installed a countersunk machine screw in order to keep the 5 × 10-inch plate from turning. I turned the jack upside down and mounted it to the bottom of the lower step with two ¼-inch carriage bolts. The jack (with the plate attached) screws down to approximately 1¼ inches, which allows the step to be folded up for travel. Depending on the type of step, some adjustment may be required as to location — forward or back — and the width of the ground plate.
DAVID L. HARDING, MABELVALE, ARKANSAS

LIQUID TAPE

An item that should be in every RV tool kit is Liquid Electrical Tape. This is a liquid, rubber-like product that seals, insulates and protects electrical connections. It's available in five different colors, and comes in a brush-top can. You simply brush it on whatever you are trying to protect; you can even dip small tool handles (like pliers) in the liquid to provide a non-slip grip.

Liquid tape is sold in the electrical section of almost any hardware store.
GEORGE CRAWFORD, BURLINGTON, IOWA

LUG WRENCHING MADE EASIER

When the unfortunate times occur that you have to use a lug wrench, it's trial-and-error to see which of the four ends fits your lug nuts. The problem is solved by a bit of spray paint or tape on the correct end.
N.A. DANTZMAN, CRESCENT CITY, CALIFORNIA

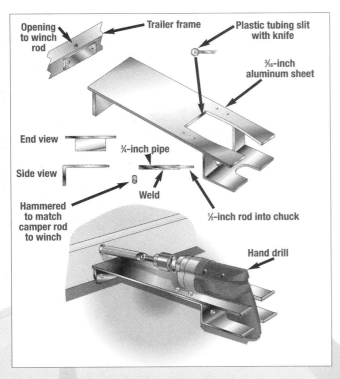

Opening to winch rod — Trailer frame — Plastic tubing slit with knife

³⁄₁₆-inch aluminum sheet

End view

¾-inch pipe

Side view

Weld

Hammered to match camper rod to winch

½-inch rod into chuck

Hand drill

STRAIN RELIEF

We have a tent trailer, and we learned from fellow campers that we could use an angle-head drill motor to mechanically lift the top during setup. This is OK for most people, but at age 75, holding on to a high-torque drill motor can be hard on my shoulders, arms and hands, especially in the Florida summer heat. I came up with a bracket that holds the drill motor in place, making the job much easier. I use a Milwaukee drill with a 5.5-amp motor rated at 850 rpm; this is a high-torque, low-rpm unit.

Granted, this project may take a little time, but in the end it's worth it. The main section is made of a ³⁄₁₆-inch aluminum sheet; the size will depend on the model of drill motor used. A section is cut out to accommodate the body of the drill motor. Two 90-degree bends are made to another piece of aluminum and sections are cut out to accommodate the drill-motor handle and lower part of the body. These two sections are attached using ¼-inch bolts and locknuts. The edges in the cutout openings are covered with plastic tubing, which was split with a knife.

The entire bracket is stabilized to the trailer, using another piece of aluminum, with spacers on the ends, which was bolted to the trailer frame. The spacers create a "notched-out section" for an end piece that is attached to the end of the bracket. You can attach this piece using glue or it can be welded (this would require special equipment). The handle is made from a piece of ¾-inch pipe welded to a ½-inch rod. The end of the handle is hammered into shape to match the end of the winch.

WILLIAM MACKRELL, FT. LAUDERDALE, FLORIDA

DEVICES & GADGETS

TOWING
ACCESSORIES
SANITATION
DOORS, HATCHES
& HANDLES
CLEANING, PROTECTING
TOOLS

LIVABILITY
SAFETY
APPLIANCES
MAINTENANCE
AUTOMOTIVE
IN CAMP
SYSTEMS
STORAGE

A Clip Tip

My husband and I came up with an idea on how to keep our map book marked and easily opened to where we need it. We took the clips from plastic hangers and snapped them on the pages we wanted to mark. These clips also work well as money clips, chip and bread-bag clips, and they even keep shoes together.

Janie Thompson, Simpson, Louisiana

All-Purpose Hanger

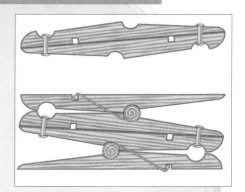

A unique way to attach items to your awning is using specially modified clothespins. Take two wooden clothespins (plastic is OK) and separate them at the spring. Attach the two halves without springs back to back in the opposite direction. Drill a hole at each end in the groove and attach the two using a soft rivet or binding clip. Make sure the head of the rivet fits into the groove so that it does not interfere with the closing of the clothespin when completed. Reinstall the clothespin halves with the springs and your hanger is ready to use.

Joe Nice, Laurel, Maryland

Awning-Rod Helper

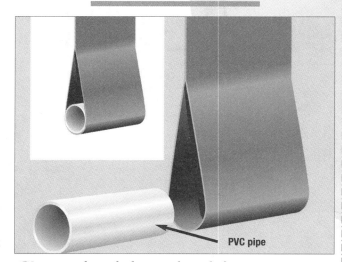

PVC pipe

Sooner or later, the loop on the end of your awning strap will collapse. Try as you may, the awning rod won't slip through without your having to get out the ladder and apply some hands-on maneuvering.

I bypassed the camping-supply store's $6 solution and improvised with a 2-inch slice cut from a ¼-inch piece of PVC pipe. I inserted the cut cylindrical piece into the collapsed rubber reinforcement piece. The PVC was secured by looping a 6-inch piece of lightweight wire through the cylinder and around the fabric. Another way would be to spot-glue it in place with a hot-glue gun. Leave the ladder stored. This fix is quick and inexpensive, and it works great!

Brenda Boyd, Livingston, Texas

◆ CLOSEUPS ◆ CLOSEUPS ◆ CLOSEUPS ◆

B U N G E E - B A L L R E L E A S E

**W**hen the bungee-ball cord is wrapped tightly around an object, like a television cable, it is often difficult to release. Tie a string around the loop at the opposite end of the ball. The string gives you an easy grip to pull the cord over the ball, releasing the object.

Charles R. Goodman, Boerne, Texas

◆ CLOSEUPS ◆ CLOSEUPS ◆ CLOSEUPS ◆

◆ CLOSEUPS ◆ CLOSEUPS ◆ CLOSEUPS ◆

A S H O E L A C E T O T H E R E S C U E

**I** had trouble finding the end of my electrical power cord after tucking it into my outside storage locker. The end always seemed to work its way down into the midst of the cord pile. I took a white shoelace, about a foot long, and tied it to the end of the cord just behind the plug. Now I open the storage door, grab the white shoelace, and pull out the cord, plug first!

James Southwick, Lemon Grove, California

◆ CLOSEUPS ◆ CLOSEUPS ◆ CLOSEUPS ◆

Awning Hooks

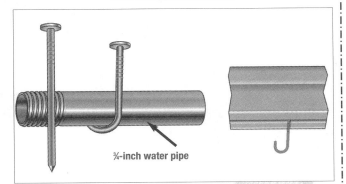

¾-inch water pipe

Here's an inexpensive way to suspend items, such as plants, lights and knick-knacks, from the awning roller. Bend 16-penny nails into a hook configuration. The bending can be done by using an old piece of ¾-inch water pipe as an anvil. The head of the nail slides securely, but easily, into the standard awning roller slot. I finished the project by spraying the bent nails with aluminum paint. Cost is a mere fraction of those awning hooks available in accessory stores. Be sure to use box nails and not standard nails.

FREDERICK A. SPENCER, COLLINSVILLE, ILLINOIS

Clearer Vision

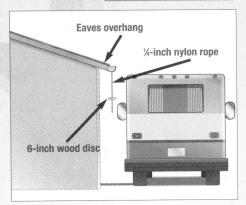

Eaves overhang

¼-inch nylon rope

6-inch wood disc

If you store your RV alongside your house, you know that the overhanging eaves can be difficult to see using the side mirrors; they are too high for the normal line of sight. With a piece of rope and a 6-inch wood disc attached at the farthest outward point, adjusted to mirror height, I can now see where the overhang ends without messing with the mirror adjustment. Use a ¼-inch nylon rope and paint the wood disc white for best possible visibility. Drill a hole in the end cap of the gutter and tie one end of the rope; drill a hole in the center of the disc so the other end of the rope can be threaded through. Use knots in the rope to adjust disc height so that it's level with the mirrors. When the mirror makes contact with the disc, you should also have 3 inches of clearance between the end of the overhang and mirror.

RANDY BRIEN, BOTHELL, WASHINGTON

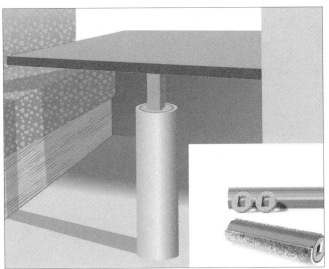

Cats Do Scratch

My wife and I and our two cats just completed a seven-week trip to the West Coast. Every time I moved around in the motorhome, I would trip, stumble and/or fall over the cats' scratching post. My daughter-in-law came up with a terrific solution. The new-and-improved post slips over the existing dinette-table leg. The post consists of a piece of 3-inch plastic pipe, two ends cut from 1-inch foam insulation and a piece of carpet. The 1-inch foam insulation is cut in a circle to fit inside the plastic pipe, and a cut is made in the center of the foam circle to fit the shape of the table leg. The carpet is cut to fit around the plastic pipe. The ends are glued in place with silicon cement, and the carpet is held in place with contact cement.

It works great. The cats love it!

LARRY BONHAM, ELLSINORE, MISSOURI

A U T O M A T I C W A S H I N G   M A C H I N E

CLOSEUPS • CLOSEUPS • CLOSEUPS •

*W*hen we go camping, we take along a 44-quart plastic container. Aside from the obvious storage uses, we put it in the back of the pickup, fill it with dirty clothes, water and laundry soap and secure the lid. After exploring the countryside or a day's outing, all I have to do is rinse the clothes and hang them to dry. When one of our grandchildren travels with us, it becomes his or her bathtub, since we only have a shower in our trailer.

META LILLIE, WICHITA FALLS, TEXAS

CLOTHESPIN MODIFICATION

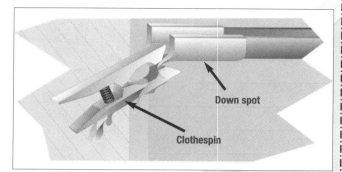

Down spot

Clothespin

Roof down spouts always seem to leave black streaks along the trailer wall because the spout is too short. After trying metal down-spout extensions and small PVC tubing, which all eventually came off, I found the simplest and most effective solution: clip on a clothespin at the end of each down spout. The water wets the wood and runs off at the end of the clothespin well away from the side wall of the trailer. The clothespin trick works on controlling morning dew drips to major downpours. Remove the clothespins when traveling.
TED BALESHTA, SIDNEY, BRITISH COLUMBIA, CANADA

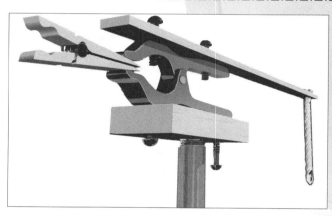

THE CURSED "BLACK STREAK," REVISITED

When we bought our new RV, we found the gutters' down-spouts (or lack thereof) allowed the runoff to create the infamous "black streak." After settling in at our campsite, I improved on a fix used by many campers: I got out my ladder and pinned a clothespin to each downspout. I soon saw it was going to be a hassle hauling out the ladder twice at each stop and stretching for the 11-foot reach.

The illustration shows my solution. The device screws to the end of the extension handle used to wash the rig, lets the operator stay on the ground and takes only minutes to complete the task.
FRAN WHITAKER, COOS BAY, OREGON

CLOTHESPIN MODIFICATION II

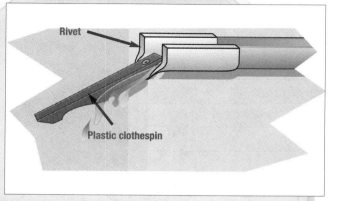

Rivet

Plastic clothespin

I have been using clothespins attached to my RV's down-spout to avoid black streaks for the last couple of years. However, I have a fifth-wheel trailer and installing and re-moving the clothespins was a real hassle every time I wished to travel, so I simply left then on. As you would expect. Each time I traveled, I lost one or two of the clothespins, which meant I would have to get the ladder out to reinstall them. After doing these three or four times, I tried some-thing different.

I use plastic clothespins that have a hole in one end of each leg of the pin. I separated the two sides, disposed of the spring and after drilling a ⅛-inch hole near the end of each down spout, I attached one leg of the clothespin to the bot-tom of each down spout with aluminum Pop rivet. One leg works just as well as a whole clothespin. I haven't lost one since then, and I use half as many clothespins. If one should get caught on a low branch, it simply turns toward the rear of the fifth-wheel, and is easily straightened using the awning rod — and no need to wrestle with the ladder.
DUANE F. ALBRECHT, PAWNEE, ILLINOIS

CORNER PROTECTION

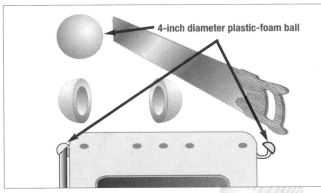

4-inch diameter plastic-foam ball

The final step in winterizing our trailer is to cover it with a plastic tarp. I use an inexpensive blue tarp that can be purchased at any building supply or hardware store, although my tip will work just as well for covers that are designed specifically for RVs. After the first or second winter's use, the tarp wears through at the top where it rests on the awning posts on one side and on the ends of the rain gutters on the other. This is usually due to the wind causing the tarp to move and abrade at these sharp pressure points. I purchased two 4-inch-diameter semi-smooth-surface plastic-foam balls from a craft store for 49 cents each. I sawed each in half, pressed them on at these pressure points, then hollowed out the inside at the indentations using a jackknife. I then press-fit these half-balls into place on the protrusions and secured them with a length of cloth tape. No more holes in the tarp.

J. BARD ANDERSON, LONG GREEN, MARYLAND

DRINK IT

There is a hole on the side of my fifth-wheel that is used to insert the crank to lower the landing gear. It's a perfect place for bugs, etc., to enter the trailer. I uncorked a bottle of my favorite wine, then inserted the cork in the crank hole; a perfect fit. No more bugs! Of course, my wife and I had to drink the wine...

DAVID WATKINS, POMPANO BEACH, FLORIDA

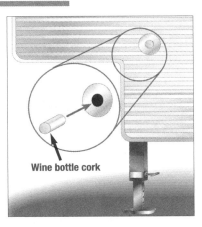

Wine bottle cork

BUMPER-PLUG RETAINER

Since losing the two end caps from my trailer bumper, and almost losing my sewer hoses, I devised a way to ensure that the end camps stay in place until I reach my destination. Although there are commercial devices marketed to solve this problem, they cost more than my solution, which is a little more than $1. All you need are two locking cotter pins, a drill, a small drill bit and five minutes of your time.

Drill a small hole through the top of the bumper and into the end cap. Place a locking cotter pin through the hole and secure the clasp on the pin. Your end cap will not come off again unless you remove it. I have used this arrangement for several trips and have not lost an end cap since.

KEVIN V. ARATA, WEST POINT, NEW YORK

DOG-DISH HOSE HANGER

The natural place to store our water hoses is the 60 × 36 × 10-inch outside access compartment in our slideout, just forward of our water connection. Our plan was to hang the hoses on a clothes hanger just like the ones you use at home. Unfortunately, the house-type hanger was too big. To properly hang a coiled 25-foot hose in the narrow compartment, a hanger about 10 inches in diameter and 3 to 4 inches deep was needed. Our golden retriever's food dish was the answer. Before screwing the bottom of the dish to the inside vertical wall of the storage compartment, we converted the empty "food" part of the dish into a small storage bin for loose hose nozzles, water thief, etc. We laid a 4-inch high scrap of Plexiglas across the lower half of the opening. (Leave a small gap between the bottom of the Plexiglas and the bottom of the dog dish for a clean-out slot or to allow water to drain.)

We also had to prepare the compartment for hose storage. The inside vertical wall of the compartment was the typical ⅛-inch thick panel, not strong enough to support the hose hanger. We added a 1 × 6-inch, 5-foot-long piece of pine board across the back of the compartment, to which we fastened the hanger.

We then cut a piece of plastic floor runner for the floor of the compartment and painted the mounting board and the inside of the compartment with a clear wood sealer.

JIM HENKEL, KING GEORGE, VIRGINIA

EASIER AWNING PULL-STRAP LOOPS

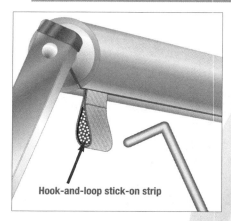

Hook-and-loop stick-on strip

My husband was always complaining about how difficult it was to get the awning wand into the pull-down strap loops, since they seem to always be stuck together. I took the fuzzy part of a hook-and-loop stick-on strip and cut it into two strips. I then placed one of these pieces in the curve of each loop. Now the wand goes into the loop, which is held open by the hook-and-loop stick-on strips.

Lorie DiNicola, Livingston, Texas

FISHING-ROD STORAGE

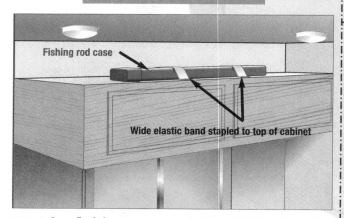

Fishing rod case

Wide elastic band stapled to top of cabinet

We love fly-fishing, so we travel with at least four fly rods in our fifth-wheel. Because we don't have basement storage, finding a safe but easily accessible place for the fly rods was a problem. Our fifth-wheel has an open area above the cabinets that are overhead, along the walls, above the sofa and dinette. This was a perfect place to store the rods.

Using heavy-duty staples, we attached each end of a 2-inch-wide elastic band to the top of each set of cabinets. We cut it long enough to just span the width of the shelf and positioned it about in the middle of the cabinet section. The elastic gives just enough to slide the fly rods (in their cases) under the strap but holds them in place safely. When not in use, the straps lay flat and can't be seen. We've taken some pretty bumpy backroads to our favorite fishing spots and the elastic straps hold the rods securely to the top shelves.

Rita Daniels, Sundance, Wyoming

ELECTRIC-JACK COVER

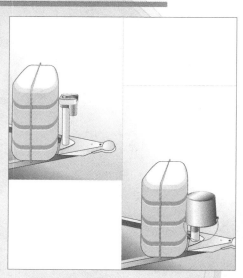

Ifound an inexpensive way to protect my electric jack from the weather and store my plastic water bucket at the same time. The bucket fits snugly upside down over the jack. The LP-gas-cylinder-bottle cover is close enough to secure the bucket in place while traveling. A bungee cord from the bucket handle to the trailer frame would be extra insurance against an updraft flipping the bucket off.

Gary Nokes, Del Rio, Texas

FETCHING WATER

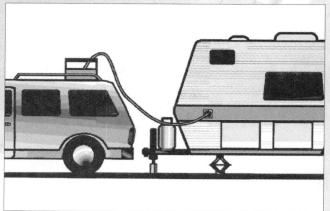

Don't you really love getting to camp and setting up in a space without hookups only to find out that you forgot to fill the freshwater tank? The first time we made that dumb mistake, we figured out a way to get enough water without breaking camp. We positioned two clean 18-gallon Rubbermaid storage containers with lids on the roof of our Suburban and filled them with water. We then drove to the trailer and used the white hose to siphon the water into the tank. Blankets were used to prevent the containers from scratching the roof paint.

William Bouma, Wildwood, Illinois

FUNNEL IT UP

To make a funnel for adding engine oil that's also easy to store, use an empty quart-size plastic oil container as the basis. Cut the container in half and you're done. The upper half of the container is now your funnel; the neck fits nicely into the engine-oil-fill access. When done, screw the cap back on and slide the bottom section that was cut off over the top for dust protection. Store the "funnel" in a corner in the engine compartment until needed.

JAMES PARISH, CHANDLER, ARIZONA

FILL 'ER UP

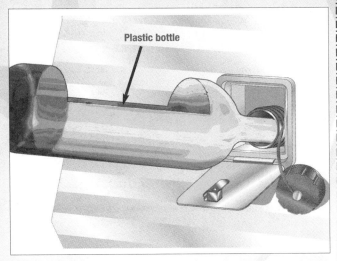

Plastic bottle

The ideas generally presented for adding water to the tank when boondocking are two-person filling gadgets that require one person to hold the funnel and a strong person to hold the water container at about head level. I submit that it ought to be self-evident that a no-person funnel held at that level of the tank inlet is far superior. The tapered neck of a large (1.75-liter) plastic liquor bottle is just right for jamming solidly into the filler opening, where it will stay in place without being held and without leaking.

ROBERT W. BATES, IDAHO FALLS, IDAHO

NOODLE WEDGIES

Swim noodle

We have just started full-timing and found that swim-noodle water toys can be easily cut with a sharp knife to any length and wedged in the refrigerator or in the cabinets to hold things in place while on the road. They are lightweight, inexpensive and work great.

DONNA MANN,
VERO BEACH, FLORIDA

FOR ROAD AND HOME

Whether it's used for a drill, a caulking gun or a container of polish, this holster, mounted on the side of your ladder, makes maintenance a lot safer. The section of PVC tube is 2 inches in diameter, or larger as needed, and is secured with heavy-duty nylon-wire ties. Small screws and hex nuts would also do the job nicely.

FRANK WOYTHAL, ANDOVER, NEW YORK

◆ CLOSEUPS ◆ CLOSEUPS ◆ CLOSEUPS ◆

GAINED YOUR MARBLES?

Many cleaning fluids come in bottles that, when full, are top-heavy and tend to fall over while the RV is on the road. To solve this problem, put a layer of marbles in the bottom of each bottle.
GINA REED, MIAMI, FLORIDA

◆ CLOSEUPS ◆ CLOSEUPS ◆ CLOSEUPS ◆

GUTTER TRICKS

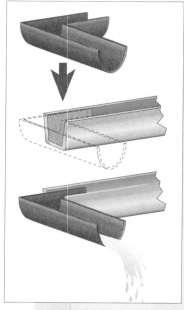

I found an easy and permanent solution to extending the rain gutters on our fifth-wheel so that the rain does not run down the sides. I used a product made by the Wiremold Company called Cord-mate. This is a plastic version of the metal Wiremold commonly used to hide wiring on the surface of the walls. I used the flat elbow, product no. C6, which is ⅜-inch wide and off-white in color; it fits perfectly into the rain gutter. These parts cost $1.39 each at my local hardware store.

Using a rubber roof sealant, such as Dicor 501-LSW, as bedding, I set this elbow in the end of the gutter with a slight downward tilt to facilitate drainage. After seating the elbow, be sure to clean any excess sealant from the gutter so that the rainwater will flow freely. The elbow is 1⅛ inches long, which gives a sufficient extension from the rig's side wall. The rubber-roof sealant is easier to remove than many other sealants; if one elbow breaks off, I can easily remove the piece and install a new one.

TOM HELM, DURANGO, COLORADO

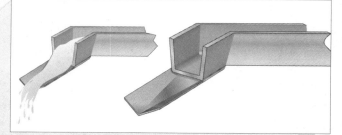

My rain-gutter-downspout extenders are made of flexible, clear plastic, from an empty 2-liter soda bottle. They are flexible and safe on the highway, and they are almost invisible — not an eyesore like a clothespin or the like. They help you recycle plastic soda bottles, too. They are fun to make and simple enough that the kids can do all the work.

Take a clean 2-liter soda bottle and cut the clear midsection into strips slightly wider than the width of your RV's spouts. You can make them as long as you like, but I've found that 3 to 4 inches is sufficient for most rigs. You'll need a clear plastic strip for each gutter spout on your rig. Next, crease the very end of each plastic strip with your thumb and forefinger (do not crease the entire length of the plastic strip). The end should look like a "V." Bend and shape the other end to match the contour of the underneath portion of the downspout. Put a dab of silicone sealer underneath the downspout and press the plastic strip into place. The plastic strip is light enough to hold itself in place until the silicone dries. Now wait for the next big rainstorm and you'll be amazed at how well these spout extenders work. You'll never see black streaks again, guaranteed!

MARK DENSLEY, LONGWOOD, FLORIDA

HOLD THOSE PINS

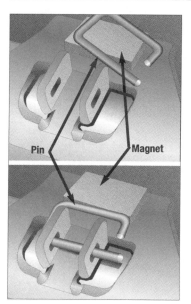

Pin   Magnet

A good solution to lost safety pins that secure the spring-bar brackets when the chains are attached is to place a rectangular heavy-duty magnet above the appropriate holes in the bracket. The magnet will hold the pins when the brackets are not in use. Magnets are available at any hardware store for about $1 each.

EUGENE L. SCHAFFNER, SKOKIE, ILLINOIS

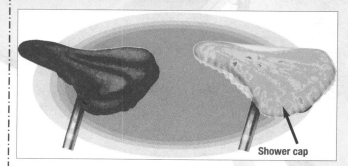

Shower cap

KEEP YOUR SEAT DRY

Stretch a shower cap over your bicycle seat to protect it from morning dew and/or rain. This works fine in the campground. While traveling in the motorhome, however, I usually put a plastic grocery bag over the bike seat and fasten it with a twist tie for added protection.

JAMES DION, NORTH SCITUATE, RHODE ISLAND

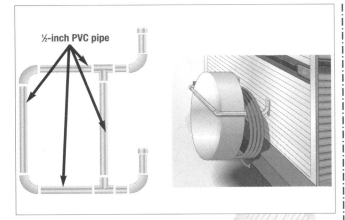

½-inch PVC pipe

HOSE MANAGEMENT

We use our 100-foot hose a lot in the spring and summer. To keep it handy and untangled, we put our spare tire into action. We made a hose holder out of ½-inch PVC pipe that slips over the top of the spare-tire holder. The length of the PVC pipe will vary as to the size of your spare. Just measure the length and width to allow the holder to sit about a third of the way down onto the spare.

MARK KUYKENDALL, PRESCOTT, ARIZONA

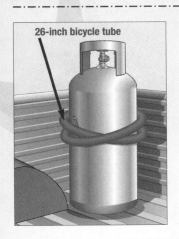

26-inch bicycle tube

LP-GAS CYLINDER SAVER

Finding a good way to transport LP-gas cylinders is always a challenge. A simple way to prevent marks on the truck and on the cylinder is to double wrap a 26-inch bicycle tube around the cylinder. Slightly inflate the tube before wrapping it around the cylinder.

COLIN CLARK, MOOSE, WYOMING

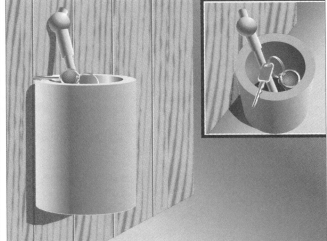

KEY STORAGE NO. 1

I was forever misplacing the keys to our motorhome door. One day it occurred to me to keep the keys near the door, so I used a rubberized beverage holder and glued it on the wall next to the entrance. Now when I enter the motorhome I place the keys in the holder. I also found this to be a handy place to keep my tire gauge.

RUSSELL DEMPSEY, JUPITER, FLORIDA

KEY STORAGE NO. 2

Need a place to keep extra keys and small flashlights? The cabinet box I made is 9 × 9 inches. I used 1 × ¾-inch oak for the frame and ³⁄₁₆-inch plywood for the back panel and front door. The hinges go on one side, and a magnetic latch keeps the door closed. A small section of ¼-inch wood strip was mounted near the inside top with cup hooks screwed in to hold the extra keys. A piece of ³⁄₁₆ × 1-inch plywood was placed on the bottom, forming a storage area for small flashlights and other items. By placing a piece of plastic sheeting over the door front, you can use it to display pictures.

JIM COMPARONI, PALO ALTO, CALIFORNIA

LADDER CADDY

Plastic drain gutter

I purchased a folding ladder to use around my fifth-wheel, but I didn't want to store it outside. I found a good place to store it inside a compartment, but all the other belongings seem to get piled around the ladder, making it difficult to remove when needed. I got a 1-foot plastic drain gutter and end caps from a hardware store and mounted my newly configured holder to the floor of the compartment, right up against the wall. The gutter is screwed into the compartment wall using sheetmetal screws. Now the ladder is stored inside the gutter and it's easy to slide in and out, regardless of what's on top of it.

L. Jerry Rigg, Lawrenceville, Illinois

NIFTY GROMMETS

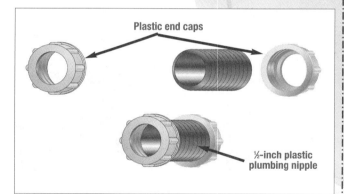

Plastic end caps

½-inch plastic plumbing nipple

I recently installed a solar panel on my travel trailer. The installation required routing a 10-gauge wire through the side of the trailer, behind cabinets and through the floor. I was unable to find grommets that could accommodate the thickness of these fixtures, especially the floor. I finally hit on the idea of using a ½-inch plastic plumbing nipple with two plastic bushing end-caps. Plumbing nipples come in a variety of sizes and are easily cut to the correct size with a coping saw. The nipple is placed in the hole and the end-caps screwed tightly down from both directions, thus giving a finished look to any project of this type. The two end-caps and nipples can be bought in any hardware store for less than $1 for the three units.

Tim Staats, Milwaukee, Wisconsin

MAGNET MAGIC

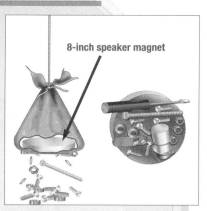

8-inch speaker magnet

I found that a magnet makes a great catch-all for small parts and tools. I use the magnet out of a defective speaker — an 8-inch magnet, which is very strong, is best. I then put the magnet on the engine, the hood or any other metal surface near the work site. As I remove bolts, screws etc, I put them on the magnet for safekeeping. It works well for holding small tools, too.

I also put one magnet on a mechanic's towel, which is tied to a string. If I happen to drop a part in the dirt, I drag the towel on the ground, picking up the parts. This also works for picking up nails and crud in the driveway — much better than using a rake or broom.

William F. Albon, Blair, Oklahoma

NO MORE FLAPPING CURTAINS

While driving with the motorhome windows open, my wife and I were tired of hearing the front curtains hitting the window screens. To solve this noisy problem, she removed the existing narrow strap and replaced it with a full-length strap made from a leather-like vinyl.

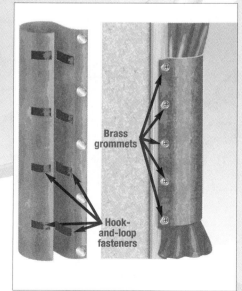

Brass grommets

Hook-and-loop fasteners

I installed five brass grommets along one vertical side to accept the screws that hold the new strap to the wall. Then hook-and-loop fasteners were installed on both vertical edges of the straps. Now the curtains are held along the entire length; no more flapping!

John Theobald, Des Plaines, Illinois

ROLL-AWAY LADDER

When we bought our new motorhome, I had plenty of room to store my 6-foot ladder, but I didn't want to tear the carpet by sliding it in and out of the basement compartment.

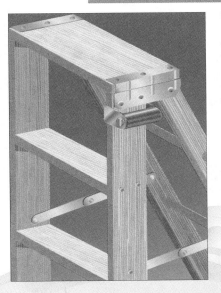

I solved the problem by fabricating a roller and attaching it to the top of the ladder. I just lay the ladder on its side and roll it into the basement.

The roller was built from a 3-inch piece of copper tubing and a piece of metal strap that can be purchased at any hardware store. Bend the strap into a "U" (with square corners) a little wider than the piece of copper tubing. Drill a ¼-inch hole in each end, and use a ¼-inch bolt, long enough to reach from one end of the bracket through the other side, to act as the axle. I used a piece of nylon tubing inside the copper tubing to act as a bearing.

WILLIAM ORMAN, KALAMAZOO, MICHIGAN

PEEK-A-BOO

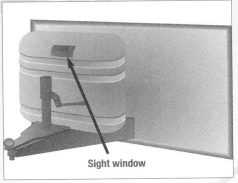

Sight window

The hard plastic covers for LP-gas cylinders are excellent protection from the elements, but they are a nuisance to remove and replace each time you want to check the indicator on the automatic changeover regulator. A sight window at a strategic location can be cut out of the cover using a razor knife. A matching piece of clear plastic from a large soda bottle can be cut and glued in place behind the opening. The hole does not have to be too large; only big enough to allow sight of the indicator flag in the regulator. Make sure you use a glue designed to work on plastic.

WILLIAM R. SVIRSKY, LONGWOOD, FLORIDA

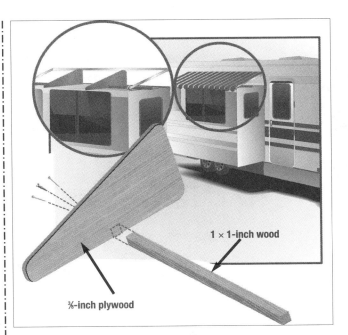

1 × 1-inch wood

⅜-inch plywood

NO MORE AWNING SAG

After considerable expense to repair the outer wall of the slideout in our fifth-wheel, it was recommended that we invest in a topper awning to prevent any future problems of water leaking into the rig. We immediately noticed that after any considerable rain, the water would gather and sag the center of the awning fabric. Using materials I readily had around the house, I erected portable supports, which I slide under the awning, ensuring that tension of the fabric is maintained and allowing rain water to run off. The materials and tools needed are: a tape measure, a pencil, ¾-inch-thick plywood, 1 × 1-inch wood (I used a 1 × 2-inch piece and cut it), wood glue, two wood screws, four finishing nails, a screwdriver, a hammer, a power saw and sandpaper.

I measured the length of the awning (in order to try to have the supports more or less evenly distributed), then measured the width of the opening (from the side of the fifth-wheel to the inside roller of the awning) and the height at both ends. Laying the measurements out on the ¾-inch plywood, I cut out the pieces, rounding the upper corners. Then I sanded all the edges. I made the 1 × 1-inch wood "handles" the length of one-third the width of the awning, plus 1½ inches, so that a portion of the wood would remain sticking over the edges of the slider to remind me to remove the supports before I retract the room.

Attaching the handles to the center at the bottom of the finished plywood was done by applying wood glue to the end before securing with a wood screw (a pilot hole was first drilled to prevent splitting). I then used a nail on each side of the screw to keep the handle from twisting. The handles allow the supports to be positioned with little effort.

ALLEN L. CLEMONS, POPE VALLEY, CALIFORNIA

POSITION MARKER

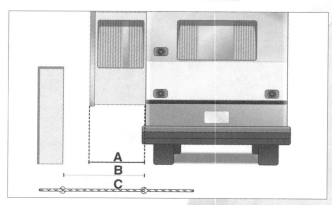

At times I find it challenging to pull into a campsite with the correct driver's side clearance for my slideout. I either pull too close to the utility pole and have to move and re-align the motorhome, or I am too far away and have less area on the opposite side for outdoor activities. So I came up with a way to make my site alignment a little easier. My method is inexpensive, is easily stored and requires no drilling or attachments to the motorhome body.

In an open area, extend the slideout and measure the distance from the edge of your extended slideout to the side of your vehicle (length "A" in the diagram). Cut a piece of rope a foot or so longer than this length. Seal the ends of the rope to prevent fraying. Make a handle at one end by tying a half-hitch knot in the rope. Then, measure the clearance distance from this knot, plus as much additional distance as you need to give you peace of mind (length "B" in the diagram), and tie another half-hitch knot at this point, making sure you don't shorten this clearance distance (rope measurement "C").

Before you pull into a new campsite, measure your own custom clearance from the utilities or any other obstruction with your knotted rope and mark this point on the ground. Pull your motorhome in, aligning the driver's side with this mark, and you'll have adequate clearance for your slideout.
Daniel Dolan Jr., Layton, Utah

ONBOARD STABILIZING BLOCKS

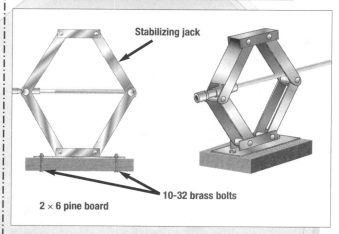

Stabilizing jack

10-32 brass bolts

2 × 6 pine board

Here's an idea that will prevent you from leaving your stabilizing blocks at the campground. Attach a 2 × 6-inch pine board to the bottom of each stabilizing-jack pad using two or four 10-32 brass bolts and nuts. I use brass because it does not rust. If you only want to use two bolts and nuts, install them diagonally from each other. Use two C-clamps to hold the board to the stabilizer jack pad while drilling the holes for the bolts. Don't forget to use a good pair of goggles for eye protection while drilling.
Joe Nice, Laurel, Maryland

SECURE HANDRAIL

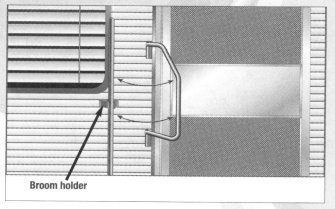

Broom holder

We have a folding handrail next to the entry on our fifth-wheel and when in the travel position, up against the side of the trailer, it bangs into the sidewall and window. To eliminate this, I mounted a broom holder on the side of the trailer. When we travel, the handrail is held in place firmly, and does not bang into the trailer or window. When at the campsite, this holder also doubles as a place to keep a broom handy by the door.
Duane Van Dyke, Oak Harbor, Washington

PIN COVER

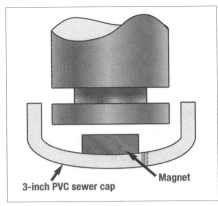

3-inch PVC sewer cap — **Magnet**

Ihave problems with grease getting on me as I go under the kingpin of our fifth-wheel trailer. To solve the problem, I use a 3-inch PVC sewer cap (the white caps are more visible) and attach a magnet to the inside with epoxy glue. After the magnet is secure, drill a small hole (1/16-inch) to facilitate drainage. I used a magnet from an old speaker. Easy to install, easy to remove; no tools necessary.

LESTOR CHAN, VICTORIA, BRITISH COLUMBIA, CANADA

SPILLING DILEMMA

Finding a place to store bottles of cleaning supplies can be difficult. Most of us have had the experience of cleaning up spilled chemicals, especially from bottles that overturned way in the back of cabinets. I took a 2½-gallon drinking water bottle, cut out sections on top and found it holds my cleaning supplies perfectly. And there's a built-in handle to carry the newly cut "carry-all" around. If you make a mistake cutting the bottle, don't sweat it; just keep in drinking and when the next bottle is empty, try again.

EMMETT TUDEL, LAYTON, UTAH

PULL THAT PIN

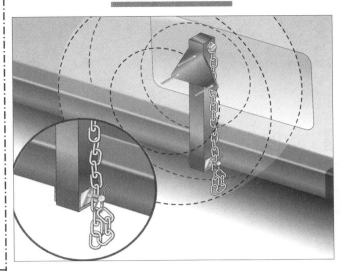

Here is a labor-saving idea for people who have a tip-down spare tire and find it hard to pull the locking pin, be it a hairpin, a cotter pin, a Joslyn clip or whatever.

Put the pin through a link at one end of a short length of small chain. The length of the chain will depend upon the configuration of your vehicle. On the other end of the chain, thread a bolt and nut to act as an anchor.

This arrangement makes pulling the pin a lot easier, and if it is dropped on the ground it is easy to locate.

J. FULTON, TERRE HAUTE, INDIANA

TAME THAT STRAP

Ihave found a way to get that pesky awning strap out of our way. I used a 35mm film canister to make a storage container.

Remove the cap from an empty canister and cut a slit in the side of the canister from the open end to the bottom. Roll your strap in a tight roll until it is high enough to be out of your way. Put the roll into the canister, allowing the remaining strap to slide into the slit cut in the side of the canister. Replace the cap on the film canister, and now there's no more pesky awning strap.

LARRY HILL, MEMPHIS, TENNESSEE

RUNAWAY PAPER TOWELS

To stop a paper towel from unrolling while traveling...

Just stick a straight pin through a few layers of paper.
ROBERT F. PERRY,
ROBERTSON, WYOMING

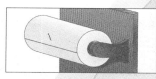

Lay an empty cardboard roller (from an empty roll) between the top of the remaining paper towels and the wall; it acts like a wedge.
JUNE C. HARTLEY,
SAN BENITO, TEXAS

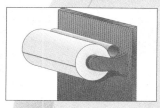

Simply snap open a clothespin and press one jaw between a few layers of the roll and the other jaw over the loose end of the roll. Use a plastic clothespin in a color that complements the decor of your rig.
MILTON F. WATTS,
LINEVILLE, ALABAMA

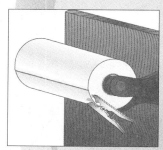

When installing the roll in its holder, merely give it a squeeze to crimp the cardboard core. It doesn't take much. This way the roll may bounce, but it doesn't unroll.
TOM METZGER,
SAN RAFAEL, CALIFORNIA

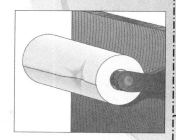

SAVE YOUR AWNING

After losing two awnings from two different motorhomes and suffering numerous other near-misses in high winds at highway speeds, I hit upon the following quick fix. Remember to wear safety goggles at all times.

1. Drill a small hole 1 inch from each end of your rolled-up awing, as high as you can get (top dead-center).
2. Widen the gap in one hook of a 5- or 6-foot bungee cord so it will fit snugly in the hole you drilled.
3. Wrap the bungee cord 1½ turns around the awning roller, in the same direction as the awning's roll-up direction (to make the roll-up even tighter).
4. Stretch the bungee cord in the same roll-up direction down to the end of the awning's arm.
5. Place the other hook in the awning arm's foot. Repeat the steps for the other end of the awning.
   This method has held up for many miles.
JIM DICKINSON, WICKENBURG, ARIZONA

NEAT AND CLEAN

Here is a way to help keep your hands and clothes clean. On the trailer hitch ball, place a water bottle with the bottom cut out. Just try different size bottles until you find one that fits. To cover the little ball that connects the sway-control friction bar, I took a plastic 35mm film container and cut the side in two places on the opposite sides just to the bottom. I put a rubber band around the container so it would easily slip on and off the ball and still stay in place.
RICHARD WARD, SUN CITY, ARIZONA

SLIP NO MORE

Does your shower head sometimes not point the way you want it to? I have found an easy, fool-proof solution.

Just cut a piece of non-slip rubber matting to about 2 × 4 inches and slip it in between the shower head and the shower-head holder (mounted on your RV shower wall). Now you can point your shower head wherever you want and it will stay put, not swivel around while you are taking a shower.

The rubber matting is the same stuff used to keep your plates from sliding around inside your cabinets. It can be purchased at discount, hardware and camping-supply stores.
PAT PULLUM, ROGERS, ARKANSAS

STORAGE PROTECTION

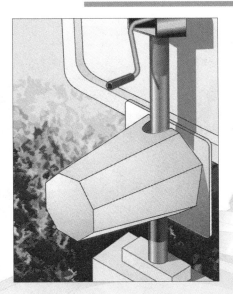

I use a nose cone to cover my A-frame coupler and safety chains during storage. Simply cut out one side to accommodate the jack post, which is 2³⁄₁₆ inches in diameter. A piece of cord wrapped across the nose-cone base and around the jack post will keep it securely in place — rain or snow.
BOB JONES, NILAND, CALIFORNIA

STORAGE PROTECTION II

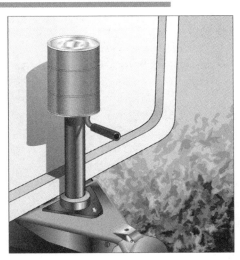

The problem was how to keep water from seeping into the gear case at the top of my trailer A-frame jack (primarily during winter storage). I tried plastic bags, but they were short-lived. The solution was an inverted coffee can.
BRUCE TRUDGEN, WILLIAMSBURG, MICHIGAN

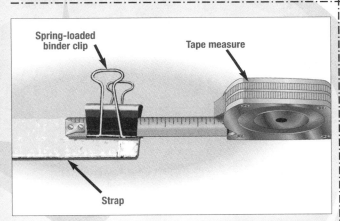

Spring-loaded binder clip

Tape measure

Strap

TAPE MEASURE TO THE RESCUE

To put the cover on our motorhome, we have to fasten the sides down by running five 10-foot straps attached to the bottom edge of one side underneath the coach to the clip on the bottom edge of the other side. Getting the straps easily from one side to the other was the challenge.

It was a very tiring exercise; we would tie the end of a strap to a block of wood and then throw it underneath to the person on the other side, who would then have to untie the strap and throw the block back. Finally, I thought of using a tape measure.

Extend the tape underneath the coach to the person on the other side, who uses a big spring-loaded binder clip to fasten the loose strap end to the end of the tape measure. Retract the tape, and the strap comes right along. This has saved a lot of time and hassle
RICK STRICKLAND, LAGUNA WOODS, CALIFORNIA

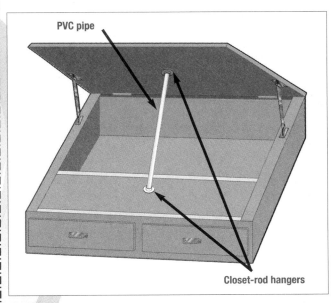

PVC pipe

Closet-rod hangers

UNDER-BED SUPPORT

The gas struts, which support the under-bed storage cover (on which the mattress lays), were getting weak and would no longer give enough support. To solve this problem, I bought a length of PVC pipe and a pair of closet-rod hangers.

Fasten one closet-rod hanger to the floor of the storage compartment and the other to the underside of the compartment cover (directly over the lower one). Cut the PVC pipe to a length long enough to hold the cover open to the height you desire. Store the pipe under the bed when not in use.
MARK KUYKENDALL, PRESCOTT, ARIZONA

THREE QUICKIES

1 When our outdoor rug is wet and/or dirty, it makes a mess in the storage compartment. To solve this problem, I purchased a 5-foot length of 6-inch PVC pipe (8-inch would have been better, but it would not fit in my compartment). I just roll up my dirty rug and slide it into the pipe. At home or wherever, I remove the rug and clean it and the pipe.

2 My motorhome has a telephone connection for use at an RV park, and the long telephone wire ended up being a tangled mess. I use an old tennis-ball tube to contain the excess wire for storage.

3 I tow a car, and like many who don't have a rear camera to watch it on the road, I rely on my sideview mirrors. I have some window-mount flags. I removed the flags and modified them so the rod would extend horizontally. Then, I placed a plastic golf ball on the end of each rod. Now, as I drive down the highway, I can see those little white balls sticking out in my mirror line of sight. It gives a visual warning if my "little pusher" has a problem.

JOHN KRILL, HENDERSON, NEVADA

THERE'S NO ESCAPE

Now that we live in our motorhome several months at a time, there is still one thing we just can't get away from: the laundry! I try to make it as quick and painless as possible.

Carrying the large soap containers and measuring out the soap, fabric softener, etc., was always a nuisance. Then I came up with an idea. Using the measuring cap from the detergent bottle, I poured one measure of water at a time into a clear plastic soap bottle (the kind with a squeeze cap). After each measure, I drew a line on the side of the squeeze bottle with a magic marker.

Now it is very easy to squeeze out just enough detergent for one wash load. This method is also good for spot cleaning, and you don't loose track of how much soap you have used. It works just as well with bleach or softener.

Any size bottle is good as long as it's clear, so you can see the contents. I keep all the laundry supplies in a vinyl tote bag, ready for use.

MARIE HASKINS, DERRY, NEW HAMPSHIRE

TWO APPROACHES TO AWNING NOISE

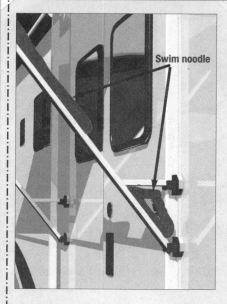

Swim noodle

Our awning-support arms always used to rattle in the breeze.

By cutting small wedge-shaped pieces from a swim noodle, I was able to create silencing wedges, which I inserted where the support arm meets the rafter arm. It was cheap, and now it's quiet!

MARK KUYKENDALL, PRESCOTT, ARIZONA

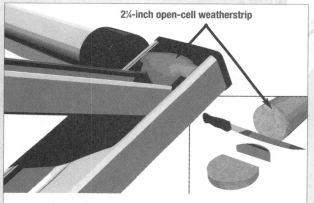

2¼-inch open-cell weatherstrip

To stop the very loud and annoying wind noise from the front arm of our motorhome's awning while driving, I went to a hardware store and bought two packages of 2¼-inch open-cell foam weatherstrip, made for window air conditioners.

From one piece of foam, I cut a length to fit in the awning-arm channel, from the top to a point where the brace connects when in the closed position. From the second piece of foam, I cut a length to fit from the bottom of the channel to the bottom of the first piece. I wedged these pieces of foam into the channel and closed the awning. All the wind noise is now stopped while driving.

To open the awning, I fold down the bottom piece of foam, so the brace that holds the awning can be fastened in place. To put the awning up, I reverse the procedure. The locking pin can be pushed through the foam to lock the awning arm for travel.

DARYL MCINTIRE, MOUNTAIN HOME, ARKANSAS

TENNIS ANYONE?

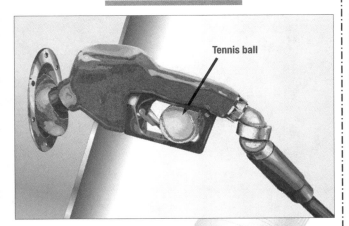

Tennis ball

Have you ever pulled into a gas station and got all set up to pump 75 or more gallons of fuel, only to find that the nozzle trigger latch is either missing or doesn't work? Use a tennis ball to wedge the lever open. It fits perfectly and allows you to wash your windows and/or check fluid levels instead of holding on to the nozzle.

BILL NORHINGTON, REDONDO BEACH, CALIFORNIA

UMBILICAL-CORD PROTECTION

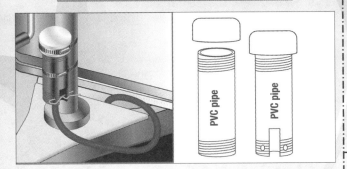

PVC pipe

PVC pipe

To keep my umbilical cord out of the snow and/or rain when not in use, I devised this storage place. I use a 6-inch-long section of 2-inch-diameter PVC pipe with a 2-inch cap on the top end. I cut a 1½-inch-deep slot across the bottom of the PVC pipe wide enough to accept the "ears" on the connector. A ³⁄₁₆-inch hole is drilled toward the lower part of the slot cut in the PVC pipe to accommodate a ³⁄₁₆ × 3½-inch-long hitch pin clip.

To use, push the umbilical-cord connector up into the bottom of the pipe with the "ears" going into the slots. While holding the cord in the pipe, insert the hitch-pin clip into the hole you drilled, so that the hitch-pin clip passes under the cord connector holding it up in the pipe.

Although this unit could be mounted almost anywhere, I mounted mine to the jack post with two hose clamps.

LELAND THOMPSON, KENT, WASHINGTON

UNIQUE BEARING

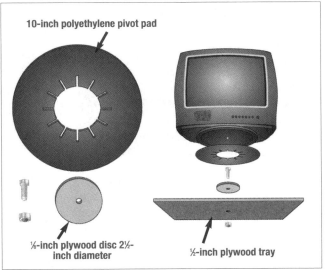

10-inch polyethylene pivot pad

⅛-inch plywood disc 2½-inch diameter

½-inch plywood tray

When I set out to build a swiveling television tray, I hit upon the idea of using a polyethylene pivot pad as a bearing surface. This is the pad that is used on fifth-wheel hitches to eliminate the need for grease between the hitch saddle and kingpin box. These pads are available from almost all RV-supply stores and they make great turntable bearings. They usually come in 8 or 10-inch diameters and are simply a molded disk about ³⁄₁₆-inch thick with an asterisk-like hole in the center.

I used the 10-inch version and cut a ⅛-inch-thick plywood disk 2⅞ inches in diameter to fit in the center and keep the pad centered. The tray is made of ½-inch plywood and pivots on a bolt in the middle of the tray. A lock nut and washer, accessed from the underside of the cabinet, can be used to set the desired pivot friction. A similar arrangement can be used to make corner turntables in cupboards.

TONY HOWARD, MONROE, WASHINGTON

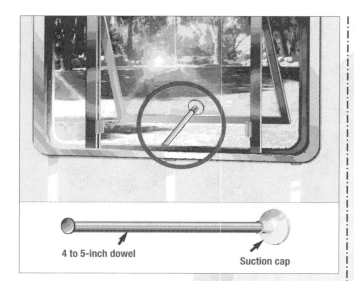

4 to 5-inch dowel

Suction cap

WINDOW BRACE

We like a lot of cross-ventilation in our fifth-wheel's bedroom, but the streetside window is an emergency exit and there is no way to hold it open. To prop it open, I took a short piece of dowel (4 to 5 inches long) and put a suction cup on one end and a rubber bumper on the other. The suction cup is stuck to the window and the rubber bumper rests on the frame, holding the window open. If a strong gust of wind causes the window to swing open wider, the dowel falls, but the suction cup keeps it attached for easy retrieval.

RAY SANER, PEORIA, ARIZONA

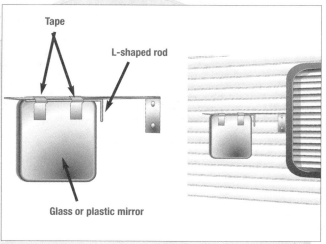

Tape

L-shaped rod

Glass or plastic mirror

VIEW IT

Our fifth-wheel trailer doesn't have any windows looking forward. Being curious (or nosy), I like to see who or what is at the front of my parking space. Here is my simple solution, and it's easy to remove for storing while towing.

I mounted a simple angle bracket at the rear of my dinette window. Use a bracket that has two holes in each leg. I took a pegboard hanger, about 8 inches long, and trimmed some of the "peg legs," leaving an L-shaped piece of rod. This rod is placed in the rear hole of the bracket and a piece of soft wire is twisted over the rod and through the other hole, keeping the rod secure.

An inexpensive vanity mirror (glass or plastic) is hung from the rod with tape. Thin strips of cloth tape will work fine. Now, while seated at the dinette table (facing to the rear), I am able to see what's going on at the front of my rig.

MARK KUYKENDALL, PRESCOTT, ARIZONA

◆ CLOSEUPS ◆ CLOSEUPS ◆ CLOSEUPS ◆

TOILET-PAPER TUBE USES

I have discovered an easy and inexpensive way to keep electrical cords from tangling. I use empty toilet-paper tubes. Simply fold the cord and insert it in the tube. The tube can be covered with contact paper or decorated. If you need a more durable holder, cut thin-wall PVC pipe into 4-inch lengths. This holder can be used to control extension and electrical appliance cords.

MANDA EDWARDS, HUNTINGTON, TEXAS

I always keep the ends of my Eaz-Lift spring bars properly greased. After disconnecting the travel trailer, I use cloth-tape-reinforced toilet paper tubes to cover the greasy ends of the spring bars. It keeps grease in and the dirt out.

DOUGLAS P. PILIEN, SANTEE, CALIFORNIA

◆ CLOSEUPS ◆ CLOSEUPS ◆ CLOSEUPS ◆

VALVE EXTENSION

I purchased a used motorhome that was missing the valve extension for an inner dual tire. I could not reach through with my hand, pliers or anything to remove the valve cap. I took a length of wood dowel about the same diameter as the valve cap and wrapped a piece of cloth tape around the end of the dowel, letting about a ½-inch extend over the end. Then I placed the end over the cap and used an awning hook to rub the tape tight on the cap. It took three tries, but I got the cap off and screwed on a new extension. It saved the time and expense of removing the outer wheel.

GLENN E. FEAR, TIPTON, IOWA

UP ON THE ROOFTOP

My rooftop AM/FM antenna, like most others, has as its base a spherical piece of cast metal, split in the middle and joined by a screw. I could never tighten the screw sufficiently to keep the two pieces of metal from rotating whenever the antenna struck a low-hanging tree limb in transit. Of course, when I got to a campground, the antenna would be flat against the roof, affecting the radio's reception.

To remedy this situation, I tried grooving the surfaces where the two pieces joined, and I tried using various lock- and serrated washers. Nothing I tried allowed the shock spring to do its job. Finally, I purchased a ¾-inch hose clamp at the hardware store and tightened it around the entire spherical section of the antenna. This clamp permitted the proper tightening and allowed the antenna spring to absorb the shock from low-hanging branches.

HARRY FLICK JR., LANCASTER, PENNSYLVANIA

UNIQUE GROMMETS

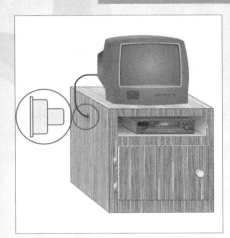

My fifth-wheel has a recess for the VCR below the television counter. I did not want to drill a hole in the Formica countertop to route the two VCR cables, so I drilled a hole in the side of the cabinet. Due to the fact that the cabinet is double-wall construction, there was a ragged edge left in the wood where the drill bit exited the side. I tried to find a grommet that would accept the two cables and seal the opening, but could not locate one. So my wife convinced me to purchase a package of baby-bottle nipples at the dollar store and just cut the end off to make an instant grommet. It turned out to be pliable enough to accept the two cables and easily fit the drilled opening. The package contained tan and white nipples, so you can choose a color.

ROBERT DEANGELIS, LEBANON, NEW JERSEY

WATER FILLER

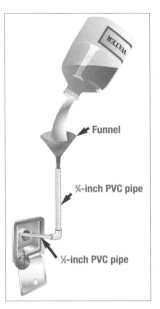

Funnel

¾-inch PVC pipe

½-inch PVC pipe

We often camp in the desert without hookups and require additional water supplied by carry-along containers. We needed a method to pour the water into our fifth-wheel's tank without spilling. Using about 1-foot lengths of ½- and ¾-inch PVC pipe, we made a simple filler device. The two sections of PVC are connected by an elbow and a funnel is used at the top. A flat-sided funnel costs about $1, and the PVC pipe and elbow are less than $2.

ROBERT J. THOMAS JR., CAVE CREEK, ARIZONA

CLOSEUPS ◆ CLOSEUPS ◆ CLOSEUPS

TWO USES FOR THE SAME MATERIAL

1 The dinette seat cushions in our motorhome had the annoying habit of sliding forward when we leaned backward because they have a smooth vinyl bottom and because there is no raised edge along the front of the seats. After trying several futile approaches, including hook-and-loop material, I found a simple but very effective solution.

Using an ordinary paper stapler, I stapled two pieces of Slip Stop, each about a foot square, to each plywood seat surface. I found it necessary to use many staples to hold the material, and to put the staples in firmly to avoid a rough surface that could wear the bottom of the seat cushion. Now we can lean back without sliding forward.

JOSEPH SHAPIRO, ST. PAUL, MINNESOTA

2 When using a public shower, take two squares from a roll of Slip Stop — one to stand on to undress, and another to stand on while in the shower.

JUDY WINTER, MIDLAND, MICHIGAN

(Editor's Note: *Slip Stop washable vinyl-coated mesh is sold by the roll and is normally used to keep dishes from sliding inside RV cabinets.)*

WATER-HEATER QUICKIES

1 Many of us have experienced the frustration of pulling into a campground to find that we've lost our water-heater door while on the road. To ensure that doesn't happen again, I use two cable ties to secure the door. One tie is threaded through the cool-air-inlet part of the door vent; the second is threaded through the first cable tie and the spring-loaded clamp. If the clamp should turn 90 degrees due to vibration, the door will remain fastened to the motorhome.

2 When draining a water heater, the removal of the drain plug often allows water to drain in the recess of the water heater and run down the side of the vehicle. To prevent this from occurring, I use a threaded 6-inch section of PVC pipe (from the hardware store) to project the stream of water out and away from the vehicle. It does take a little skill to remove the drain plug and insert the PVC pipe simultaneously, but the results outweigh the alternative.

LARRY EY, BEL AIR, MARYLAND

THE $1 SOLUTION

A s with most travelers, we find the center console on our pickup truck very useful for resting our arms, stowing items inside and putting maps and directories on the outside top surface. Unfortunately, with nearly every stop, the whole pile of stuff ends up on the floor of the cab.

The $1 solution was to buy a length of 1-inch elastic band and wrap it completely around the console's lid and fasten the ends together (forming a giant "rubber band"). We found that two bands, separated by a few inches, around the lid solved the problem for us and allowed more storage on top of the lid. The bands do not interfere with the normal closure and locking of the lid.

ROBERT CORDY, NEW MEADOWS, IDAHO

10-Minute Tech / **171**

THE BEST OF TECH TOPICS: VOLUME I
Bob Livingston

Over the years, thousands of RVers have corresponded with Bob Livingston through his monthly *Tech Topics* column in *Highways* magazine. *The Best of Tech Topics* includes their most important and most asked questions along with no-nonsense answers and solutions to pressing RV problems. Whether you are working on your own RV or in the RV trades, you'll find the job-tested information you need right here.

5½ × 8½, 98 pages
$12.95 ISBN: 0-93478-55-9

100 MILES AROUND YELLOWSTONE
Jim and Madonna Zumbo

This book is a comprehensive guide that focuses on the sights and activities within a 100-mile radius of Yellowstone National Park. It is a valuable guide for travelers who choose Yellowstone as their destination, but don't want to miss out on the many sights and activities nearby. Particular emphasis is made on RV travel and information in this area.

7⅜ × 9¼, 288 pages
$34.95 ISBN: 0-93478-52-4

PLEASE DON'T TAILGATE THE REAL ESTATE: SCOUTING THE BACK ROADS AND OFF-RAMPS TO FIND TRUE LOVE AND HAPPINESS
William C. Anderson

A hilarious collection of insights, observations, and travel adventures of noted author and Hollywood screenwriter, William "Andy" Anderson, gleaned from more than 30 years of RV travel with his wife and family in their rig, *Rocinante*. Andy is a rare combination of gifted humorist and warm-hearted observer whose hilarious accounts of the twists, turns, quirks, and challenges of life on wheels comes from his own personal experience.

5½ × 8½, 224 pages
$16.95 ISBN: 0-934798-51-8

These books are available at fine bookstores everywhere. Or, you may order directly from Trailer Life Books. For each book ordered, simply send us the name of the book, the price, plus $3.95 per book for shipping and handling (CA, CO, IN residents please add appropriate sales tax).

Mail orders to:
Trailer Life Books
64 Inverness Drive East
Englewood, CO 80112

You may call our customer-service representatives if you wish to charge your order or if you want more information. Please phone, toll-free, Monday through Friday, 6:30 A.M. to 6:30 P.M.; Saturday, 7:30 A.M. to 1:30 P.M., Mountain Time, **(800) 766-1674.**
Or, Visit us online at **tldirectory.com**

OTHER BOOKS BY TRAILER LIFE

RV HANDBOOK — 3ʳᴰ EDITION

This "no fluff" comprehensive guide for both novice and seasoned RVers has thousands across the U.S. and Canada reaching for this book as a constant source of reference. It has become the "bible" for the RV road warrior. Features hundreds of proven RV tips, tricks and techniques to save you time, money and maybe even your sanity. Packed with user-friendly technical advice, checklists, schematics, photos and charts. You simply won't find this level of detail covered in any other RV book.
8½ × 10¾, 275 pages
$29.95 ISBN: 0-934798-66-4

TRAILER LIFE'S RV REPAIR & MAINTENANCE MANUAL, FOURTH EDITION
Bob Livingston

This revised edition presents recreational-vehicle owners with all the up-to-date practical knowledge needed for diagnosing problems, making repairs and communicating with mechanics. Filled with detailed troubleshooting guides and checklists, hundreds of comprehensive illustrations and photographs and easy-to-understand step-by-step instructions for repairing, replacing and maintaining systems.
8½ × 11, 500 pages
$34.95 plus $3.95 shipping and handling ISBN: 0-934798-70-2

10-MINUTE TECH THE BOOK

The first volume in this series features hundreds of easy-to-do, money-saving tips taken from *Trailer Life* magazine's *10-Minute Tech* and *MotorHome* magazine's *Quick Tips* — the most widely read and talked-about self-help column for RVers. This handy book features clever ways to help you improve the RV's livability, plenty of towing tips, procedures for cleaning and maintaining the rig, user-friendly tips on fixing your appliances, great ideas for storage and much more. Filled with easy-to-follow illustrations that will help turn RVers into savvy do-it-yourselfers.
7¾ × 9½, 219 pages
$29.95 ISBN: 0-934798-59-1

COMPLETE GUIDE TO FULL-TIME RVING: LIFE ON THE OPEN ROAD, THIRD EDITION
Bill and Jan Moeller

This best-selling how-to-do-it book covers a broad range of subjects of interest to full-timers, those considering a full-time lifestyle or seasonal RVers. New and expanded chapters including working full-timers, remodeling your RV for full-time living and widebody RVs, in addition to chapters on costs, choosing the right RV, safety and security and more.
7⅜ × 9¼, 548 pages
$29.95 ISBN: 0-934798-53-2